THE POLITICS OF REPRODUCTION

FORMATIONS: ADOPTION, KINSHIP, AND CULTURE
Emily Hipchen and John McLeod, Series Editors

The Politics of Reproduction

Adoption, Abortion, and Surrogacy
in the Age of Neoliberalism

Edited by
Modhumita Roy and Mary Thompson

THE OHIO STATE UNIVERSITY PRESS
COLUMBUS

Library of Congress Cataloging-in-Publication Data is available online at catalog.loc.gov.

Cover design by Nathan Putens
Text design by Juliet Williams
Type set in Adobe Minion Pro

♾ The paper used in this publication meets the minimum requirements of the American National Standard for Information Sciences—Permanence of Paper for Printed Library Materials. ANSI Z39.48-1992.

We dedicate this volume to the memory of our fathers,
Richard E. Thompson Jr. (1924–2011) and
Birendra Narayan Roy (1926–2011), and to our mothers,
Barbara J. Thompson and Pranati Roy,
with love and thanks.

CONTENTS

ACKNOWLEDGMENTS

WE ARE indebted to many whose support and encouragement have made this volume possible. We want to express our deep gratitude, even if we are unable to name them all here.

At Ohio State University Press, our editor, Kristen Elias Rowley, has provided guidance, support, and advice throughout the process. The book would not have been possible without her enthusiasm and encouragement from the start. We thank her for her help in seeing this project through to completion. Sincere thanks to Tara Cyphers for her keen eye and sound advice in the final stages of the book's preparation. We would like to thank our anonymous reviewers, who understood the political and intellectual stakes of the volume, for their generous and perspicacious feedback, which pushed us to answer our questions and to galvanize the volume's focus.

Our collaboration would not have been possible without the Motherhood Initiative for Research and Community Involvement (MIRCI), and that organization's founder and force of nature, Andrea O'Reilly. We are grateful for her capacious understanding of "mothers, mothering, and motherhood" that includes all facets of reproduction.

We wish to acknowledge the generous support of our departments and deans' offices at James Madison University and Tufts University. We thank JMU College of Arts and Letters Faculty Mini-Grants and Faculty Research

---

Awards Committee Grants-in-Aid, Tufts University, for providing funding for manuscript preparation.

We are indebted to the contributors to this volume for their hard work and commitment to reproductive politics. Special thanks to Kate Walters for allowing us to use her evocative painting for the cover, and to Matthew White for his meticulous work on indexing the volume.

Modhumita would like to thank her "middle-aged brigade," Pilar Bartley, Goizane Suengas, and Heiddis Valdimarsdottir, for always being there. A very warm thank you to her sister, Anindita Raj Bakshi, who broke the rules first and showed the way. Thanks also to comrade and mentor Malini Bhattacharya for her encouragement, and to Paromita Chakravarti for her irreverent wit and sustaining friendship. And, of course, the late, great Jasodhara Bagchi, fiery feminist and friend, whose work continues to inspire. A grateful thank you to Abha Sur for filling her with delicious meals and provocative ideas. Modhumita also wants to thank friends and colleagues at Tufts University, especially Sonia Hofkosh and Elizabeth Ammons, for enriching her intellectual and personal life. Sincere thanks to Douglas Riggs, Jennifer LeBlanc, and Wendy Medeiros, in the English office, for their patience and help with temperamental computers and other sundry machines and for many everyday acts of support and kindness.

Mary would like to thank her inspiring coworkers at The Center for Choice (1983–2013) for their fearless dedication to abortion access, boundless compassion, and bawdy/body humor. Gratitude is also due to Carol Yoder, her running partner, for her generous spirit, good humor, and for lending an ear—mile after mile. She also thanks her feministy colleagues and friends—Jessica Davidson, Dawn Goode, Kristin Wylie, Becca Howes-Mischel, Debali Mookerjea-Leonard, and AJ Morey—for their sustaining conversations and support. Last but not least she thanks Olive the pit bull, and sweet, loyal Blondie, who ungrudgingly awaits—from her position directly behind the office chair—a promised walk.

And, finally, we would like to express our love, gratitude, and thanks to our families, and especially, to our mothers, Barbara J. Thompson and Pranati Roy, to whom this volume is dedicated.

INTRODUCTION

MODHUMITA ROY AND MARY THOMPSON

"WHAT SEPARATES and what connects the lives and stories of women imagined within the capacious borders of the global? . . . How are we simultaneously intertwined with one another and made separate through relations of power, of position, of geography and history?" ask Cindi Katz and Nancy Miller in their "Editor's Note" to a special double issue of *Women's Studies Quarterly* (11). *The Politics of Reproduction* seeks to answer their questions by focusing on the entangled politics of abortion, adoption, and commercial surrogacy, as they play out in the "capacious borders of the global." The essays in this collection are attentive particularly to the "diverse instantiations" (to borrow Wendy Brown's phrase) of neoliberalism's reshaping of economies and intimacies. Our aim here is to analyze and understand the dynamics of "simultaneously intertwined" reproductive politics as they unfold in specific instances of family creation, choice, and labor. Consider these three recent reports in the news that center on reproduction and reproductive choice:

> In October 2017, a 17-year-old undocumented immigrant from Central America, "Jane Doe," having received a judicial bypass of the state parental consent law in Texas, sought to have an abortion. Her action sparked a federal lawsuit, and a Court of Appeals' three-judge panel (including then-member Brett M. Kavanaugh) initially blocked her request and compelled her to receive antiabortion counseling from a local crisis pregnancy clinic.

1

Ultimately, the full Court of Appeals for the D. C. Circuit overturned the panel's decision (6-to-3), and Jane Doe was able to terminate the pregnancy (Chappell).

In November 2017, a gestational surrogate in California, Jessica Allen, gave birth to twins and handed them over to the commissioning couple, the Lius, who had travelled from China. In a rare phenomenon known as "superfetation," Allen had ovulated and become pregnant after being implanted with the Lius' embryo, making one of the twins biologically unrelated to the Lius (Ridley). The Lius reportedly returned the non-biological child to the agency to adopt out. However, since Mrs. Liu's name appeared on the birth certificate, making her the legal mother of the twins, in order to gain custody of the child to whom they were biologically but not legally related, the Allens were initially asked to repay part of the surrogacy fee, in addition to incurred legal fees and the processing charge from the agency.

In his January 2018 State of the Union address, President Trump introduced an adoptive couple, the Holets, as his special guests. Ryan Holet, a police officer, had apprehended a pregnant woman injecting herself with heroin and, in that moment he claimed, "God spoke to him," prompting him to persuade the woman to let his family adopt her baby. While the intended point of this anecdote was the altruism of the adoptive Christian couple, Trump's account neglected to report what happened to the birthmother.

These three alarming vignettes might appear, on one level, to reflect quite different concerns: abortion, surrogacy, and adoption. But a closer look reveals some deeper connections, and it is these deeper, more insidious connections that this collection of essays explores: the asymmetrically distributed privilege and precarity within which reproductive choices are made, the confluence of different degrees and kinds of desperation that force particular decisions, and the biopolitics that regulate not just biological life but the very conditions of the regeneration of life.

To unravel the "simultaneously intertwined" lives and concerns, we might begin by making deceptively simple observations about transnational movements of bodies and resources. In the instances cited above, Jane Doe, for example, having recognized the demand for eldercare in the US, had come to seek a nursing degree. The wealthy and geographically mobile Lius were attracted by the legalized commercial surrogacy industry in California, where Jessica Allen was looking for opportunities to supplement her income as an eldercare worker. In looking deeper into their movements and what necessitates them, we probe the larger issue of neoliberalism's global restructuring of economies, which has produced extreme inequalities, authorized the dismantling of welfare provisions, and increased the vulnerabilities of populations already at risk. To ask why Jane Doe traveled to Texas or the Lius to California is to detect also the effects of economic reorganization on social institutions as much as in our intimate lives. This volume, in other words, is attentive to the effects of "macroeconomic intervention in the micropolitics of family relations, reshaping people's private, everyday lives" (Davies 28). In a radically altered economic and social landscape, the desires of one class of women for reproductive labor—baby-making and eldercare—are legitimated and serviced by another class of women who are driven by the need to survive.

A related series of observations arise when we focus on the entanglement of reproduction, motherhood, and the state. We might usefully ask, when do regulations protect women and when do they increase their vulnerability? The California surrogacy example lays bare the challenges that arise from the splitting apart of reproductive labor into discrete components—genetic, gestational, legal, and social—and which dispersal necessitates an attendant redefinition and understanding of *motherhood*. It is the complicated context of medical advances—particularly the breakthroughs in biotechnology in the arena of assisted reproduction—refracted as they often are through existing ideologies of race, family, and citizenship, that give rise to the *problem* faced by the Lius. These new biomedical technologies also have bolstered the state's interest in regulating reproduction and necessitated legal redefinition of human life, of motherhood, and of kinship. Those interests are equally constituted through and shaped by social frameworks of race, class, and citizenship, which we can see when efforts to restrict all women's access to abortion begin by impacting socially vulnerable women, as in the case of undocumented Jane Doe. Here we see how social policies reflect the fears of conservative groups (and others) about race, immigration, *family values,* and national belonging.

A final constellation of observations arises over the complexly sedimented issue of *choice.* The question of *choice* is particularly urgent in a political and ideological climate that encourages individual solutions to intractable social problems, especially in the context of unprecedented economic disparities. Whose choices are amplified in the use of new biomedical technologies that assist in human reproduction? We are discouraged from seeing the economic motivations behind the *choices* to surrender a baby for adoption or to become a surrogate or to seek an abortion. Most consequential for this volume are the political and social constructions of *good* and *bad* choices. How do we resist seeing Jane Doe, the Lius and Allens, and Baby Holet's birth mother in terms of *good* and *bad* choice-makers?

These are urgent concerns for this collection of essays. In this introduction, we focus more fully on them and the three areas of concern they exemplify to set the stage for making and exploring connections not only between the women in the three vignettes but also between and among the essays in this volume. Our work, and that of the essays collected here, is profoundly indebted to and influenced by existing scholarship—on neoliberalism, reproductive politics and justice, and the discourse of *choice*—which this introduction also acknowledges and explores.

Neoliberalism's "Slow Violence"

Most commentators agree that from the 1970s on, there was a decisive historical economic and ideological shift from what has been referred to as the postwar consensus; that is, we can trace a move from a commitment to redistribution of resources and the creation of social safety nets for all to the rise of speculative finance, deregulation, and fetishizing of the so-called free market. Coined by South American theorists to describe such economic restructuring and reforms, *neoliberalism* serves as a shorthand for free trade through deregulation and the exploitation of natural resources and the environment, austerity programs imposed by the IMF and World Bank that have dominated the life of so-called developing countries, and a general prioritizing of profit over human rights and well-being of populations. Neoliberalism, according to David Graeber, is the brainchild of "financiers philosophically opposed to the very idea of public goods" (8). This redesign of entire social systems is directed toward value extraction to benefit the few, what David Harvey rather more bluntly than most calls "accumulation by dispossession." For Harvey, the phrase accurately describes the worldwide transfer of resources, raw materials, and value from the poor to the rich (that is, from the 99 percent to the 1 percent); this ruthless transfer, in his estimation, is "the new imperialism." One of the striking features of this iteration of global capitalism is that it is more than the rearrangement of the economy. In an interview with Timothy Shenk for *Dissent,* Wendy Brown rightly insisted that we understand neoliberalism not just as a set of economic policies but as a "broader phenomenon of governing rationality" (Shenk) through which forms of human activity, even those once thought to be outside market logic and exchange—intimate bodily labor such as reproduction, for example—are brought into its orbit and reconstrued in market terms (Brown, *Undoing the Demos*). The commercialization of all areas of life and the privatization of public goods—education, healthcare, natural resources—not only generate "extreme inequalities of wealth and life conditions," they lead to "increasingly precarious and disposable populations" (Shenk). Perhaps what is most dangerous and sinister about neoliberalism is that it "does profound damage to democratic practices, cultures, institutions and imaginaries" (Shenk). Across the world, despite local variations, neoliberalism shares the common features of intensified inequality and the commercialization of everything. This ferocious move toward privatization and commoditization was conjoined with an older, more uncompromising ideology of social conservatism. As Melinda Cooper, among others, has maintained, "neoliberalism and the new social conservatism . . . [are] the contemporary expression of capital's double movement" (18). Their symbiosis has produced the ideology of "private family responsibility" and transformed welfare from a "redistributive program into an immense federal apparatus for policing the family responsibilities of the poor" (21). The common agenda of neoliberalism and neoconservatism has been to "arrange things so that [social] needs are satisfied in as small and private a unit as possible" (Davies 28). In virtually every country in the world, now, this *logic* has become commonsense: "a simultaneous emphasis on personal self-realization for the affluent, and of 'personal responsibility' for the poor" (Graeber 8).

One of the most detrimental effects of this restructuring has been the collapse of welfare provisions across the world. The standard prescriptions of the IMF and World Bank, with their insistence on austerity programs, have pushed large numbers of people into precarious living conditions. Precarity—the "politically induced condition in which certain populations suffer from failing social and economic networks of support" that render them "differentially exposed to injury, violence, and death" (Butler ii)—is produced by a neoliberal philosophy that solely prioritizes investment and profit. In the global South, draconian Structural Adjustment Programs (SAPs) imposed radical curtailment of domestic spending, including agricultural and food subsidies, education and health, all of which disproportionately impact the poor, and especially women. The economic ravages of austerity measures (as well as war and environmental disasters) push more and more people to seek out desperate "alternative circuits of survival" (Sassen 515). The result of such immiseration, to borrow an evocative phrase from Rob Nixon, is "slow violence." It is, as he describes, "an attritional violence"; a violence that "occurs gradually and out of sight . . . dispersed across time and space" (Nixon 2).

The damage to the social fabric is disproportionately borne by women, especially poor women and women of color. Feminist scholars such as Briggs, Ghosh, Glenn, Brown, McRobbie, Kabeer, Pareñas, and Duggan (among others) have written extensively on the effects of neoliberalism, paying particular attention to its globalized redesigning of socialities and intimacies. As Briggs notes, the term *globalization* oversimplifies the effect that neoliberalism has had on reshaping not just markets and economies but also politics, households, and individuals. Nevertheless, the term helps in understanding how we relate to one another "through relations of power, of position, of geography and history" (Katz and Miller 11). Arjun Appadurai in his introduction to an anthology simply titled *Globalization* observed that though we appear to live in a "world of flow" (5), which includes "ideas and ideologies, people and goods, images and messages, technologies and techniques" (5), such a world is not "coeval, convergent, isomorphic, or spatially consistent" (5). The unequal relations, or "relations of disjunction" (5) within which objects—ideas, persons, images, and so on—flow produce "problems of livelihood, equity, suffering, justice, and governance" (6). This volume is mindful of such variable effects and iterations of the macroeconomic interventions in the micropolitics of family-making and choice.

As in the rest of the world, in the US, too, neoliberalism signals not simply an economic turn but also a reshaping of political ideologies and institutions. Beginning in the late 1970s, financial and corporate interests "reset government priorities to shrink spending on the well-being of actual humanbeings—from schools to housing to child welfare programs like AFDC—in order to keep corporate taxes low and profits high" (Briggs, *How All* 8–9). Both Democrats and Republicans oversaw the dismantling of the social safety net, much of which had existed since the Great Depression. After all, it was Bill Clinton, a *new* Democrat, who took credit for ending *welfare as we know it* with the passage of the Personal Responsibility and Work Opportunity Reconciliation Act of 1996. The debate that preceded the passage of the bill reignited the racialized and gendered moral panic of the 1980s, which had demonized working-class, black, Latino, and indigenous women through discourses of *crack babies, welfare cheats,* and *welfare queens* (Briggs, "Foreign" 59). Sometimes aligned with conservative values and sometimes with new Democrats like Clinton, neoliberalism has fed and been nourished by the US culture wars that, as Briggs notes, were not simply about "God and gays (which is to say, the proper form of the family and reproductive labor)," but instead were "a campaign to shift the relationship of government, personal responsibility and economy" (Briggs, *How All* 14).

The fallout of these debates and policy changes hits hardest close to home in the institution of the family and in households—that is to say, in our relation to each other and in our practices of family-making. Economic austerity programs have restructured paid productive and unpaid reproductive labor. As wages stagnate or drop and more individuals enter the workforce, the socially necessary labor required for what Adrienne Rich described as "the activity . . . of world repair" has continued to be viewed as women's work, and women as the natural providers of such labor (xvi). Put less poetically, the quotidian *reproductive labor* of homemaking, eldercare and childcare, and child-rearing, has become *double shift* for a great many women. Other women, who have the financial ability, outsource the labor of care-giving to under-privileged women: immigrants, with or without documents, like Jane Doe; or women like Jessica Allen, who, forgoing the care of their own families, have had to step in. Arlie Hochschild has characterized this "wrenching trend" as a "care drain"—that is, "the importation of care and love from poor countries to rich ones" (186). Indeed, Evelyn Nakano Glenn and others have alerted us to the "long history of *extracting* caring labor from women of color as part of a larger system of coerced labor" (49). These forms of "stratified reproduction," a term coined by Shelle Colen, contain within them "global processes . . . in local, intimate, daily events in which stratification is itself reproduced" (178). Thus, inequality and power differentials are themselves *reproduced* in the very processes of nurturing and caretaking, and in the labor of social and biological reproduction. These issues are critically important to this collection of essays as we consider how some women are encouraged to view their labor and reproductive options as expanding and discouraged from identifying with women whose decisions are constrained or compelled. Even as various opportunities to work in the paid labor force and to make families reflect *some* women's amplified options, they also indicate *other* women's desperation, even coercion, which too often remains unvoiced and frequently overlooked.

It is in this context of the reorganization of productive and reproductive labor in the age of neoliberalism that *The Politics of Reproduction* considers how we might reassess our understanding of vulnerable women's "alternative circuits of survival" (Sassen)—such as an individual's decision to mine her biocapital to extract value. Jessica Allen, for example, recognized that surrogacy—renting her womb—would allow her access to capital ($35,000) otherwise impossible to accumulate on a low- or minimum-wage job in eldercare, and further, she was right to determine that the payment would allow her to stay at home with her family. Under the circumstances, Allen's calculation was a *rational* one, and we can see analogous calculations at work in the growing market in reproductive bio-materials such as eggs, sperm, and breast milk. In other words, as Donna Dickenson has persuasively argued, in this neoliberal era, the body itself has become a thoroughly commoditized entity. Perhaps of greater moment, this "multi-sited female-centered commerce . . . in body bits," in the current conjuncture, is held out as signs of autonomy and *choice* (Chavkin and Maher). The ever-increasing, ever more normalized vicious-ness of austerity and privatization create vulnerable subjects—"resource-less women" (Solinger, *Beggars*)—who are compelled to turn over their reproductive capacities to service those who, in comparison, are more economically secure. Pat Brewer reminds us that "in the neoliberal universe, reality itself is simply whatever you can sell. The same sense of fragmented individuals left with nothing but their own capacities for self-marketing echoed on every level of the emerging culture of the time" (8). Commoditization and self-marketing, as Dickenson is quick to point out, was neither inevitable nor is it irreversible: It not only "can be resisted, it is already being resisted in many parts of the world" (vii). However hopeful Dickenson's assessment of the resistance may be, it is certainly the case that traditional forms of political mobilization and resistance are being challenged, even undone or "disarticulated," to use McRobbie's term (*Aftermath* 24).

The Politics of Reproduction

Beyond "the simple facts of pregnancy and birth" (Briggs, *How*)—one aspect of the reproductive labor historically performed by women—*The Politics of Reproduction* is attentive to the complexly intercalated political, symbolic, economic, and ideological connotations of the process. The three narratives about Jane Doe, the Allens and Lius, and Baby Holet's birth mother highlight the construction and reconstruction of pregnancy and motherhood. In each case, we cannot but see pregnancy as a "biosocial experience" and motherhood as a "historically specific set of social practices" (Hartouni 31). The essays in the volume, too, challenge the commonly held belief that reproduction is our most private and intimate activity; they examine, instead, the various ways in which reproduction is "in fact, deeply a matter of public concern . . . subject to considerable regulation" (Joffe and Reich). Reproduction is an economic, social, biological, and now technological phenomenon, with multifaceted personal and social implications and consequences, and the *politics* of reproduction have long been a volatile terrain—not just for feminist analysis. Rickie Solinger, in *Reproductive Politics: What Everyone Needs to Know*, argues that female fertility and its regulatory regimes—laws and policies—"have provided mechanisms for achieving immigration, eugenic, welfare, and adoption goals as well as supporting or hindering women's aspirations for first-class citizenship" (xvii). Though Solinger is describing the state of reproductive politics in the US, her observation is equally, though not identically, applicable to the rest of the world. Female fertility, its regulation, cultural constructions, and economic and political consequences, are all part of what is to be understood by *reproductive politics*.

Around the world, one aspect of reproductive politics in particular—abortion—has remained an "indexical issue" for feminists and the opponents of the right to choose (Barrett and McIntosh 14). Abortion continues to be a touchstone in the battle over rights, agency, bodily integrity, and control. It is on the issue of a woman's right to terminate a pregnancy that we see the state's intervention most clearly. Whether in the global South or in the North, the biosocial ideology of *motherhood*—both that women are *naturally meant* to have children and that it is their religious, national, or familial duty to do so—remains strong, even if the *ideal* reproducing body is a racially restricted one. Women who try to prevent reproduction, either via birth control or abortion, are deemed "unnatural, frivolous, even depraved creatures" as they are perceived to be denying "their destiny as mothers" (Gordon 311). They can be strongly stigmatized as *failures* (Thompson, "Misconceived" 132) and shamed by antiabortion rhetoric (Ludlow). Advances in technology that allow us now to chart the development of the fetus have exacerbated, in part, the instrumental view of women's bodies. The iconography of the "free-floating fetus," aggressively promoted in anti-choice propaganda, especially in the US, has been effective in expunging the pregnant woman and her needs "in favor of the perceived needs of her fetus" (Latimer 319). As such, the concern for the welfare of the fetus legitimizes the close scrutiny, even surveillance, of the pregnant woman's behavior, and not just by medical institutions. The virtual "sonographic fetus" is granted an "independent and natural subjectivity" to the detriment of the pregnant female body, whose only value is now reduced to her function as a carrier (Latimer 319). It ought not to surprise us, then, that birthmothers in commercial surrogacy arrangements are similarly reduced, referred to as "hosts," "environments," and "interchangeable fetal carriers" (Roy, "Foreign" 57).

In the US, the *Roe v. Wade* (1973) decision, which safeguarded abortion access for some women, was immediately followed by lawmakers' serious attempts to curtail or overturn its provisions. The Hyde Amendment (1976), for example, ensured that there would be no universal access to abortion. The enduring support for Hyde (or lack of awareness about it) points to an unwillingness on the part of most Americans to fight on behalf of reproductive equality for Medicaid recipients. Universal access continues to be limited by the subsequent backlash of decisions and policies, including *Webster v. Reproductive Health Services* (1989), *Planned Parenthood v. Casey* (1992), and the recent Targeted Regulation of Abortion Providers ("TRAP") laws. Poor, young, immigrant, and mostly nonwhite women's bodies have become the battleground upon which the state's unremitting interest in denying middle-class (mostly white) women access to reproductive freedom has, since *Roe,* been fought. Policies that restrict women's access to abortion impact first and most powerfully the populations who are the least able to resist them. Numerous

challenges to abortion rights—waiting periods, parental consent or notifica-
tion laws, mandatory counseling or ultrasound policies, and proposed bans
on selective abortions—impact women differently depending on income, age,
geography, race/ethnicity, disability, immigration, and incarceration. If the
long-term goal of conservative lawmakers is to curb middle-class and white
women's access to abortion, their policies are felt most immediately and dev-
astatingly by young women of color living in poverty in the US and, increasingly, globally. Chikako Takeshita reminds us that the Global Gag Rule—that
is, the denial of funding from the US Agency for International Development
(USAID) to nongovernmental organizations (NGOs) that provide abortion
referrals, counseling, or reproductive services—is a clear indication of how
the US's attempt "to restrain abortion, contraception, and women's sexuality
in general, has an impact on women beyond the United States" (Sreenivas,
"Roundtable" 108). As we have already noted, though, governments around
the world restrict access to abortion based on a hegemonic pronatalism that
goes beyond the influence of—or pressure by—the US.

The legalization of abortion in the US sometimes has been blamed for the
shortage of *desirable* (white) babies for adoption domestically. In actual fact, a
constellation of other factors, both domestic and international, prompted middle-class interest in transnational adoption (Briggs, *Somebody's*). Complicated
adoption processes (and conversely, lax regulations elsewhere) are often cited
as salient factors for US couples looking abroad to adopt. But transnational
(and quite often transracial) adoption lays bare the fundamentally unequal
positions of women and provides, as Rickie Solinger argues, a "very accurate
index of the vulnerable status of women in the country of the birthmothers"
(*Beggars* 67). Instead of viewing adoption as a *choice* that birth mothers make
to give up their babies, Solinger urges a focus on the "abject choicelessness
of some resourceless women" (67). International adoption, thus, ought to be
seen as another instance of what Arlie Hochschild terms "care drain" or what
Solinger explains as "the transfer of babies from women of one social classification to women in a higher social classification or group" (67). Adoption,
too, then is no simple desire for family-making and is, instead, a marker of
the vulnerability of some women and the extension of choice for others. The
availability of so-called *surplus babies* ought also to be seen as the end result of
state policies that accelerate the destitution and vulnerability of certain populations, which inevitably undermines the ability of poor and working-class
women to mother their children.

In the US, this "transfer of babies" is facilitated by the unspoken belief that
impoverished women are "too poor to parent" (Burroughs). Thus, mothers
who live in poverty are more susceptible to having their children removed by

the state and placed in foster care even when there are no signs of abuse or intentional neglect. Here, economic class and race intersect, such that African American children in the US are twice as likely as white children to enter the foster care system, and Latino and Native American children are also disproportionately overrepresented. The problem, Dorothy Roberts argues, lies in a system that shows greater interest in child removal over family support. In her analysis of safe haven laws, which encourage birth mothers to surrender newborns without question or penalty, Laury Oaks challenges policies that target young, impoverished (usually nonwhite) pregnant women with messages to surrender the children they are assumed to be incapable of mothering: "We need to place newborn surrender within the context of the unequal support available to women and girls in this country and how we come to think about good mothers versus potentially bad mothers" (3). The work of these scholars turns conventional thinking about adoption on its head to reveal the state-facilitated vulnerability of some birth mothers and overprivileging of certain adoptive families. Trump's State of the Union speech praising Officer Holet and his wife, in effect, *disappeared* the birth mother from his narrative and national consciousness. His focus instead on the Holets' Christian altruism reflects the brutality of the neoliberal state, fused as it is now with neoconservative ideologies, that favors specific forms of family-making (middle class, heteronormative, and two-parent) over protections for the human right to parent and public support for comprehensive addiction treatment.

The terrain of surrogacy economics and politics is just as messy. Commercial surrogacy, which Anne Phillips categorizes as one form of "intimate bodily service" (66), is now a multi-billion-dollar industry of transnational scale. Globalization, new reproductive technologies, and the increasing commoditization of the body (identified by Kimbrell in his 1994 title, *The Human Body Shop*) have made possible types of "newly emergent and highly unequal reproductive exchange" (Rudrappa and Collins 939). And yet, this "ability of the affluent to buy eggs and sperm, to create embryos, rent poor women's wombs, to make babies at a cut rate" (Roy, "Labor" 184) is often rationalized by commissioning parents through "moral frames of compassion and altruism" and characterized as a double gain, "a win-win" for all concerned (Rudrappa and Collins). A closer look reveals, however, that poor women, lacking resources to begin with and made more vulnerable by the programs of neoliberal states, are the providers of bio-materials and of the necessary labor in the reproductive process.

What undergirds this flourishing and mostly unregulated trade in baby-making is the ideology of *familialism*. As Michèle Barrett and Mary McIntosh in their classic *The Anti-Social Family* argued, the "currently dominant model of the family is not time-less and culture-free" (33). Indeed, the family is a historically specific social and economic institution with enduring ideological resonance: "In many ways the institution and the ideology are reciprocally related, enjoying mutual reinforcement" (8). One reason why the institution has proved so durable, they were quick to remind us, is that "the family offers a range of emotional and experiential satisfactions not available elsewhere in the present organization of social relations" (21). Family, thus, is "at one and the same time . . . seen as *naturally* given and as socially and morally desirable. The realm of the 'natural' and the socio-moral are nowhere so constantly merged and confused as in our feelings and thoughts about the family" (26). This condensation of the ideological, social, normative, and *natural* accounts for *baby hunger* experienced by many—perhaps especially by the childless—and fuels the global trade in commercial surrogacy. The technological interventions in the production of the baby hold out the possibility of detecting in the offspring what Barrett and McIntosh call "outward tokens of similarity, familiarity, and belonging" (23). It is surely the strong pull of the biosocially produced idea of kin and family that was the central reason for the Lius' rejection of the nongenetic twin carried by Jessica Allen. The market in bio-materials—the buying of eggs and sperm to make one's *own* baby—paradoxically both undermines and reaffirms the ideological attachment to reproducing *family resemblance*. It may well be that the attachment to the "outward tokens of similarity," now made more negotiable through technology and market forces, encourage some to bypass the option of transnational (transracial) adoption, which appear to challenge the "cultural fetishes of blood and kinship" (Kawash 982).

These new reproductive politics and commerce associated with artificial reproductive technologies (ARTs)—the buying and selling of reproductive materials, for example, as well as access to expensive procedures and treatments—"reflect[] pronounced class- and race-based inequalities" and provide "a prime example of stratified reproduction" (Inhorn and Birenbaum-Carmeli 179). In reviewing the scholarship on the effects of ARTs on social life, Inhorn and Birenbaum-Carmeli concluded that "technologically assisted reproduction is largely restricted to global elites, whereas the infertile poor, who are at the highest risk of infertility, are devalued and even despised as reproducers" (179). Equally troubling are the ethical issues surrounding the expectation of perfectibility that have arisen with the advent of prenatal and genetic testing, fetal screening, and buying eggs and biological materials to correct or eliminate the possibility of perceived imperfections (Rothschild). Concern over what has been called *neo-eugenics* has arisen in relation not only to the creation of so-called *designer babies* but also the suppression of the rights of nonwhite and poor women to have children. In her introduction to a *Frontiers* special issue on reproductive justice, Mytheli Sreenivas reminds feminists that "whether 'old' or 'new,' there is no automatic trajectory—either progressive or regressive—between reproductive technology and struggles for reproductive justice" (Introduction vii).

The concept of reproductive justice informs much of the work in *The Politics of Reproduction.* Since the late 1980s, the reproductive justice movement has challenged the normalization of stratified reproduction. An activist movement arising from a coalition of organizations concerned by the unavailability of healthcare in communities of color (African American, Latina, indigenous, and Asian), reproductive justice decenters middle-class and white norms informing traditional campaigns for birth control and abortion access. The movement is grounded in an awareness of historical race-based oppressions—including forced childbearing, sterilization abuse, denial of parenting rights, eugenics, medical abuses, and environmental threats—and advocates for policies that both enhance access to birth control *and* prioritize life within oppressed communities. According to Ross and Solinger, the movement is guided by three tenets: "the human right to not have a child, the human right to have a child, and the human right to parent children in safe and healthy environments" (169). Elsewhere, Ross places the reproductive justice movement squarely within the campaign for human rights by reminding feminists that intersectionality—the recognition of our different locations within interlocking oppressive systems—is not an end in itself and, instead, "is a process; human rights is the goal" (Ross et al. 14).

Yet another approach to redress reproductive injustice is reflected in Martha Fineman's notion of *vulnerability* as an alternative to the thinking about "traditional equal protection analysis." The concept of vulnerability focuses not only "on discrimination against defined groups, but [is] concerned with privilege and favor conferred on limited segments of the population by the state and broader society through their institutions." This approach, she argues, "has the potential to move us beyond the stifling confines of current discrimination-based models towards a more substantive version of equality."

No Choice Other Than to Understand Ourselves as Choosing

The first two decades of the twenty-first century have witnessed intensified interest in definitions and understandings of reproduction in the US and around the world. Much less discussed, however, have been those narratives that problematize the normalized scripts of reproductive desire, choice-making, and creation of families. In their useful introduction, Joffe and Reich reassert the core feminist belief that control of their fertility is "essential for women to gain full citizenship, and to be able to participate in 'public' as well as private life" (3). While they are right to cast the tension as between "women's own desires regarding reproduction and the demands of the nation state" (3), we wish to broaden the analytical frame of reproductive politics to include the complex dynamics of desire and choice and to scrutinize the often unnamed ideology of pronatalism. Furthermore, a closer, critical look reveals the division of labor that separates those who desire and those who are instrumental in satisfying such desires.

The obvious target—and justifiably so—of feminist critiques has often been state regulations of reproduction; however, we might also look to how regulation and incitement of reproductive desire has been internalized and the social mechanisms that have accomplished this turn. The unquestioned hegemony of pronatalism, which recasts the human decision to have children as a biological imperative, has long stymied inquiry into this presumed natural yearning for families of genetically related children. So deep is this ideological investment that we struggle to identify who is allowed to yearn, whose desires are condemned, and how the absence of such desires is demonized as unnatural. We must investigate the social and ideological frames within which such aspirations are formulated. This collection of essays considers how, in the rush to fulfill reproductive desires, exploitation is rebranded as empowerment, desperation is presented as choice. We must undertake this investigation, for, as Solinger has argued, neoliberal representations of women as empowered reproductive choice-making *consumers* obscure the lack of protections for women's reproductive health and rights as full *citizens* (*Beggars*).

Our aim in this anthology is to explore legal, ideological, social, cultural, and economic grounds upon which the concept of *reproductive choice* is constructed. A lot of feminist work has gone into promoting *choice* in terms of abortion, availability of birth control, family planning measures, and so on. Furthermore, Rayna Rapp reminds us, women must now add to this list *unwanted choices* as a result of new technologies such as genetic testing and fetal surgery. In *The Politics of Reproduction* we are interested in the less obvious, perhaps more treacherous, construction of choice into moral categories of good, bad, dangerous, and outside the pale. The essays that make up this collection all pay close attention not only to the construction of the moral categories within which women's choices are evaluated but also to the very real consequences to (actual) women's lives. The essays are also attentive to the invasion of the logic and language of the marketplace into the very idea of choice-making.

"What happens," Solinger pointedly asks, "when the special guarantee for all women—the promise that all women can decide for themselves whether and when to be mothers—is expressed by the individualistic, market-place term 'choice?'" (*Beggars* 6). Solinger's connection of *choice* to the marketplace leads us inevitably back to the economic and political restructuring of neoliberalism. As individuals are encouraged, when not forced, to self-regulate under neoliberal regimes, the consequences of the unavailability of social benefits like healthcare, housing, and childcare may appear to originate in individual *bad* decisions. Disciplined by an aversion to "mismanaged life" (Brown, *Edgework* 42), the neoliberal subject is hailed as an entrepreneurial actor, who reflects what Denbow calls "*proper* self-governance" (3). An older understanding of the concept of autonomy, *proper* self-governance, she argues, reflects alignment with existing social norms; failure to successfully align oneself "demonstrates that one is not deciding rationally" (3).

Bad choice-maker is not a harmless label; in fact, it signals consequential social significance. On the level of social policy, it is used to explain away and even justify inequity. Indeed, Brewer remarks that in the current conjuncture, "systematic inequality and an accumulation of disadvantages are presented as the consequences of individual choice or lack of diligent application" (8). The belief that inequality is better understood as a question of moral fiber, rationality, and personal responsibility has been successfully promoted by various entities—media, right-wing think tanks, politicians, public intellectuals—in defense of "a whole raft of policies designed to improve the conduct of persons and supplant welfare regimes" (McRobbie, "Reflections" 63). The belief that every woman is an independent agent making free choices mistakes the conditions for and qualities of real freedom, and "it becomes difficult to recognize limitations on the reproductive 'choices' of nonwhite and low-income/poor women and easier to mistake the women themselves as 'bad choice'-makers" (Thompson, "Juno" 167). Trump's State of the Union address, for example, made no mention of the coercive context in which the birth mother of baby Holet, caught with narcotics by a police officer, made her *choice* to surrender her baby. Trump's account sought instead to present an oversimplified parable of a *bad* mother who tacitly redeemed herself by surrendering her baby to a *good* family.

As noted above, the reproductive justice movement has exposed *choice* as, at best, a flimsy concept when compared to an ethics of *justice* that accounts for women's different sociohistorical locations. Without economic, social, and political restructuring, as Solinger concludes, *choice* is "a hollowed out promise" (*Beggars* 11) and "a remarkably unstable, undependable foundation for guaranteeing women's control over their own bodies, their reproductive lives, their motherhood, and ultimately their status as full citizens" (7).

Contrasted with *bad* choice-makers, those women who make *good* choices—specifically good *reproductive* choices—are celebrated as symbols of the freedom promised by neoliberal regimes. As McRobbie observes, however, a *good* choice-maker identifies as an entrepreneurial individual who, in order to claim the promise of freedom, must disavow feminism and collective political organizing (*Aftermath*). Rather than resisting structural oppression and the incitement to choose, this woman must identify reproductive choices—her own as well as others'—as either the reflections of freedom or the "failure to navigate the impediments to prosperity" (Brown, *Edgework*). The essays in this volume interrogate women's experiences of this neoliberal paradox succinctly defined by David Harvey: We have no choice but to think of ourselves as making choices. These nonchoices, this collection suggests, threatens to redefine our very understanding of freedom.

The essays in *The Politics of Reproduction,* therefore, renew the call for a feminist coalitional vision—one that recognizes our differences as well as our accountability to each other. They call for a more responsive and responsible state, one that provides regulation and the return of a social safety net. These essays reject the facile replacement of *citizen* with *consumer* in our public sphere. Finally, these essays argue for the recognition and protection of all women's bodily sovereignty and humanity.

This Volume

We began this introduction with three vignettes that highlight the differential impact of the technologies, ideologies, policies, and practices of reproductive politics on women. These are the overarching concerns of this volume as a whole, as it also pays attention to the asymmetrical effects of neoliberalism's rearticulation of both the public and the private. We trace the fallout—not just in the US but also in various parts of the world—to make visible neoliberalism's deployment of the discourse of choice, which, in point of fact, exploits as it also obscures, the vulnerability of some women and the privilege of others. An early (but ultimately discarded) title of our project—*Mad, Bad, and Dangerous*—referred to this collection's awareness of the social *construction* and *reconstruction* of women's vulnerabilities as moral categories, always already appalling and wrong.

The Politics of Reproduction uniquely brings together abortion, surrogacy, and adoption as sites that need to be considered as a whole. In one sense, these concerns are related in very literal ways: Policies discouraging abortion seek to encourage adoption; the desire for genetically related children, however, promotes surrogacy over adoption; the by-products of the surrogacy process often result in abortion; abortion is credited—accurately or not—with decreasing the number of desirable white babies available for adoption, which drives the surrogacy market; and so on. But our interest lies in the connections that are less tangible. We focus on these issues because they reflect new ways of constructing family and changing definitions of motherhood in an era of expanding reproductive freedoms and choices that are available, particularly to women. And yet, even as these sites reflect some women's amplified options, they also indicate other women's unvoiced desperation and coercion. Taken together, abortion, adoption, and surrogacy point to larger questions about shifts in global economies, political life, our gendered and raced vulnerabilities, the ways we make and understand family, enduring feminist challenges, and our accountability to each other when our world invites us to reject difference and misidentifies the threats to our safety and existence.

The entangled politics of adoption, abortion, and surrogacy are global in scope. The essays in this collection reflect a particular, although not exclusive, focus on the Americas, but the economies and intimacies that have been rescripted by neoliberalism include—perhaps even more visibly—the geopolitics of African and Asian countries. In Nigeria, for example, *child harvesting* and *baby factories/farms* are proliferating. These illegal institutions, where unmarried pregnant women—mostly young and often rape survivors—are promised medical care only to have their infants taken from them, supply the black market in adoption. Some mothers and children are trafficked, while babies are adopted by international families (often from the UK) who are attracted by lower black market prices (Makinde). Furthermore, a 2018 issue of *The Nation* reports how the US international adoption market—"one of the most unregulated industries in America today" (Cavell 13)—in part drives fraudulent international adoption agencies. Believing that they are merely agreeing to have their children's educations sponsored, Ugandan mothers—most of whom do not speak or read English—discover they have been tricked into signing over their parental rights to their children. Adoptive families in the global North adopt *paper orphans* (children who have biological parents—usually mothers) whom they fight to retain using any first-world means available to them. In Asia, the problem is more visibly with commercial surrogacy. Dubbed "the womb of Asia," for example, Thailand, until 2015—when it banned international commercial surrogacy—was a prime market for Australian prospective parents. The well-known incident involving Baby Gammy in 2014—a case in which Australian prospective parents rejected a child with Down syndrome who was carried by a Thai surrogate—pointed to unanticipated problems with new technologies and laws that have the power to redefine motherhood and parental rights.

The Politics of Reproduction reflects this pattern of privileged women and families (primarily from the global North) having their reproductive desires fulfilled by less privileged women (primarily in the global South), who make their reproductive decisions under harsh socioeconomic conditions. The constellations of countries shift at each instantiation, but the dynamic of desperate *choice* and disavowed accountability remains constant.

The essays in this volume reflect the many academic fields where feminists have sought to question the hegemony of neoliberalism. They are drawn from a wide range of disciplinary and theoretical perspectives and are attentive to the historical, cultural, and ideological conjunctures of reproductive politics. *The Politics of Reproduction* reflects the work of legal scholars, medical anthropologists, as well as literary and cultural critics who examine the normalization of power via cultural forms. This blend of interdisciplinary work is called for, as feminist scholars seek to get their arms around the new and pervasive challenges that neoliberalism poses to women.

We have refrained from dividing the essays into sections or even categorizing them in any way. Instead, we have loosely paired the essays based on their investigations of similar issues. It is our hope that, read together and without additional categorization, the essays will clearly, for the reader, reach across these assemblages to each other as we see them doing.

The Essays

The first two essays in the collection consider how the demands of neoliberalism, wedded with conservative values, cast nonnuclear family structures as *illegitimate* and a danger to the social order—rather than seeing them as *endangered by* the ideology of patriarchal familialism. In her close reading of Jesmyn Ward's acclaimed Katrina novel, *Salvage the Bones,* Mary Thompson analyzes Ward's depiction of the racialized biopolitics that shape access to birth control and abortion. Black women, the novel reveals, are denied access to abortion but are condemned or penalized for having children to whom the state might have obligations. Thompson examines the stigmatization of unwed, teenage African American sexuality and reproduction to reveal the neoliberal state's abdication of responsibility to its most vulnerable members: children of color living in poverty. These are the very children that Valerie Stein argues are of particular interest to evangelical religious groups. Stein considers how the children of single mothers, deemed *fatherless,* are targeted

by the evangelical orphan care movement in their promotion of transnational adoption. The movement's interest in the *rescue* of so-called fatherless
orphans, she shows, is not only in service to the preservation of heteronormative family structure; as she also argues, it privileges the needs of adoptive families over those of birth families. We must, as Stein maintains, ask
ourselves the question, "Whose interests are being served and promoted by
the claim of a biblical mandate for adoption?" And further, "What economic,
political, and social agendas are linked with the rise of the evangelical orphan
care movement?" One of the outcomes of following the biblical mandate is the
transfer of children via adoption from the socially vulnerable to the economically privileged. As other essays in the volume do, Thompson and Stein illustrate well the rise under neoliberalism of *private* solutions to *social* problems.

A second pairing of essays reflects Appadurai's idea of "flow," specifically
in the case of reproductive tourism in Mexico. In her analysis of pre-2016
Mexican surrogacy websites advertising to a US clientele of gay prospective
parents, Heather Mooney examines how these sites appeal to their audience
through the rhetoric of choice, ease, and inclusivity of "all families" while rendering Latina surrogates invisible: "Though camouflaged by the intersecting
neoliberal discourses of volunteerism, choice, and commerce," Mooney writes,
"a clearer vision of a raced future emerges when looking across different formations of racialized labor and transnational flows of bodies, body parts, and
capital." While Mooney's essay considers the "flow" of desire for children from
the US to Mexico, Rosalynn Vega weighs the unintended impact in Mexico
of reproductive tourists' dollars on the economy of midwifery. Drawing on
twenty-eight months of research across thirteen Mexican states, Vega analyzes
how "the emergence of Seguro Popular [Mexico's universal health insurance]
has inadvertently rendered midwifery difficult to practice and inaccessible to
women who do not purchase medical services in the private health sector."
Furthermore, her analysis reveals that "midwives are forced to choose between
economic insolvency or selling their services to affluent Mexicans and reproductive travelers seeking *humanized birth*" in the private sphere. These essays
ask us to recognize the deleterious if sometimes hidden consequences of
reproductive tourism that is nonetheless marketed via the rhetoric of *helping*
local economies, impoverished women, and childless couples.

Another pair of essays does important work in analyzing the role cultural
representations play in normalizing power. In their essays, Zarena Aslami and
Diana York Blaine analyze contemporary narratives that reflect the shift to a
cultural regime of what Lauren Berlant called "public intimacies." It is through
the loss of a political public sphere that we now understand our freedom in
terms of the once-private choices we make about sexuality, reproduction, and

family-making. Aslami's essay explores the residual anxiety produced by the contradiction inherent in choice under neoliberalism. Returning to Lisa Belkin's inflammatory 2003 *New York Times Magazine* essay, "The Opt-Out Revolution," Aslami argues, "The women who quit fast-track jobs cast their decision to leave as choice rather than as being an overdetermined bid to save aspects of their lives for which they felt solely responsible." She concludes that the women who opted out demonstrated that "they had *no choice* other than to think of themselves as taking an option. To admit otherwise, and maintain their sense of self, would be unthinkable." Blaine's essay expands the historical scope to our understanding of neoliberalism by considering the twenty-five-year span separating the teen-pregnancy dramas *Fast Times at Ridgemont High* (1982) and *Juno* (2007). Her essay reflects upon the erosion the of public sphere and the normalization of neoliberal values. How is it, she asks, that the tacit acceptance of abortion in *Fast Times* has been replaced by *Juno*'s dramatized rejection of abortion in favor of having her baby adopted by "the lovely couple"?

Many essays in this volume point to the rhetoric of choice's role in obfuscating biopolitics and, specifically, the specter of eugenics. Two essays, in particular, highlight the conflicted and entwined technologies and politics of reproduction and neo-eugenics, which we understand to mean not only human enhancement but also regulated populations. In her essay recounting the forced sterilization of thousands of indigenous and poor Peruvian women under the auspices of the Reproductive Health and Family Planning Program—an allegedly *progressive* social policy promoted by President Fujimoro as empowering women—Julieta Chaparro-Buitrago considers how even blatant examples of eugenics are authorized by the powerful and powerfully alluring discourse of *choice* under neoliberalism. The racial logic beneath a state-sponsored sterilization program, analyzed by Chaparro-Buitrago, takes on new significance when read alongside of Karen Weingarten's exploration of the abortion debate within feminism and disabilities studies. Weingarten's close reading of Emily Rapp's 2013 memoir *Still Point of the Turning World* provides a focal point for her discussion of "how intersected women's reproductive lives are with fears about disability." Weingarten surveys how eugenics haunts the politics of abortion and disability by juxtaposing the 2016 Zika virus outbreak in South America with the introduction in the same year of legislation in Indiana "forbidding abortion in cases where a fetus was diagnosed with a disability."

Two additional essays explore how social service and healthcare workers navigate, negotiate, and disseminate neoliberal values about family-making.

Melissa Hardesty's essay examines the role of social workers in normalizing the economics of adoption and allaying the anxiety produced by the perceptions of "paying for babies." Starting with Elisabeth Landes and Richard Posner's polemical "Economics of the Baby Shortage" (1978) and Viviana Zelizer's *Pricing the Priceless Child* (1985), Hardesty extends the analysis of adoption to its economic implications. By contrasting private and agency-based national and international adoptions with foster care adoption, Hardesty probes the anxiety produced by the obvious role wealth plays in adoption and the function of social workers in that process. Healthcare workers in Oaxaca, Mexico, on the other hand, must mediate between the interests of the state and the desires of their clients. Rebecca Howes-Mischel's essay attends to healthcare workers who, under Seguro Popular, encourage rural and indigenous Oaxacan women to limit their childbearing. Howes-Mischel reveals, through her fieldwork, how nurses and doctors are enlisted in the deployment of the concept of *choice* in service to state-sponsored family planning programs. Her analysis questions the "promotion of consumer choice-making as feminist aspiration" and concludes that "an *incitement* to choose does not always accompany the *ability* to choose."

Finally, although each essay in this collection is sensitive to the precarious and vulnerable positions of women under neoliberalism, the final two essays of this collection trace the contours of this vulnerability as depicted in fiction and as lived through law. Rachel Fenton provides an important application of Martha Fineman's theory of "vulnerability" to laws governing (or failing to govern) transnational surrogacy. Agreeing with Fineman that "an adherence to formal equality has seemingly eclipsed our moral and political aspirations for *social justice*," Fenton explores what "aspirational social justice and well-being might look like in the context of ARTs." While Fenton's essay proffers the promise of remedy, Modhumita Roy's essay exposes its dire need. Roy's essay takes up the idea of *precarity*—a term which, as Tavia Nyong'o has rightly noted, has seen a "sudden acceleration" in academic writing. Keeping in mind, Nyong'o's justifiable worry that the overuse of this term threatens to generalize precarity as ubiquitous and therefore an undifferentiated human condition, Roy reads Michael Robotham's thriller *The Night Ferry* (2007) as a vivid instantiation of the production of vulnerable subjects via war (Afghanistan) and displacement. The novel skillfully links the *precarity* of abject lives to the exploitative violence of reproductive labor (surrogacy), which then is connected to *baby hunger*—that is, the desire for genetically related offspring in the making of a *normal* family life.

Works Cited

Appadurai, Arjun. *Globalization*. Duke University Press, 2001.

Barrett, Michèle, and Mary McIntosh. *The Anti-Social Family*. Verso Books, 1982.

Brewer, Pat. Introduction. *The Origin of the Family, Private Property and the State,* by Frederick Engels, Revolution Books, 2004, pp. 7–23.

Briggs, Laura. "Foreign and Domestic: Adoption, Immigration, and Privatization." *Intimate Labors: Culture, Technologies and the Politics of Care,* edited by Eileen Boris and Rhacel Salazar Parreñas, Stanford University Press, 2010, pp. 49–62.

———. *How All Politics Became Reproductive Politics: From Welfare Reform to Foreclosure to Trump*. University of California Press, 2017.

———. "Reproductive Technology: Of Labor and Markets." *Feminist Studies,* vol. 36, no. 2, Summer 2010, pp. 359–74.

———. *Somebody's Children: The Politics of Transracial and Transnational Adoption*. Duke University Press, 2012.

Brown, Wendy. *Edgework: Critical Essays on Knowledge and Politics*. Princeton University Press, 2005.

———. *Undoing the Demos: Neoliberalism's Stealth Revolution*. Zone Books, 2015.

Burroughs, Gaylynn. "Too Poor to Parent?" *Ms. Magazine,* Spring 2008, www.msmagazine.com/spring2008/tooPoorToParent.asp.

Butler, Judith. "Performativity, Precarity, and Sexual Politics." *Revista de Antropología Iberoamericana,* vol. 4, no. 3, September–December 2009, pp. i–xiii.

Cavell, Anna. "'Those Kids Are No Longer Yours': How Parents in Uganda Lose Their Babies to Adoptive Families in America" *The Nation,* vol. 5, no. 11, November 5, 2018, pp. 12–17.

Chappell, Bill. "Jane Doe Has An Abortion in Texas after Battle with Trump Administration." *The Two-Way,* NPR, 25 Oct. 2017, www.npr.org/sections/thetwo-way/2017/10/25/560013894/jane-doe-has-abortion-in-texas-after-battle-with-trump-administration.

Chavkin, Wendy, and JaneMaree Maher, editors. *The Globalization of Motherhood: Deconstructions of Biology and Care*. Routledge Press, 2010.

Colen, Shellee. "Like a Mother to Them: Stratified Reproduction and West Indian Childcare Workers and Employers in New York." *Conceiving the New World Order: The Global Politics of Reproduction,* edited by Faye Ginsburg and Rayna Rapp, University of California Press, 1995, pp. 78–102.

Cooper, Melinda. *Family Values: Between Neoliberalism and the New Social Conservatism*. Zone Books, 2017.

Davies, William. "Against Responsibility." *London Review of Books,* vol. 28, no. 21, 8 Nov. 2018, pp. 28–30.

Denbow, Jennifer. *Governed through Choice: Autonomy, Technology, and the Politics of Reproduction*. New York University Press, 2015.

Dickenson, Donna. *Body Shopping. Converting Body Parts to Profit*. One World Publications, 2008.

Duggan, Lisa. *The Twilight of Equality? Neoliberalism, Cultural Politics, and the Attack on Democracy*. Beacon Press, 2003.

Fineman, Martha. "The Vulnerable Subject: Anchoring Equality in the Human Condition." *Yale Journal of Law and Feminism,* vol. 20, no. 1, 2008, article 2, digitalcommons.law.yale.edu/yjlf/vol20/iss1/2/.

Glenn, Evelyn Nakano. "Caring and Inequality." *Women's Labor in the Global Economy: Speaking in Multiple Voices,* edited by Sharon Harley, Rutgers University Press, 2007, pp. 46–61.

Ghosh, Jayati. *Never Done and Poorly Paid: Women's Work in Globalizing India.* Women Unlimited, 2009.

Gordon, Linda. "Fetal Politics." *History Workshop Journal,* vol. 73, no. 1, 2012, pp. 309–17.

Graeber, David. "Neoliberalism, or the Bureaucratization of the World." *The Insecure American: How We Got Here and What We Should Do about It,* edited by Hugh Gusterson and C. Besteman, University of California Press, 2010, pp. 79–96.

Hartouni, Valerie. *Cultural Conceptions: On Reproductive Technologies and the Making of Life.* Minnesota University Press, 1997.

Harvey, David. "The 'New' Imperialism: Accumulation by Dispossession." *Socialist Register,* vol. 40, 2004, www.socialistregister.com/index.php/srv/article/view/5811.

Hochschild, Arlie Russel. *The Commercialization of Intimate Life. Notes from Home and Work.* University of California Press, 2003.

Inhorn, Marcia, and Daphna Birenbaum-Carmeli. "Assisted Reproductive Technologies and Culture Change." *Annual Review of Anthropology,* vol. 37, 2008, pp. 177–96.

Joffe, Carole, and Jennifer Reich. *Reproduction and Society: Interdisciplinary Readings.* Routledge Press, 2015.

Kabeer, Naila. *Reversed Realities: Gender Hierarchies in Development Thought.* Verso, 1994.

Katz, Cindi, and Nancy Miller. "Editor's Note." *The Global and the Intimate,* special issue of *Women's Studies Quarterly,* vol. 34, no. 1/2, Spring/Summer 2006, pp. 11–12.

Kawash, Samira. "New Directions in Motherhood Studies." *Signs,* vol. 36, no. 4, 2011, pp. 969–1003.

Kimbrell, Andrew. *The Human Body Shop: The Engineering and Marketing of Life.* Harper Collins, 1994.

Latimer, Heather. "Reproductive Technologies, Fetal Icons, and Genetic Freaks: Shelley Jackson's *Patchwork Girl* and the Limits and Possibilities of Donna Haraway's Cyborg." *Modern Fiction Studies,* vol. 57, no. 2, Summer 2011, pp. 318–35.

Ludlow, Jeannie. "Love and Goodness: Toward a New Abortion Politics." *Feminist Studies,* vol. 38, no. 2, 2012, pp. 474–83.

Makinde, Olusesan Ayeodeji, et. al. "Baby Factories Taint Surrogacy in Nigeria." *Reproductive BioMedicine Online,* vol. 32, no. 1, Jan. 2016, pp. 6–8.

McRobbie, Angela. *The Aftermath of Feminism: Gender, Culture, and Social Change.* Sage Press, 2009.

———. "Reflections on Feminism, Immaterial Labour and the Post-Fordist Regime." *New Formations,* vol. 70, no. 4, 2010, pp. 60–76.

Nixon, Rob. *Slow Violence and the Environmentalism of the Poor.* Harvard University Press, 2011.

Oaks, Laury. *Giving Up Baby: Safe Haven Laws, Motherhood, and Reproductive Justice.* New York University Press, 2015.

Parreñas, Rhacel Salazar. *Servants of Globalization: Women, Migration, and Domestic Work.* Stanford University Press, 2001.

Phillips, Anne. *Our Bodies. Whose Property?* Princeton University Press, 2013.

Rapp, Rayna. *Testing Women, Testing the Fetus: The Social Impact of Amniocentesis.* Routledge, 1999.

Rich, Adrienne. "Conditions for Work: The Common World of Women." Foreword. *Working It Out: 23 Women Writers, Artists, Scientists, and Scholars Talk about Their Lives and Work,* edited by Sara Ruddick and Pamela Daniels, Pantheon, 1977, pp. xiii–xxiv.

Ridley, Jane. "I Rented Out My Womb, and They Almost Took My Own Son." *The New York Post,* 25 Oct. 2017, nypost.com/2017/10/25/i-rented-out-my-womb-and-they-took-my-own-son/.

Roberts, Dorothy. *Shattered Bonds: The Color of Child Welfare.* Basic Civitas Books, 2002.

Ross, Loretta, et al. *Radical Reproductive Justice: Foundations, Theory, Practice, Critique.* The Feminist Press, 2017.

Ross, Loretta, and Rickie Solinger. *Reproductive Justice: An Introduction.* University of California Press, 2017.

Rothschild, Joan. *The Dream of the Perfect Child.* Indiana University Press, 2005.

Roy, Modhumita. "Foreign Babies/Indian Make: Outsourcing Reproduction in the Age of Globalization." *Locating Cultural Change: Theory, Method, Process,* edited by Partha Pratim Basu and Ipshita Chanda, SAGE India, 2011, pp. 54–72.

———. "Labor Pains: 'Nannygate,' Undocumented Workers and the Social Cost of Mothering in Contemporary Cultural Texts." *Mothers and the Economy: The Economics of Mothering,* special issue of *Journal of the Motherhood Initiative for Research and Community Involvement,* vol. 3, no. 1, Spring/Summer 2012, pp. 182–202.

Rudrappa, Sharmila, and Caitlyn Collins. "Altruistic Agencies and Compassionate Consumers: Moral Framing of Transnational Surrogacy." *Gender & Society,* vol. 29, no. 6, 2015, pp. 937–59.

Sassen, Saskia. "Women's Burden: Counter Geographies of Globalization and the Feminization of Survival." *Journal of International Affairs,* vol. 53, no. 2, Spring 2000, pp. 503–24.

Shenk, Timothy. "What Exactly Is Neoliberalism? Interview with Wendy Brown." *Dissent,* 2 Apr. 2015. www.dissentmagazine.org/blog/booked-3-what-exactly-is-neoliberalism-wendy-brown-undoing-the-demos.

Solinger, Rickie. *Beggars and Choosers: How the Politics of Choice Shapes Adoption, Abortion, and Welfare in the United States.* Hill and Wang, 2001.

———. *Reproductive Politics: What Everyone Needs to Know.* Oxford University Press, 2013.

Sreenivas, Mytheli. Introduction. *Reproductive Technologies and Reproductive Justice,* special issue of *Frontiers: A Journal of Women's Studies,* vol. 34, no. 3, 2013, pp. vii–xiv.

———. "Roundtable: Laura Briggs, Faye Ginsburg, Elena Guitierrez, Rosalind Petchesky, Rayna Rapp, Andrea Smith, and Chikako Takeshita." *Reproductive Technologies and Reproductive Justice,* special issue of *Frontiers: A Journal of Women's Studies,* vol. 34, no. 3, 2013, pp. 102–25.

Thompson, Mary. "Juno or Just Another Girl?: Young Breeders and a New Century of Racial Politics of Motherhood." *Twenty-First-Century Motherhood: Experienced, Identity, Policy, and Agency,* edited by Andrea O'Reilly, Columbia University Press, 2010, 158–69.

———. "Misconceived Metaphors: Irene Vilar's *Impossible Motherhood: Testimony of an Abortion Addict.*" *Frontiers: A Journal of Women's Studies,* vol. 35, no. 1, 2014, pp. 132–59.

Wang, Amy. "Surrogate Mother Forced to Give Away Own Child after Surprise Twin Pregnancy." *The Independent,* 3 Nov. 2017, www.independent.co.uk/news/world/americas/surrogate-mother-pregnant-twins-own-baby-jessica-allen-omega-family-global-san-diego-a8034901.html.

CHAPTER 1

Precarity and Disaster in Jesmyn Ward's *Salvage the Bones*

A Reproductive Justice Reading

MARY THOMPSON

IN 2005, the effects of Hurricane Katrina, compounded with an inadequate federal response, devastated African American communities along the Gulf Coast and specifically in New Orleans, prompting a strong outcry from black leaders.[1] The antiabortion movement, which is dominated by white religious groups, has for more than a decade appropriated African American politics to malign abortion, but its theft of this particular tragedy was striking. In the weeks following August 2005, antiabortion groups alleged that satellite pictures of Katrina resembled ultrasound images of the fetus in utero, and, according to Carole Sanger, they claimed that the hurricane reflected divine punishment for US abortion-friendly policy. This outrageous claim can be seen as part of a pattern of racialized appropriations. As Laurel Raymond of the online news site *Think Progress* documents, abortion opponents have for many years sought to link slavery and abortion (calling it "black genocide"), recast Margaret Sanger as a racist,[2] referred to abortions as "womb lynchings," and sponsored Southern billboards that read, "The most dangerous place for

I would like to thank my department writing group—David Babcock, Allison Fagan, Mollie Godfrey, Dawn Goode, Dennis Lo, and Sofia Samatar—for feedback on a version of this essay.

1. See Sandalow.

2. Dorothy Roberts's *Killing the Black Body* provides a nuanced discussion of Sanger's adherence to eugenics and the absence of racist ideologies in her writings. Loretta Ross similarly defends Sanger against charges of reproductive racism ("Trust Black Women").

an African American is in the womb." More recently, they have launched a campaign for #UnbornLivesMatter, mimicking the Black Lives Matter movement and deflecting its critique of police violence. Despite professing the desire to "protect . . . black life," Raymond notes, these groups remain shamefully mute on black women's historical lack of reproductive control and on violence against black women and children. Meanwhile, these same groups urge policymakers to defund Planned Parenthood even as African American rates of unplanned pregnancy remain higher than white rates.[3] Reproductive justice and human rights activist and scholar Loretta Ross contends that the motivation behind the stated interest in "protecting black life" by abortion opponents is the goal of curbing *all* women's reproductive freedom. "It is about re-enslaving Black women," she remarks, "by making us breeders for someone else's cause" ("Re-Enslaving").

Salvage the Bones, Jesmyn Ward's acclaimed 2011 Katrina novel, explores reproductive precarity and the threat of "re-enslavement" under a neoliberal state that is alternately indifferent and hostile to the lives of poor, rural African Americans. Set on the Gulf Coast of Mississippi as Katrina approaches, *Salvage the Bones* tells the story of Esch Batiste, a fifteen-year-old African American girl who discovers she is pregnant. Esch, whose mother has died prior to the novel's action, prepares for Katrina's onslaught with her older brothers Randall and Skeetah, their younger brother Junior, and their alcoholic father in The Pit, their maternal family's ransacked land in the heart of Bois Sauvage. *Salvage the Bones* explores the neoliberal racialized biopolitics of Esch's pregnancy through imagery of Katrina bearing down on the coast (as a woman might in childbirth) and the metaphors of storms, natural/national disasters, and Mother Nature. In place of her mother, Esch derives courage from the maternal figure of China, her brother's pure white pit bull whose labor as both fighter and breeder helps to support the family. Through this affiliation, the novel rehabilitates ("salvages") and rehumanizes the concept of the *bitch* for Esch as a badge of black maternal empowerment. What follows is a consideration of neoliberalism and the controlling images of black women's reproductivity, leading to an analysis of the novel's symbolic juxtaposition of China's whiteness and Esch's blackness as a comment on racially stratified reproduction. Within this framework, the novel's triumph is the humanizing

---

3. Abortion rates for African American women are disproportionately higher than rates for white women (who nevertheless procure the greater number of abortions), and this statistic reflects higher rates of unplanned pregnancy for black women (double the rate of white women), which, as Susan Cohen points out, arise from poor access to birth control.

of Esch despite a preponderance of dehumanizing stereotypes about pregnant black teens.[4]

Salvage the Bones and Biopolitics

Biopolitics, as Foucault introduced the term, describes the infusion of social power into biological processes, the end result of which is the regulation of populations. Pregnancy and childbirth are still thought to be among the most natural of human actions; however, as many feminists have sought to show, it remains highly constructed and contested cultural terrain. *Who* is authorized to reproduce—*when* and *with whom*—and who is condemned for reproducing reflect biopolitical operations that are obscured by the language of *choice*. Neoliberalism promises the expansion of reproductive choice for women, but its reality reflects stratified reproduction—greater choice for already privileged women and desperate nonchoices for women on the social margins.

As the introduction to this collection of essays shows, neoliberalism is an economic and political theory that discourages reliance on the state and encourages individual entrepreneurial agency. It fosters stratified reproduction through what historian Rickie Solinger calls a new morality of "good and bad choice-makers" (7) that promotes self-sufficient motherhood and discourages state-dependent motherhood. These categories of *good* discipline and of alleged *bad* mismanagement rely on the demonized figure of the pregnant black teen as a *natural/national disaster*. In the cultural imaginary, negative representations of African American women and mothers have historically included the hypersexual jezebel, the lazy welfare queen, and the *breeder*—the woman who reproduces with animalistic indifference and equal disregard for both social mores and her resulting offspring. These pejorative figures—what Hill Collins refers to as "controlling images" (76)—have been deployed throughout policy debates and cultural representations and serve as cautionary, disciplinary tales to all women.[5] The pregnant (black) teen *breeder* is expected to fail at parenting, to be a drain on social resources, and through her sexual *excesses*, to overrely on abortion as *a form of birth control*. In opposition to this image, *good* choice makers—the "top girls," as McRobbie names

---

4. Glenn Jellenik has argued that the novel abstains from polemic, proffering instead a "universal" story and eliciting a compassionate response from its audience (221). I disagree and argue for a reading of the intersectional biopolitics of race, poverty, and gender. Contrary to Jellenik's assertion, the novel's "universal" appeal rests in the specificity of Esch's racial and gender identity and her resistance to dehumanizing stereotypes.

5. Dorothy Roberts's *Killing the Black Body* provides a discussion of how controlling images of nonwhite women are deployed in the disciplining of all US women's reproduction.

middle-class, twenty-something, mostly white women (54)—obtain *good* abortions that are defensible because they reflect and enable a lack of reliance on the neoliberal state.

When asked about contemporary media such as *16 and Pregnant* and the portrayal of teen mothers as simultaneously vilified and celebritized, Ward observed, "The figure of the black teen mother continues to loom large in our public consciousness, and we're not willing to speak about the ethnic and class stereotypes associated with it because they're still too useful to some" (265). "My country needs me," Hortense Spillers ironically noted two decades earlier in her groundbreaking essay on the ideological work of racist and sexist images of African American women, "and if I were not here, I would have to be invented" (65). Reflecting on the condemnation of the black matriarchal family by Moynihan and others, Spillers's essay traces how slavery obscured the systemic violation of black women, denied the violence of white paternity, and positioned black women as the symbolic fathers of their own children. Spillers speculated that the un-gendering of both black men and women under slavery positions them outside patriarchal notions of gender and family, a marker of Otherness that nevertheless holds radical potential for black women who claim their "monstrous" power to name (80) and for black men who recognize the feminine Other within themselves. Although Ward's interview does not mention Spillers's essay, *Salvage the Bones* shares an interest in the subversion of patriarchy through its alternative kinship arrangements, as will be discussed later in this essay.

Storm and hurricane imagery, allusions to Mother Nature and Medea, and the rhetoric of natural/national disasters provide the figurative language for exploring and subverting the stigmatization of African American teen pregnancy in *Salvage the Bones*. Esch's father, for example, explains the danger of the approaching hurricane to his family by repeating the popular myth that the worst US storms have all been named for women—a myth that includes the (incorrect) explanation that these storms are underestimated (Samenow). Ironically, as Esch's father makes these proclamations, he is unaware that his daughter is pregnant. Katrina threatens everyone with its life-altering force, a power that is metaphorically granted to Esch's youthful pregnancy. Storm imagery invokes simultaneously women's power to create and to destroy. At one point, Esch likens her body to a "storm drain" (41), an abortive image that suggests her body's inability or unwillingness to contain a pregnancy. In a different scene, she looks into the swirling waters of a flushed toilet and names it a "baby storm" (146), suggesting her lost romantic hopes and future, her lost mother, or a "lost baby" as in the Lucille Clifton poem of that title. Esch—unloved by Manny, the father of her pregnancy—also claims kinship with Medea, the mother from Greek mythology who murders her children when she is rejected by her lover: "Here is someone that I recognize. When Medea falls in love with Jason, it grabs me by the throat. I can see her . . . I know her" (38). These textual moments connect the images of the hurricane with pregnancy, and the awesome power of Mother Nature with mothers to imply destruction and waste, the exact meaning of which is unclear: Will Esch claim a fearsome maternal power and abort her baby like waste? Is Esch's future wasted? Or are Esch and her unborn black child seen as a waste of social resources? Will they be discarded as waste? Through Katrina metaphors, the novel explores the negative double bind faced by African American mothers of unplanned pregnancies: unsanctioned, unwed childbearing or stigmatized abortion.

The text subverts the controlling image of unwed, African American teen pregnancy as a national disaster by identifying *real* precarity, including the constraints on reproductive control and health that are confronting all American women but impacting rural and poor women of color first and most drastically. Precarity, according to Butler, "designates that politically induced condition in which certain populations suffer from failing social and economic networks of support and become differentially exposed to injury, violence, and death" ("Performativity" ii). Esch's mother, for example, has died in a non-elective home birth before the story's action. This loss is Esch's personal tragedy but also one that points to the troubling rise in the national black maternal death rate, which, according to the Centers for Disease Control and Prevention (CDC), is three times the rate of maternal death for white women. Furthermore, the novel's setting during the chaotic period preceding and following Katrina reveals the precarious position of populations already marginalized by the logic of neoliberalism and extends this consideration to include gender. In opposition to the popular refrain, "Why didn't they *just* evacuate?" that—in neoliberal fashion—blamed victims of the storm for what appeared to be mismanaged lives and poor decision-making, Ward's novel portrays the *choices* that are (un)available to impoverished populations. Readers are shown how Esch and her family lack the resources to leave The Pit and thus fall back on perfected strategies for enduring storms. Including gender in its awareness of precarity, the novel also reveals—through Esch's poignant isolation with her secret pregnancy—how Katrina exacerbated threats to the safety and reproductive health of underserved women. In her discussion of women's greater vulnerability during Katrina, Ross observes that a failure to take into consideration gender means that "women become doubly victimized—by the disaster and by the response to it" ("A Feminist Perspective" 11). Ross goes on to point out, "Mississippi already had only one abortion provider before the storm. Women traveled from Louisiana or Alabama for services. What will an already under-served region do to help women receive reproductive healthcare?" (12).

How is it, we might additionally ask, that women's gender-specific needs—for protection from gender-based violence or for reproductive healthcare, for example—come to be ignored or dismissed under neoliberalism? Wendy Brown explains that when the neoliberal state prioritizes the market, citizens are "interpellated as entrepreneurial actors" (42) whose agency is expressed and determined through *self*-care. Young women like Esch do not experience state protection of their rights (to healthcare and to reproductive control) as citizens; instead, they are expected to behave like consumers and neoliberal actors. *Choice* has replaced rights, leaving women who already experience race- or class-based oppression continually exposed, as Ross observes, to gender-specific threats and double victimization.

Looking more specifically at precarity and abortion access, we see that *Roe v. Wade* ensured that some women have access to abortion, but universal availability has been curtailed by the subsequent backlash of decisions and policies, including the 1976 Hyde Amendment, which prevents federal funding (Medicaid) from going to abortion services. As antiabortion legislation mushrooms, the situation for all women worsens. Across the country there are now contraceptive and abortion *deserts* that lack adequate, if any, reproductive healthcare or clinics (Power to Decide). Indeed, the Trump administration promises to tighten the noose on women's reproductive rights by cutting funding to Planned Parenthood and appointing antiabortion judges to the Supreme Court in an effort to see *Roe v. Wade* overturned. In an interview shortly after the 2016 election, Trump articulated his desire to see abortion decided state by state, and when asked what women seeking abortions should do if they live in states prohibiting it, he dismissively suggested that "they go to a state where it is legal" ("President Elect Trump Speaks"). Trump's off-the-cuff remark reflects the brutal cynicism of neoliberalism as it applies to abortion politics: Women are *free* agents who have *choices,* but it is not the state's role to protect reproductive rights. If you are too poor or too young to participate in this new regime, that is not *the state's* problem; *you* should have chosen better.

Narrated through Esch's triply marginalized perspective, Ward's novel offers an aesthetically powerful text for contemplating the havoc caused by the hegemony of neoliberal values and the need for reproductive justice. Esch's situation exemplifies the threat of "re-enslavement" described by Ross. Admitting that she lacks a prescription and money for birth control pills, Esch ponders her *choices* thusly:

The girls say that if you're pregnant and you take a month's worth of pills, it will make your period come on. Say if you drink bleach, you get sick, and it will make what will become the baby come out. Say if you hit yourself really hard in the stomach, throw yourself on the metal edge of a car and it hits you low enough to call bruises, it could bring a miscarriage. Say that this is what you do when you can't have an abortion, when you can't have a baby, when nobody wants what is inside you. (102)

She contemplates these forms of physical harm before concluding, "These are my options, and they narrow to none" (102). Esch's terrifying musings point to what some critics claim is becoming a frequent occurrence in the US: women who attempt to self-induce miscarriage (Dreweke). Confronted by her non-choices, Esch keeps her pregnancy secret until "none of us have any choices about what can be seen, what can be avoided, what is blind, and what will turn us to stone" (88). Her ambiguous silence marks either a failure to become or a rejection of the neoliberal entrepreneurial actor.

Salvage the Bones's depiction of neoliberal racialized biopolitics—including stigmatized sexuality,[6] the lack of access to birth control, unplanned teen pregnancy, inaccessible abortion, black maternal death in childbirth, and socially stigmatized unwed motherhood—lays bare the reality of reproductive precarity. In doing so, it exposes how the logic of a neoliberal entrepreneurial *actor*, who is able to choose between desirable options to maximize her outcomes, fails women who are young, poor, and/or black. By portraying a state that in no way concerns itself with Esch's reproductive rights, health, or subsequent endangerment, *Salvage the Bones* implicitly raises awareness of the need for reproductive justice to remedy precarity—an ethical demand that encompasses prenatal care, birthing options, and the right to parent in safe environments *in addition to* birth control and abortion.[7]

---

6. Unlike Erica Edwards's important reading of Ward's novel, which focuses on what she calls the "surplus" of Esch's "avaricious young black female sexuality" (161) and its disruptive potential, I focus on motherhood in the novel. Edwards's reading borrows Clyde Wood's concept of *blues epistemology*, "'an ethic of survival, subsistence, resistance, and affirmation' that sustains networks of labor and kinship throughout the Mississippi Delta region" (qtd. in Edwards 156). She contends that rather than resisting institutions of power, Esch and her family exist simultaneously parallel to and in a relationship of surplus to normative structures. To build on Edwards's *blues epistemological* reading of the novel, I consider Angela Davis's observation "that blues*women* found the cult of motherhood irrelevant to their realities" (239; my emphasis). Davis's comment attends to race, epistemology, *and motherhood* to remind us that reproductive subjugation constrains all women, but it affords privileges to some while seeking to annihilate others. Esch confronts motherhood as a blues*woman* in Davis's sense.

7. See Ross and Solinger.

Teen Pregnancies and Pit Bulls: Black and White *Breeders*

Salvage the Bones probes the urgent threats to black women and children posed by neoliberalism. It does this through the implicit questions that it asks about the relative valuing of human and nonhuman, as well as black and white life. The novel's plot concerns itself with Esch's response to the non-choice of having a baby: Will she embrace or reject unsought motherhood in a world that does not value her or her child? These questions are answered through Esch's identification with China, her brother's pit bull whose fighting and breeding labor supports the family financially. Read literally, the figure of China depicts the mistreatment of dogs in illegal dogfighting and breed-ing, but as a *literary device,* the meanings attached to her figure multiply and comment on women's exploitation and devaluation, maternal ferocity, and—through her *whiteness*—the racialized biopolitics of stratified reproduction. What follows here is a consideration of how Esch subverts this stratification by *salvaging* the idea of *the bitch* to create her own ferocious black motherhood. Rather than dehumanizing her, *the bitch* creates a subversive space of kinship with nonhuman China that simultaneously celebrates Esch's maternal power and rejects the artificial devaluing of her black child.

The novel's bold, disturbing linking of an animal with a black woman pur-posefully invokes historical, dehumanizing stereotypes. The novel associates Esch and China as *breeders*—literally they are both pregnant females—and, because neither chose to reproduce, the text implies a gendered solidarity between them. However, the symbolism of China's *whiteness* and the artificial overvaluing of her offspring compared to Esch's unwanted black child disrupts this solidarity. China gives birth to a litter of puppies valued at eight hundred dollars, and, ironically, while no one wants to claim Esch's pregnancy (includ-ing Esch herself), everyone wants one of China's puppies. This ironic juxtapo-sition of their offspring exposes the stratification of reproduction aggravated by precarious conditions of displacement, racism, youth, and poverty.

Perspective on the artificial labeling and valuing of human and nonhu-man life is offered by Patricia Williams. In her essay "On Being the Object of Property," she addresses the long tradition of dehumanizing African American mothers and their children. Beginning with an account of the sexual exploita-tion of her enslaved, preteen great-great-grandmother, she extends this per-sonal history to contemporary debates over forced sterilization, surrogacy, and the devaluing of black children. Black mothers and their children have histori-cally been assigned little to no social value except during the period of slavery, when enslaved women were compelled to produce more property for white slaveholders. Williams writes,

> Whether something is inside or outside the marketplace of rights has always been a way of valuing it. . . . Thus when black people were bought and sold as slaves, they were placed beyond the boundaries of humanity. And thus, in the twistedness of our brave new world, when blacks have been thrust out of the marketplace and it is white children who are bought and sold, black babies have become "worthless" currency to adoption agents—"surplus" in the salvage heaps of Harlem hospitals. (164–65)

Williams links the overvaluing of the white child sought through surrogacy to the devaluing of black children, who have moved from being valued nonhumans to valueless humans.

In a similar fashion, *Salvage the Bones* provocatively connects the overvaluing of the nonhuman puppies of a *white* mother to the disavowal of Esch's black, human, *surplus* child. Certainly, in other contexts, pit bulls are *surplus*, to use Williams's term; indeed, the American Humane Society shelters are filled with unwanted pit bulls. However, within the world of the novel and the economy of Bois Sauvage, China and her litter exist within the marketplace, and their artificial value is symbolized by her *whiteness*. China and Esch's gendered and maternal solidarity is challenged by this reminder of their *racial* difference, even as this reminder prompts consideration of why a nonhuman puppy is valued more than a human child whose *genocide* antiabortion groups have so earnestly sought to prevent.

Exploiting this irony, Ward's novel masterfully plays with "controlling images" of both black mothers and pit bulls. As a malleable figure of alterity, pit bull mythology can be adopted and deployed in different contexts and with different meanings. Pit bull symbolism was on full display, for example, during the 2008 presidential campaign, when Sarah Palin notoriously declared, "I love those hockey moms. You know, they say, the difference between a hockey mom and a pit bull—? Lipstick." Palin's reference to *hockey* moms coded her remark about laudable maternal ferocity as specific to *white* motherhood. However, in the shared cultural imaginary, pit bulls metaphorically stand in most often as "racialized figures of deviance" (Edwards 157)[8]—and specifically African American *male* deviance. The actor Michael B. Jordan recently invoked pit bull mythology to describe his portrayal of slain Oscar Grant: "Black males, we are America's pit bull. We're labeled vicious, inhumane and left to die on the street. . . . We get branded a lot for being vicious, not human" ("Fruitvale Station"). For Jordan, the pit bull represents the injustice

---

8. Pit bulls also serve in the popular imaginary as metaphors of sexual deviance (see Weaver).

of stereotypes and the dehumanization of African American men.[9] However, placing Palin's comment side by side with Jordan's reveals how black women remain invisible in these popular images of superhuman white motherhood or dehumanized black masculinity. Esch's identification with China, therefore, presents an overlap within the Venn diagram of Palin's and Jordan's symbolic invocations of pit bull mythology.

Although disquieting, the novel's linking of its African American characters with animals purposefully destabilizes dehumanizing stereotypes by erasing the distinction and hierarchy of values assigned to human and nonhuman. Dogs serve as the novel's valued figurative and literal currencies: Junior hides under the house with stray dogs (114); the siblings fight over the bones of a meal (6); the boys sleep in canine-like fashion wherever fatigue overtakes them "in the backseats of cars, the old RV, the porch" (10); Manny dries himself by shaking "like a dog" (55); Esch thinks her unusual corkscrew hair is "like a Doberman come out white" (7); Skeetah pulls on Esch's wrist "as if he can make me heel" (72); and Esch longs for Manny to touch her tenderly "as he would a pit puppy with pedigree papers" (9). These comparisons do not degrade the human characters because the novel carefully reassigns value to the nonhuman. Another such revaluing is the novel's embrace of *savagery*. In the novel's paratext, Ward notes: "The word salvage is phonetically close to savage. At home [Mississippi], among the young, there is honor in that term. It says that come hell or high water, Katrina or oil spill, hunger or heat, you are strong, you are fierce, and you possess hope" (264). Taking the *black* heart of Bois Sauvage ("wild woods") and its savage and animal inhabitants as the normalized center of the novel, the outlying areas populated by whites become unfamiliar, "pale arteries" (34). This reversal of center and margin is extended through depictions of white people as zombie-like in appearance and behavior (28). White *normative* society is dead, nonhuman, and alien, its own "tangle of pathology" (Spillers 66).

The textual pairing of China and Esch, in particular, invokes gendered solidarities even as it subverts non/human and *racial* differences. Throughout the novel, China is anthropomorphized as Skeetah's adoring and adored lover, and his status is enhanced by this relationship: "She has eyes only for him" (2); "he is focused on China like a man focuses on a woman when he feels that she is his, which China is" (3); and she is described returning to him like "a woman

---

9. This image is further complicated by the negative association of African American men and dogfighting, which arose in 2007 due to football player Michael Vick's conviction in a dogfighting ring. In response to the condemning media coverage of Vick, his surrendered dogs were quickly adopted, according to *Sports Illustrated* (see Gorant), even though pit bulls are usually "surplus" in many US animal shelters.

approaching her partner on the dance floor" (101). Like a doting spouse, he constructs a home with a linoleum floor for her (28–29, 103), allows her in the family house (211), buys only the best pet food for her and eats it himself while the family lives on Ramen noodles and scavenged eggs (193), and, contrary to their father's prohibition, longs to allow her on his bed (161). Skeetah declares, "Between man and dog is a relationship . . . [e]qual" (29). Her value to Skeetah is amplified through her symbolic whiteness, which is invested with several contradictory meanings and values: cocaine or "china" heroin (addictive; reflective of wealth and excess); the family china (valued heirloom and household good); a china doll (porcelain, whiteness, beauty fragility); Chyna (the World Federation Wrestler turned porn star from 1990s); and the nation of China—to which Junior suggests Esch send his rejected breakfast when she admonishes him that people are starving in Africa (25).

China's real value, however, is in her labor as a breeder and fighter, without which she would have no place in the Batiste family. She is bred with Kilo, another fighting dog who is owned by Manny's cousin, and sexually, she dominates and mates with the same aggression she displays while fighting. About their mating, Esch observes, "There was blood on their jaws, on her coat, and instead of loving, it looked like they were fighting" (8); "she'd drawn blood: he hadn't" (95). China proves to be a resilient breeder although she is devoid of mercy. As China whelps, Esch observes, "What [she] is doing is fighting, like she was born to do. Fight our shoes, fight other dogs, fight these puppies that are reaching for the outside" (2). Previously, China has cruelly killed other mothers—notably the family's laying hens (210)—but Esch marvels at her ability to nurture: "I don't know what I thought she would do once she had [her litter]: sit on them and smother them maybe. Bite them. Turn their skulls to bits of bone and blood. But she doesn't do any of that. Instead she stands over them, her on one side and Skeetah on the other like a pair of proud parents, and she licks" (17). She is a shrewd and ruthless mother, driving off one puppy that becomes sick (40–41), fighting off her litter when they have nursed sufficiently (109), and merciless when, unprovoked and in a Medea-like gesture, she kills the puppy that looks like Kilo (192).

An undefeated champion, her labor as a competitive fighting dog contributes to the family's security, wealth, and status. She and the other fighting dogs are sources of income through the side betting that takes place during the fights, but she also arbitrates, defends, and supports the siblings like a surrogate mother. She intimidates treacherous Manny, who fearfully observes, "China don't like me" (101), and Daddy, who drunkenly assails his children (105–6). After Skeetah has stolen dewormer from a local farmer, the siblings are pursued by his dog until China murderously intervenes (81). Additionally, when Manny's cousin (the owner of Kilo) insists on taking the pick of the litter as stud fee, Skeetah defends his claim to the puppies by fighting China in her postpartum, debilitated state. Over Randall's objections at jeopardizing a nursing mother's well-being, Skeetah pits China against Kilo, the father of her litter: "*How are you going to fight her? She's a mother!*" Randall asks, to which Skeetah responds, "*And he's a father, and what the fuck difference does it make? . . . We all fight. . . . Everybody*" (169). China's fight not only denies the cousin's claim on a puppy but also defends Esch's honor, as the conflict over the stud fee coincides with Manny's realization and rejection of Esch's pregnancy. In this scene, with both families present, Manny's cousin observes with double meaning to Skeetah: "I heard your bitch had our puppies" (148). China's victory over Kilo defends the family's resources and honor, and later, Randall ends his friendship with Manny when he suspects "you dogging my sister" (201). As these moments suggest, China, as a lover, mother, and fighter, is linked with Esch—at times, as Manny attempts, to dehumanize and devalue her, and at other times to suggest her fierce potential.

Although Esch identifies with China, she is not like her initially. With Manny, Esch is a passive lover, painfully aware of his devaluation of her. As her family prepares for Mother Nature's onslaught and she grapples with impending motherhood, the most threatening disaster, in her eyes, is her inability to win his love. Before Manny, Esch has sex with numerous boys because it was easier than telling them no (23). She notes her "girly heart that, before Manny, I'd let boys have because they wanted it, and not because I wanted to give it" (16). Manny also demands her passivity. She actively desires him, but sensing his conditional attraction—"You know it ain't like that" (56)—she does not dare to voice it. Manny has only contempt for female "weakness" (11, 96) although he simultaneously demands it from Esch and his normative-feminine girlfriend. Manny, a neoliberal agent with entrepreneurial choices of his own to make—namely, whether or not to claim fatherhood—ultimately rejects both Esch and her pregnancy, scorning the social *disadvantage* of being associated with a mother, a child, a dependent. He represents a black masculinity that is alienated from the "blues epistemology," an ethic that values communal survival over individualism (Edwards).

Esch's passivity extends to her approaching identity as a mother. It is hard to say that Esch *chooses* motherhood any more than China does. Birth control is available to Esch only in the form of condoms (30), and she is unable/unwilling to demand their use with Manny for reasons already noted. Although she wonders wistfully if ending the pregnancy would make Manny love her (102–03), abortion is too distant geographically and financially. As mentioned above, her only act of agency is *not* to reveal her pregnancy. Ironically it is Skeetah, the expert dog breeder who knows the most about mothers, who carefully scrutinizes Esch's body to learn her secret. Disputing Manny's observation about China (made in the presence of Esch) that giving birth weakens females ("price of being female," Manny declares), Skeetah objects, "You serious? That when they come into they strength. They got something to protect. . . . That's power" (96). And it is Skeetah who, in a mothering gesture, assures Esch, "Everything need a chance" (214), indirectly encouraging her to fight for her child.

The formidable figure of China prompts Esch to confront not only her pregnancy but also Manny. Esch passively awaits his love until his rejection of her pregnant body compels her to fight. When Manny disowns the pregnancy, claiming it could be any boy's, Esch attacks him with explosive violence—"I am on him like China" (203)—while he fights back, calling her "stupid bitch" (204). Recognizing the injustice of the double bind of expected and devalued feminine weakness, Esch awakens to her identity as *a bitch* and assaults Manny "like China," no longer denying her resilience and strength.

Ironically, the novel's radical message of hope arrives in the end when China is lost. Esch, her brothers, and her father survive Katrina, but China and her litter do not. As the hurricane floods their home, the family must climb through their roof and attempt a desperate escape to higher ground by jumping through tree limbs. In the process, Esch's pregnancy is revealed to their unsuspecting father, who, surprised, pushes Esch into the floodwaters. Although Esch's father appears to reject her, readers recall that he taught his children to swim by throwing them in, suggesting that he pushes Esch toward survival (23). Skeetah, meanwhile, abandons his hold on China to grab Esch, who drops the remaining puppies. The deceptive promise of cross-species affinity offered by the boy-and-his-dog plot is disrupted for readers by Skeetah's choice of Esch over China and her litter. The heroic pit bull is last seen swimming against the waters as the human family finds shelter in the second story of their grandparents' abandoned house. As the storm ends and the water recedes, the Batiste family is left to assess the damage and to await China's return. Esch's father resumes his parental role, telling her she needs prenatal care. Big Henry, another family friend who has steadfastly supported Esch without attempting to exploit her sexually, reassures her, "This baby got plenty daddies" (255).

The novel concludes with a displacement of the white breeder and her artificially overvalued offspring, in addition to a rescripting of nonnormative kinship roles that frame Esch's pregnancy within a context of hope. Not only has Skeetah ungendered the idea of *mothering* by serving as a mother-guide to China, her puppies, and Esch, but Big Henry's comment that Esch's child will have more than one nonbiological father suggests that *fathering* is not connected essentially to biology. The (absent) biological father is forgotten when Esch claims a decidedly not "monstrous" but rather Zeus-like progenitor relationship to her child: "I lie awake and cannot see anything but that baby, the baby I have formed whole in my head, a black Athena, who reaches for me. Who gives me that name as if it is mine: *Mama*" (219). Mothering is similarly de-essentialized by the fact that Esch, a true blues*woman*,[10] expresses no romanticized attitudes toward motherhood and must rely on her father's guidance, Randall's protection, Skeetah's support, and even Junior's readiness "to give it a bottle" (247). Esch's role models include the memories of her mother and of China, whom Esch claims as her "sister" (258) at the conclusion of the novel. This recasting of kinship (brothers as mothers, dogs as sisters, friends as fathers) changes the biopolitical field of the novel and thereby disrupts the neoliberal morality of stratified reproduction. Good/bad reproductive choice-making is interrupted by reconfigured family systems. The novel rejects the double bind of bad choices facing young African American mothers—abortion or stigmatized teen motherhood—and replaces it with a loving, supportive *blues ethic*. In place of neoliberal morality, the novel refocuses on a nonbiological family and community that cherishes the black child and values an ethic of survival. In this sense, the image of Esch as a *breeder* is replaced with a fighter and a new mythology for African American motherhood.

Conclusion

Ward's novel challenges the dehumanizing "controlling images" of black women and the artificial overvaluing of white reproduction. The novel refutes the cultural symbolism of African American *breeders* by humanizing Esch and her family and by casting the *white breeder* as a nonhuman. Ultimately, her novel subverts reproductive stratification by privileging Esch's black maternity and alternative family structure, which cherishes the black child over the marketable offspring of China. Yet this alternative family structure does not reject its Other; instead, its nonnormative definition of family—not based in patriarchal roles—privileges the relations of human and nonhuman, blood and affinity, hierarchy and interdependence, survival and violence as the structure of kinship that endures the conditions of precarity. In so doing, the novel creates a new mythology of nonpatriarchal black motherhood and alternative family structure that expands Spillers's vision.

---

10. See Davis.

What does *Salvage the Bones* tell us about reproductive politics and reproductive justice? First, the narrative helps to reverse the invisibility of African American women's reproductive vulnerability. From the initial detail of Esch's mother's death in childbirth to Esch's inability to obtain an abortion, readers are made aware of the roles that race, poverty, youth, and location have in determining the sorts of *choices* that are (un)available to poor, rural women under neoliberalism. This awareness undoes the neoliberal morality of good/bad choice-makers and the marketplace. Esch's mother does not choose a home birth because of *progressive* values but because the cost of a hospital stay and the trip there are prohibitive. Her nonchoice proves fatal. Similarly, Esch's nonchoice to have a child does not reflect bad values but rather society's abdication of its responsibility to young women. She lacks access to birth control, abortion, *and* social approbation for having a child. Second, Ward's novel asserts a nonnormative understanding of reproduction, motherhood, and kinship that affords Esch an alternative means of self-realization and survival outside/within neoliberal hegemony. Radically, her agency is expressed through her choice to love her socially vulnerable child.

China's *whiteness* exposes the injustice of stratified reproduction and what McRobbie calls the threat of "disarticulated" affinity groups—that is, the breaking apart of Esch's and China's gendered alliance. Yet the novel sustains hope for coalitional politics. As the source of Esch's inspiration, China—in tandem with Mother Nature and Katrina—represents awe-inspiring maternal strength, and thus, her return is longed for at the text's conclusion. As nonhuman property, China harkens to the not-too-distant past of enslaved women's exploitation as *breeders*. The affinity Esch feels for her suggests a gendered, maternal solidarity that persists in opposition to oppressive systems. Esch claims China as her sister in a gesture of solidarity, and while China must textually recede—along with the cult of white motherhood—in order for Esch's child to gain valuation, the narrative points hopefully to the possibility of a future that contains the children of both Esch and China. Rather than a sign of solidarity's failure, the novel's conclusion suggests the possibility of kinship and solidarity and their shared resistance to the logic of neoliberalism.

Works Cited

Butler, Judith. "Performativity, Precarity, and Sexual Politics." *AIBR: Revista de Antropología Iberoamericana*, vol. 4, no. 3, Sept.–Dec. 2009, pp. i–xii.

Brown, Wendy. *Edgework: Critical Essays on Knowledge and Politics*. Princeton University Press, 2005.

Centers for Disease Control and Prevention. "Pregnancy Mortality Surveillance System." *Centers for Disease Control and Prevention,* US Department of Health and Human Services, 9 Nov. 2017.

Cohen, Susan. "Abortion and Women of Color: The Bigger Picture." *The Guttmacher Policy Review,* vol. 11, no. 3, Aug. 2008, www.guttmacher.org/gpr/2008/08/abortion-and-women-color-bigger-picture.

Davis, Angela. "I Used To Be Your Sweet Mama: Ideology, Sexuality, and Domesticity in the Blues of Gertrude 'Ma' Rainey and Bessie Smith." *Sexy Bodies: The Strange Carnalities of Feminism,* edited by Elizabeth Grosz and E. Probyn, Routledge, 1995, pp. 231–65.

Dreweke, Joerg. "As U. S. Abortion Restrictions Mount, Issue of Self-Induced Abortion Gains Attention." *Guttmacher Institute,* 25 Sept. 2015, www.guttmacher.org/news-release/2015/us-abortion-restrictions-mount-issue-self-induced-abortion-gains-attention.

Edwards, Erica. "Sex after the Black Normal." *Differences: A Journal of Feminist Cultural Studies,* vol. 26, no. 1, 2015, pp. 141–67.

Foucault, Michel. "Right of Death and Power over Life." 1976. *The History of Sexuality: An Introduction,* vol. 1, Vintage, 1990, pp. 135–57.

"'Fruitvale Station' Star Michael B. Jordan: 'Black Males, We are America's Pit Bull.'" *Huffington Post,* 18 Dec. 2013, www.huffingtonpost.com/2013/12/18/fruitvale-station-michael-b-jordan_n_4462009.html.

Gorant, Jim. "What Happened to Michael Vick's Dogs." *Sports Illustrated,* 29 Dec. 2008, www.si.com/more-sports/2008/12/23/vick-dogs.

Hill Collins, Patricia. *Black Feminist Thought: Knowledge, Consciousness, and the Politics of Empowerment.* 2000. Routledge, 2009.

Jellenik, Glenn. "Re-shaping the Narrative: Pulling Focus/Pushing Boundaries in Fictional Representations of Hurricane Katrina." *Ten Years after Katrina: Critical Perspectives of the Storm's Effect on American Culture and Identity,* edited by Mary Ruth Marotte and G. Jellenik, Lexington Books, 2015, pp. 221–37.

Power to Decide. "Access to Birth Control." Power to Decide, https://powertodecide.org/what-we-do/access/access-birth-control. Web.

"President Elect Trump Speaks to Divided Country." *60 Minutes,* 13 Nov. 2016.

Raymond, Laurel. "The Anti-Choice Movement Is Hijacking Black Lives Matter to Push Its Own Agenda." *Think Progress,* 12 July 2016, thinkprogress.org/the-anti-choice-movement-is-hijacking-black-lives-matter-to-push-its-own-agenda-6c580ca97da/.

Roberts, Dorothy. *Killing the Black Body: Race, Reproduction, and the Meaning of Liberty.* Vintage, 1997.

Ross, Loretta. "A Feminist Perspective on Katrina." *Off Our Backs,* vol. 35, nos. 9–10, Sept./Oct. 2005, pp. 11–13.

———. "Re-Enslaving African American Women." *On the Issues,* Fall 2008, www.ontheissues-magazine.com/cafe2.php?id=22.

———. "Trust Black Women: Reproductive Justice and Eugenics." *Radical Reproductive Justice: Foundations, Theory, Practice, Critique,* edited by Loretta Ross et al., The Feminist Press, 2017, pp. 58–85.

Ross, Loretta, and R. Solinger. *Reproductive Justice: An Introduction.* University of California Press, 2017.

Samenow, Jason. "Revision: Female Named Hurricanes Are Most Likely Not Deadlier Than Male Hurricanes." *The Washington Post,* 11 July 2017, www.washingtonpost.com/news/capital-weather-gang/wp/2017/07/11/revision-female-named-hurricanes-are-most-likely-not-dead-lier-than-male-hurricanes/?utm_term=.cf2309ddf01b.

Sandalow, Marc. "Katrina Thrusts Race and Poverty onto National Stage / Bush and Congress under Pressure to Act." *San Francisco Chronicle,* 28 Sept. 2005, www.sfgate.com/news/article/Katrina-thrusts-race-and-poverty-onto-national-2606416.php.

Sanger, Carole. "Seeing and Believing: Mandatory Ultrasound and the Path to a Protected Choice" *UCLA Law Review,* vol. 351, 2008, pp. 351–408.

Solinger, Rickie. *Beggars and Choosers: How the Politics of Choice Shapes Adoption, Abortion, and Welfare in the United States.* Hill and Wang, 2001.

Spillers, Hortense. "Mama's Baby, Papa's Maybe: An American Grammar Book." *Diacritics,* vol. 17, no. 2, Summer 1987, pp. 65–81.

Ward, Jesmyn. *Salvage the Bones.* Bloomsbury, 2011.

Weaver, Harlan. "Pit Bull Promises." *GLQ: A Journal of Lesbian and Gay Studies,* vol. 21, nos. 2–3, June 2015, pp. 343–63.

Williams, Patricia. "On Being the Object of Property." *Writing on the Body: Female Embodiment and Feminist Theory,* edited by Katie Conboy et al., Columbia University Press, 1997, pp. 155–75.

CHAPTER 2

Privileging God the Father

The Neoliberal Theology of the Evangelical Orphan Care Movement

VALERIE A. STEIN

OUR CULTURE often presents adoption as a feel-good story: Heroic adoptive parents, perhaps unable to have *children of their own,* battle the system and all of its red tape to rescue a poor, hopeless child in need of a family. In the end, everything works out and the child is where she was meant to be. These heart-warming narratives rarely show us the pain and loss experienced by the child and the birth mother. In fact, the birth mother plays at best a minor role in the story, one that highlights her supposed choices: She is given a nod for having made a loving choice so that her child could have the kind of life she could not provide, or she is disparaged as having made bad choices that make her unfit to parent.

Versions of this narrative flourish in evangelical Christian circles where adoption and foster care have become the focus of a growing movement in the new millennium. The evangelical orphan care movement is a theological trend that draws on the New Testament doctrine of adoption to promote and encourage adoption, foster care, and orphan care. Proponents argue that adoption and orphan care are at the heart of the gospel message because the work of Christ results in the adoption of Christian believers. The movement is perhaps most clearly represented by CAFO, the Christian Alliance for Orphans. The Alliance, officially incorporated in 2007, emerged from an initial gathering of thirty Christian leaders in 2004. The now annual CAFO Summit has since grown to include over two thousand participants, and the

Alliance considers itself to be the "definitive hub for the Christian orphan movement" (Christian Alliance for Orphans, private communication). CAFO seeks to coordinate the efforts of over 650 churches and almost 200 member organizations, including groups working in the areas of adoption, advocacy, foster care, global orphan care, and family preservation (CAFO, "About Us"). The Alliance also sponsors Orphan Sunday, a widely popular annual crusade held by churches across America and around the world in early November. The initiative seeks to motivate and coordinate responses to what evangelicals see as their God's call to care for the orphan. Leading evangelical groups and churches participate in Orphan Sunday, such as Focus on the Family, the Southern Baptist Convention, and Rick Warren's Saddleback Church. Many evangelical pastors, politicians, and other prominent figures have adopted themselves and are strong advocates for Christian adoption and foster care.[1]

This call to adopt is not fundamentally about providing options for infertile couples or humanitarian care for children in need. Rather, evangelical books, advocacy websites, sermons, blogs, and denomination resolutions claim a biblical and theological mandate for orphan care as a missionary activity: The adoption of orphaned children by Christian families mirrors the adoption of believers by God to be co-heirs with Christ. Adoption is the heart of the gospel.

This religious framing of adoption is not socially or politically neutral. Evangelical theology and American politics are intertwined, each continually reorienting itself in relation to the other.[2] Just as biblical authors wrote to reinforce or challenge prevailing ideologies or power structures, contemporary biblical interpretation and theological discourse are always contextual; they engage political, economic, and cultural matters, be they within the church or in society at large, privileging certain perspectives and obfuscating or dismissing others. We must ask: Whose interests are being served and promoted by the claim of a biblical mandate for adoption? Specifically, what is this narrative's role in a society in which privileged women adopt the children of women who are economically and socially vulnerable? And moreover, what economic,

---

1. Evangelical pastors and theologians Russell Moore, Dan Cruver, Tony Merida and Rick Morton, and John Piper have all adopted and promote Christian adoption as a theological mandate (see their respective works in the works cited). Kentucky Governor Matt Bevin has four adopted children and is a vocal supporter of CAFO's initiatives (Medefind). Christian music artist Stephen Curtis Chapman adopted three daughters from China and founded Show Hope, a nonprofit adoption advocacy organization that offers adoption grants and facilities orphan care centers in China (Show Hope, "Our Story").

2. For example, see Melinda Cooper's *Life as Surplus: Biotechnology and Capitalism in the Neoliberal Era,* in which she demonstrates the close relationship between evangelicalism, pro-life politics, and neoliberal free-market philosophy.

political, and social agendas are linked with the rise of the evangelical orphan care movement?

Analysis of the theological framework of the evangelical orphan care movement reveals that "God's heart for the orphan" ultimately leads churches to give preference to the needs, desires, and perspective of the adoptive parents, whose role is aligned with the evangelical Christian deity's. The birth mother virtually disappears in God's plan for the *fatherless* child and subsequently from the attention of the churches. Adoption as gospel has political implications as well, supporting a world view consistent with neoliberal ideals. Preference for private solutions, minimal government intervention, and reduction of the state's responsibility is buttressed by a religious narrative that glorifies and encourages financial support for adoption and the prospective adoptive parents but is silent about disadvantaged women and the web of social services that could support family preservation.

Rooted in the metaphor of God as father, the theology of the evangelical orphan care movement normalizes the *paterfamilias,* and thus it benefits evangelical Christian women who are in a heteronormative, two-parent family. Aligning with this metaphor of God as father, evangelical adoption theologians have a tendency to refer to the children in need as *fatherless.* The theologically advantageous use of *fatherless* intersects with the American myth of absentee black fathers to also privilege white women at the expense of women of color. The theology is further racialized due to the evangelistic role of adoption; conspicuous transracial families serve as a visual pronouncement of the gospel. In the evangelical orphan care movement, theology justifies the systemic patriarchal, racial, and economic inequities that are imbedded in the adoption industry and the foster care system.[3]

Adoption and Orphans in the Bible

The authority of the Bible is a fundamental characteristic of evangelical Christianity, and proponents of Christian orphan care claim a scriptural foundation for their view of adoption as a theological imperative. However, the Bible never advocates for adoption. In fact, the modern Western concept of legally adopting a child is virtually absent from the Bible. When the Bible speaks of orphans, there is no mention of adoption; in the New Testament's proclamation of the deity's adoption of sinners, there is no command about orphan care. While the evangelical orphan care movement points to the Bible to glo-

---

3. Laura Briggs exposes the inequities behind transracial adoption in *Somebody's Children: The Politics of Transracial and Transnational Adoption.*

rify adoption and advance a neoliberal solution to families in crisis, a critical reading of the Bible actually challenges the movement at every turn and can help reveal the sociopolitical agenda of the interpreters.

The Hebrew Bible / Old Testament contains a vast amount of legal material governing ancient Israel in religious, ethical, and social matters. Though some form of adoption of children may have been practiced in ancient Israel, there are no laws in the Hebrew Bible regulating adoption and there is no Hebrew term reflecting the practice. There is, on the other hand, legal material pertaining to orphans. Deuteronomy calls for what is essentially a social safety net for orphans—and along with them widows and immigrants. According to Deuteronomy 14.28–29, obligatory tithes of produce were to be directed to these marginalized individuals every third year. Additionally, Deuteronomy 24.19–21 commands Israelites not to harvest all the produce from fields, orchards, and vineyards, but rather to leave some behind for the orphans, widows, and immigrants.

There is attention to the plight of the orphans throughout the Hebrew Bible. The text makes it clear that the Israelite's god, Yahweh, is concerned for the orphan: He is father and helper to orphans, he upholds them and executes justice on their behalf, and in him they find mercy (Ps. 10.14, 10.18, 68.5, 146.9; Deut. 10.18; Hos. 14.3). Israelites are repeatedly commanded not to oppress orphans (Exod. 22.20–24; Deut. 24.17, 27.19; Jer. 7.6, 22.3; Zech. 7.10; Prov. 23.10). Each of the three major prophets indicts Israel based on unjust treatment of orphans (Isa. 10.1; Jer. 5.28; Ezek. 22.7).

Of the forty-two times the Hebrew word for *orphan* (*yātom*) occurs in the Bible, all but five occur in conjunction with the word for *widow* (*'almānāh*). Yahweh is also their protector, upholds them, and executes justice on their behalf. Prophetic indictments against oppressive treatment usually include widows along with orphans. The New Testament Book of James echoes the Hebrew Bible's insistence on attention to the needs of the orphans and widows: "Religion that is pure and undefiled before God the Father is this: to care for orphans and widows in their distress and to keep oneself unstained by the world" (Jas. 1.27).

The repeated pairing of orphans with widows throughout the biblical text suggests that the widows are the mothers of these children; what they lack is a father. In fact, some English translations popular among evangelicals, such as the King James Versions and the New International Version, read *fatherless* rather than *orphan*. In ancient Israel's patriarchal society, motherless children could be absorbed into the father's household, but fatherless children (and their mothers) were vulnerable and at risk. Rather than calling for the removal of these children to be placed in two-parent homes, the Bible calls for a social system that provides for their survival.

In addition to what the Hebrew Bible specifically says about what to do for and how to treat orphans, there are two stories in the Hebrew Bible in which a child is *taken in* in a way that is similar to modern Western adoption. In neither case does the story lend itself to the model of adoption upheld in the evangelical orphan care movement. The Book of Esther recounts what we might consider to be a kinship adoption: Esther's cousin raises her after her parents die. The more well-known story of Moses in Exodus has several parallels to modern Western non-relative adoption, especially international and domestic transracial adoptions.[4] Attention to the sociopolitical roles in Moses's story reveals oppression and desperation of the birth family that the evangelical orphan care theology ignores.

Moses was *adopted* by a member of the ruling class; the adoption only happened because the policies implemented by the ruling class left his birth parents unable to keep him safe. Moses was not an orphan. Given a different sociopolitical context, Moses's parents surely would have raised him. The story shares some of the complexities and ethical challenges of international adoption today. While some international adoptions allow an opportunity for truly needy orphaned or abandoned children to have a permanent family, in many other cases, demand for children increases supply. Several nations that once ranked among the top sending nations for intercountry adoption—such as China, Ethiopia, Cambodia, and Guatemala—have closed or significantly scaled back their programs after reports revealed that the Western money flowing into the adoption industry resulted in children being bought or kidnapped and birth families being coerced or tricked into giving up their children (The Schuster Institute).[5] The imbalance of power that enables the pharaoh's daughter to take Moses as her son parallels the flow of adoptees to First World nations, whose wealth has often been at the expense of developing nations. There are similar issues of power imbalance driving domestic adoptions, especially in the case of transracial adoptions. Poor women of color are more vulnerable to social and economic pressures to relinquish their children, and they are more likely to be deemed unfit and lose custody or parental rights (Laura Briggs; Solinger).

---

4. Moses was a Hebrew child born to parents enslaved by the Egyptians. The pharaoh had ordered the Hebrew midwives to kill male babies by casting them into the Nile River. Moses's mother hid him and, when that was no longer possible, put him in a basket among the reeds in the river; his older sister watched from a distance. The daughter of the pharaoh found him, recognized him as a Hebrew, and took him as her own son.

5. The US is a signatory of The Hague Convention on Intercountry Adoption, which was designed to prevent child trafficking and ensure the best interests of the child (HCCH).

Furthermore, Moses is seemingly abandoned but is meant to be found, with his sister standing at a distance to see what would happen to him. This scenario mirrors many abandonments in China, where the children—often second daughters or children with disabilities, both of whom may pose financial difficulties—are placed somewhere they will quickly be found and even watched until they are. Similarly, Moses's account resonates with adoptions from Ethiopia or Haiti, where children often have a surviving but impoverished parent who surrenders the child to an orphanage to ensure the child will live. In fact, rarely are adopted children full orphans. While UNICEF has estimated there are 163 million orphaned children in the world, it notes that most of these children have one surviving parent and that of those who have lost both, most are able to live with extended family (UNICEF).

Moses, like many transracially adopted children, struggles with identity. He does not seem to fully identify with the Egyptians: "One day, after Moses had grown up, he went out to *his* people," meaning the Hebrews (Exod. 2.11; my emphasis). But when he seeks some kind of camaraderie with Hebrews, he is rejected, and it is presumably Hebrews who report the fact that he murdered an Egyptian whom he witnessed beating a Hebrew man. Moses flees both peoples, belonging with neither, and living "somewhere between."[6]

In the story of Moses, we see an adoptee who struggles with identity even though he was given a life of privilege. He is ultimately empowered to return to his birth culture and lead his people out of slavery, thus standing up against the oppressive political regime of his Egyptian adoptive family. The idea of a returning adoptee also parallels contemporary international adoption. In many cases, poor, illiterate birth families sign away their rights to their children believing their children will return to support them after receiving an education (The Schuster Institute; Joyce).

In Moses's story, the birth family is not only included but is, as a Hebrew family, the very focus of the deity's attention. Their side is unambiguously God's side. The adoptive family is problematized as members of the ruling class, as Egyptians responsible for oppressing the people of the Israelite God. Far from glorifying adoption, the story of Moses shines a light on an oppressive sociopolitical situation in which a child is given up out of desperation.

Evangelical Christians could pair these two stories of Esther and Moses—one highlighting kinship care and the other involving an adoptive parent essentially gaining a child because of her role in an oppressive regime—with the Hebrew Bible's persistent concern for orphans and widows in order to

---

6. See the recent movie *Somewhere Between* (2011) about the identity struggles of four girls adopted from China.

advocate for just social systems that enable family preservation. Orphan care theology, however, essentially ignores these two stories and instead pairs the Hebrew Bible's attention to the plight of orphans and widows with the New Testament's adoption metaphor. The result is, as we will see, advocacy for adoption rather than social services.

The adoption metaphor in the New Testament is where we find the only explicit use of the term *adoption* in the Bible. Romans 8.15, 8.23, 9.4; Galatians 4.5; and Ephesians 1.5 use adoption as a representation for atonement, giving a concrete image to explain the salvific relationship between the believer and the deity. The believer is a sinner, unworthy, and essentially enslaved; Jesus's suffering and death restore the relationship with the deity, who is his father, and enable Jesus's status of sonship to be shared with the believer. The process changes the status of the believer to co-heir with the Christ:

> But when the fullness of time had come, God sent his Son, born of a woman, born under the law, in order to redeem those who were under the law, so that we might receive adoption as children. And because you are children, God has sent the Spirit of his Son into our hearts, crying, "Abba! Father!" So you are no longer a slave but a child, and if a child then also an heir, through God. (Gal. 4.4–7)

The New Testament adoption metaphor stands in the Hebrew Bible tradition in which prophetic texts use metaphors to envision the character of the Israelite God and that God's relationship with the Israelites. Common metaphors include king-vassal, husband-wife, judge-litigant, parent-child, and master-slave. As is generally the case with biblical metaphors that draw on analogies to human relationships, the purpose of the metaphor is to shed light on the deity by referencing a relationship that is well known or understood by the audience. To understand the metaphor's purpose and impact, we need to understand how the relationship was understood and functioned in the context in which the text was written. Both the Hebrew Bible / Jewish culture and the Greco-Roman culture serve as contextual frameworks for New Testament writings. Both shed similar light on the metaphor's implied relationship between the Christian God and believer.

In both the Hebrew Bible and the New Testament, the metaphor in which Israel becomes the deity's son references the practice of adopting an heir for the *parterfamilias* rather than providing a home for a child who needs one. Read in the context of Western society, where adoption refers to the practice of taking the child of others to raise as one's own, many English translations seem to suggest that the deity is becoming the father to children: "I thought how I would set you among my children and give you a pleasant land, the most beautiful heritage of all the nations. And I thought you would call me, My Father, and would not turn from following me" (Jer. 3.19). However, the Hebrew word often translated as *children* literally means *sons* (*bānim*), and used in this context of being given land actually implies that Israel is gaining the status of son in order to inherit land.[7] Similarly in the New Testament, the Greek Paul uses to speak of redemption points to a change of status from slave to heir. The word often translated in Galatians 4.5 as *receive adoption as children* (*huiothesían*) literally means *to place as a son*.[8]

The Greco-Roman context offers a similar reference for the New Testament metaphor of adoption. In first-century Rome adoption was driven by the need for a male heir. Childless families (or families without a boy) would adopt a male to become heir. Adoption of females was rare. The adoptees generally were not orphans nor even children. The adoption sometimes imparted a change in social status if the adoptee came from a family with a different standing.

The New Testament *doctrine of adoption* is not part of a biblical mandate to adopt orphans; rather, it is a theological metaphor that compares redemption to slaves becoming heirs. The Christian God may have a *heart for orphans,* but the New Testament adoption metaphor does not reveal it.

Evangelical Adoption Theology

Evangelical Christians misappropriate this metaphor, as well as other biblical texts, to create a religious narrative that glorifies modern Western adoption and adoptive parents. This narrative ultimately reinforces the idea of the traditional two-parent, heteronormative family as well as minimal government intervention. Accordingly, it favors evangelical Christian women who have financial and familial resources to take in a child over calling on the community to provide a welfare system that could support vulnerable women in the care of their children. The proponents of the movement seek to create a culture of orphan care throughout the church. This involves developing a theological framework that identifies orphan care as part of the core foundation of the church so that it is always a priority, but it also involves leadership,

---

7. See also, for example, Genesis 15, where the childless Abram laments that a slave will become his heir.

8. Popular English translations such as the New Revised Standard Version and the New International Version use *children* when the Hebrew and Greek refer to *sons* in order to make the biblical text sound more gender-inclusive for modern audiences.

networking, training, financial support, and structures that increase evangelical participation in and responsibility for adoption ministries, foster care, and orphan care on the local and global levels.

Kathryn Joyce has written on the success and extensiveness of the evangelical adoption movement in *The Child Catchers: Rescue, Trafficking, and the New Gospel of Adoption*. She has shown that the adoption industry is dominated by evangelical agencies and programs both in the US and in the sending countries. With multiple accounts from a wide range of countries, Joyce reveals how the evangelical adoption agenda has impacted the supply of children at the expense of impoverished families and stigmatized single mothers. In many cases, evangelical Christian organizations are even found to be acting unethically and illegally in order to obtain children for adoption. For example, Joyce recounts child trafficking in Haiti after the 2010 earthquake by a Baptist missionary group and accusations against Christian World Adoption of child harvesting in Ethiopia (1ff, 129ff).

In addition to Joyce's revealing exposé, one can also find evidence of the movement's prevalence in various online adoption communities and resources, such as those on Facebook, adoption discussion forums, blogs, and Pinterest pages, where usernames like James127 or InHisName abound. Evangelical Christians frequently reference *a call to adopt* and *God's heart for orphans*. Christian blogger Shay Shull's theological framing of her family's decision to adopt is representative: "God is calling me to step out of my comfort zone and do something to further his kingdom." She attributes the adoption to God's plan and sees it as having an evangelistic purpose. Also common are blogs filled with biblical quotes and religious references displaying pictures of large Christian adoptive families—with six, eight, and even eighteen and twenty-one children—that call to mind the evangelical Quiverfull movement where children are evidence of one's obedience to God and also a means to increasing the number of Christians in the world.[9] The Wright family blog illustrates this trend to large adoptive families as well as the role of adoption as a tool of evangelism: "[We] are a walking billboard for adoption—which I love because people it is all about God's testimony! The famous question. . . . . . are you going to adopt more children. . . . . our answer—we are open to what God has in store" (Wright and Wright). The Wrights have eight transra-

---

9. The Quiverfull movement is a conservative Christian movement in which adherents reject birth control in order to accept as many children as God bestows on them. The belief is grounded in the Genesis commandment to be fruitful and multiply (1:28) and gets its name from Psalm 127: "Children [Heb: sons] are a heritage from the LORD, offspring a reward from him. Like arrows in the hands of a warrior are children born in one's youth. Blessed is the man whose quiver is full of them" (3–5a).

cially adopted children and one child of the same race but with visible special needs. Transracial adoptions prove to be particularly suited to the evangelical agenda to spread the gospel because conspicuous families often attract attention. Thus, not only does adoption spread Christianity by acquiring a child to raise in the faith, it also provides opportunities to preach the gospel to curious onlookers.

The cost of adoption is even given theological frameworks. Chip-in buttons or links to a GoFundMe page to help pay for the adoption make rhetorical appeals to *God's will* and allow evangelicals to participate in spreading the gospel even if they are not adopting themselves. Evangelical foundations offer adoption grants for prospective parents who can demonstrate adherence to the organization's faith statements.[10]

The evangelical view of adoption is grounded primarily in the New Testament, especially in the metaphor of God as an adoptive father in Romans, Galatians, and Ephesians. As I have mentioned, this rhetorical language seeks to explain salvation with an analogy to adoption. The practice of adoption most familiar to the original audience differs from what most modern readers think about adoption. Since metaphors are connected to the social context in which they originate, they can be rejected or forgotten or ignored if they no longer make sense in a new social context. However, metaphors can also be adapted to new realities if there continues to be perceived similarities between the abstract and concrete references. While the biblical adoption imagery relies on a cultural understanding of adoption that is no longer reflected in today's context, there are enough attributes in modern Western adoption that allow the metaphor to be intelligible: For example, both practices include a change in legal status to include rights of inheritance and both often include a change in social status (in modern Western adoption, children generally move from a lesser-advantaged to a higher socioeconomic level). Evangelical leader and adoptive father John Piper cites these similarities in his published sermon "Adoption: The Heart of the Gospel." He argues there are eight comparisons between adoption of children in contemporary society and the Christian God's adoption of believers: Both are (1) costly; (2) involve a change in legal status, (3) inheritance rights, and (4) a familial relationship; (5) result in a moral transformation; (6) involve planning; (7) bring adoptees out of bad situations; and (8) involve suffering now for later glory. His list of

---

10. For example, search *adoption* on Pinterest, GoFundMe, or Facebook. Also, note the prominence of evangelical Christians on blogs and discussion boards found at sites such as Adoptive Families Circle and AdoptTogether. Organizations that offer adoption grants to Christians who adhere to their faith statement include ABBA Fund and the Ephesians 3:20 Foundation.

similarities demonstrates the theological viability of adoption as a metaphor for evangelicals.

Piper's purpose in drawing these comparisons is to promote adoption by aligning it with the will and experience of the deity. Paired with the James 1.27 passage, the adoption metaphor becomes an ideal to imitate and a social agenda to promote. The Epistle of James calls on followers to be "doers of the word" (1.22). The heart of the *word*, which is another way of referencing the gospel message, is salvation. As we have seen, one of the ways the New Testament presents salvation is as God's adoption of sinners. For evangelicals, Christians should adopt because God has adopted them (Romans, Galatians, Ephesians) and because God calls on believers to care for orphans (Jas. 1.27).[11] Christians are called on to do for orphans what God has already done for them as believers.

Coupling the James passage with the adoption metaphor suggests a new meaning for both. The New Testament metaphor does not make orphans into sons of God; it makes slaves inheritors alongside the son. By reading this adoption metaphor both in a modern Western context and through the hermeneutical lens of James 1.27, which advocates care for orphans, the metaphor seems to be referencing adoption as the practice of providing a father to the fatherless. The James passage is also given a new meaning when it is juxtaposed with the adoption metaphor. This passage stands in a long biblical tradition of public responsibility for the disadvantaged, including orphans, widows, and immigrants. James charges true believers to live out their religion with care for the orphan *and* widow. Read alongside the doctrine of adoption, the focus of James narrows even further to focus solely on orphans and further still to adoption as the means to caring for them. The passage that drew on a fundamental societal and structural responsibility for the oppressed seems to advocate instead for what is essentially a private act of *charity* in which a family adopts an orphan. An example of the conflation of the adoption metaphor with the James passage and the tradition in which it stands is clear in the advocacy materials of the Christian adoption agency America World Adoption: "The Bible references orphans and adoption over 50 times because of its importance to the Father. About half of these verses describe God's heart for this specific group of children. The other half pertain to Christians' mission to protect, give justice to and provide for 'the least of these.'" The biblical texts never use *orphan* and *adoption* together, and yet evangelical rhetoric links them as if the Bible (God) is calling on Christian families to

---

11. This pairing and justification is common: See Moore; Merida and Morton; CAFO, "Core Principles".

adopt children rather than generally to ensure that families without an adult male are cared for.

Read together, James and the adoption metaphor convert the biblical commitment to provide justice and material support for fatherless children *and* their mothers into the evangelical charge to provide a father to the fatherless at the expense of the mother. While the phrase *providing a father to the fatherless* suggests restorative measures, this is actually socially charged language that targets families of color as well as nontraditional families. The prevailing myth of failing black families with unwed mothers and missing fathers marks the children of women of color as especially in need of rescue. Women who are not raising children in a traditional nuclear family structure, including those in the LGBT+ community, are maligned by the seemingly rational appeal to provide fathers to the fatherless. The *biblical mandate* to adopt finds expression in racially coded language that is based on heteronormative assumptions and institutions.

Adoption is all the more seen as God's plan in evangelical Christianity because it functions as a missional activity. Linking the practice of adoption to the doctrine of adoption makes it an act of evangelism. The adoption movement makes clear that adoption is not simply about providing homes to needy children, as important as it may be for children to have parents. Rather, adoption is theologically foundational to the mission of the church. International adoption, especially, is seen as a *Great Commission* activity. Matthew 28.19 calls for Jesus's followers to spread the gospel across the Earth: "Go therefore and make disciples of all nations, baptizing them in the name of the Father and of the Son and of the Holy Spirit." According to David Platt, evangelical pastor and president of the Southern Baptist Convention's International Mission Board, adoption is *necessary* if one is serious about the Great Commission (Miller). Adoption as a form of evangelizing is also evident in the plea for donations on the BlogSpot of Orphan's Ransom, a Christian organization that seeks to help prospective adoptive parents fund their adoption: "Your contribution will benefit children who may otherwise never receive the gift of a family or hear the truth of Christ's love" (Orphan's Ransom). Dillon International, a leading Christian adoption agency, links adoption to evangelism in its statement of faith: "Dillon International was founded on the belief in the Great Commission of Jesus Christ." The view is also prevalent among evangelical adopters, as is shown in a comment responding to well-known Christian blogger and adoptive mom Jen Hatmaker and her discussion of ethical issues in international adoption:[12]

---

12. An atypical evangelical adopter willing to publically criticize evangelical positions, Hatmaker warns her readers that the Christian adoption narrative contributes to the flow of money from wealthy to impoverished nations in international adoption and that this money all too

Ben—May 14th, 2013 at 2:24 PM

But what of the Gospel? I have been separated from my family because I believe the Gospel . . . but I feel that I have gained everything. Is our mission to keep families together? What about in families where they'll never hear the Gospel? What is of more value? Could God not be using any of this to His Glory? Salvation requires a cost . . . to follow Jesus means leaving affections for things of this earth. My adopted son will be much better off with me . . . but it's not because of my wealth. it's because in my home he'll hear the Gospel where he probably wouldn't have with his birth parents. (Hatmaker)

This comment by an adoptive father reveals the ethical implications of viewing adoption as spreading the gospel: It associates the adoptive parents with the will of the deity and privileges adoption even in the face of moral objections. While international adoption options have diminished in recent years due to increasing restrictions by the sending countries, evangelical groups have stepped up promotion of domestic adoption and foster care as a means of essentially fulfilling the same role: a strategy for providing access to children to advance a theological agenda.[13]

Evangelical pastor and author Dan Cruver confirms that the real goal is to save the souls of children, but he also explains that adoption is evangelistic in another important way—it is an imitation of the gospel: "The *ultimate* purpose of human adoption by Christians . . . is to place them in a Christian home that they might be positioned to receive the gospel, so that within that family, the world might witness a representation of God taking us in and genuinely loving the helpless, the hopeless, and the despised" (Cruver 15). In Cruver's comments we see that not only does adoption provide a way for children to hear the gospel, it also serves as a demonstration of the gospel to others by mirroring the metaphorical adoption of believers as co-heirs with Jesus. Thus adoption is a way of living out the gospel for others to see what the Christian God does: *Saving* a helpless and hopeless orphan is a reflection of that God's redemption of believers through Jesus Christ. The family becomes a witness of the gospel, especially a conspicuous transracial family, because such a family inevitably seems to inspire questions about adoption.

Connecting adoption to the gospel message and evangelism means that adoption into an evangelical family—which is also typically a white, hetero-

often leads to corruption, such as mothers and families relinquishing their children because they were pressured or deceived.

13. In 2016, CAFO promoted Stand Sunday as one way to observe Orphan Sunday. Stand Sunday is an initiative to promote foster care as a Christian responsibility (Weber).

normative, two-parent family—is theologically the better choice than family preservation; the narrative thus supports the choices of the adoptive mother over the birth mother, privileging one kind of family over another. This theological foundation of adoption goes even further, though, than favoring the position of the adoptive parents; it implicitly maligns the birth parents, even while turning a blind eye to them. At first glance, the birth parents are simply ignored. There is no place in the metaphor for them: The only roles are God, who is played by the adoptive parents, and the new heir, whom the adoptee is cast to play. In line with the change of social status often seen in both the Hebrew Bible and the Roman adoption practice, the metaphor notes that the believer had been enslaved but is now a son. In Romans, Paul refers to humanity as formally enslaved to sin, and thus in the biblical context, the imagery of slavery is to an abstract master (Rom. 6.6, 16–20); however, according to another atonement metaphor known as the ransom theory, humans are enslaved to devil. This atonement theory views Christ's death as payment to the devil to free humanity from bondage. The ransom theory was not really developed until the third century in the work of Origen, and is rooted in a different set of biblical passages, but these atonement images and theories end up being conflated in evangelical Christian thinking, resulting in an amalgamation of ransom and adoption imagery.[14] Thus, while the impact of the adoption metaphor's reference to slavery originally would have emphasized the change in legal status, when the metaphor is read in light of the ransom theory and appropriated to support adoption of children, the lens of Christian theology suggests the birth parents as evil. Evangelical leader and adoptive father Russell Moore insists that birth parents should not be equated with Satan, but he states this because he himself draws on this theological framework to explain that adoption in Christ means a transfer from old fatherhood to a new one: "We are no longer Satan's children" (121). His very choice to use the imagery of being Satan's children ties these ideas together even as he professes to deny their association.

Additional association between adoption and the ransom theory of atonement comes from linking adoption fees with the cost of redemption. For example, the adoption grant organization Orphan's Ransom compares adoption fees to the *price* Christians were bought for and offers financial support to Christians who adopt (Orphan's Ransom). While there is no reference to Satan, there does not need to be: The contextualization of adoption fees in the ransom atonement theory suggests that the child's earlier life is one of sin and

---

14. Some find a biblical basis for the ransom atonement theory in passages such as 1 Corinthians 6:20, 1 Peter 1:18, and Mark 10:45.

darkness and the adoption is what saves the child from that darkness. Fund-raising is common for evangelical adoptions, and the church community is called on to help with this *ransom*. Russell Moore even sees the payment as part of spiritual warfare (53, 177–78).

If through adoption in Christ believers have a new identity that oblit-erates the old one, if that new identity is bought with a ransom to free the sinner from the devil, and if this metaphor is justification for and a call to the adoption of children, then the theological framework leaves its mark on our understanding of the practice of adoption. How can adoption not clearly be the better choice? Indeed, as the deity predestined believers for adoption (Galatians), did this same God not predestine these children for adoption? Adoption becomes the default choice; the association of the birth parents with the devil—however obliquely—helps reinforce the idea that God's desire must be for child removal rather than family preservation. This vilification of the birth family accords with persisting prejudices about the poor and families of color that attribute their struggles to moral failings and bad choices. This belief provides a theological justification to oppose governmental social ser-vices that might benefit such families.

While this theological framework already indirectly supports the role of the church and Christian families as a solution to the needs of these children instead of government agencies or policies, there is also unambiguous lan-guage in the evangelical orphan care movement framing the issue of orphan care as one that is the responsibility of the church and not the state. For exam-ple, in *Orphanology* evangelical ministers and adoptive parents Merida and Morton fault spiritual warfare along with "ineffectual governmental systems" for the number of "fatherless children" in the world and for the fact that the adoption process can be difficult (93). The only accepted role for the govern-ment seems to be for it to align public policy with the orphan care movement. Merida and Morton encourage political engagement if it can be discerned that government policy or action might help the adoption of orphans. As an example of how the government can help, they mention how Christian lobby-ists effected a change in US immigration policy that allowed families to adopt children with HIV from abroad (105). They offer no examples of government policies to help family preservation. Their focus is only on the orphans, and they argue that orphan care is the responsibility of the church; the state clearly needs to get out of the way.

Russell Moore argues against government involvement in *Adopted for Life*. Moore is an adoptive father as well as a leading evangelical theologian and president of the Southern Baptist Ethics & Religious Liberty Commission. He notes that Christians should both work to alleviate the poverty that sometimes is the reason for children being relinquished and at the same time take care of the children who have been orphaned. However, he never advocates for governmental programs or policies. In fact, he insists that the care of the vulnerable is the job of the church and not the government. Referring to a popular but controversial saying in the 1990s—"it takes a village"—Moore comments that it does not take a village if we mean the state. He argues that the proverb is biblically sound only if we mean the church: "The Bible's call to protect the widow and the fatherless is written to no one individual—and certainly not to Caesar's government" (115, 190–91). The focus of the evangelical orphan care movement is in line with this view, calling on the church community to care for the children and the adoptive families emotionally, spiritually, and financially. While there may be vague encouragement about working to end poverty, the clear focus is on Christian adoption rather than birth family preservation.

The Christian Alliance for Orphans (the advocacy group behind Orphan Sunday) also favors the role of churches over that of the state:

> Government can play a vital role in child protection, but government can never provide the love, nurture and sense of belonging children need to thrive. That happens only one home and family at a time. Consequently, the Church cannot outsource James 1:27. Churches possess the unique capacity, community and clear command to do this in an effective, sustainable way. Local churches must play the central role, both in embracing children and in embracing the families that embrace children. (CAFO, "About Us")

We see in this passage both the privileging of adoptive parents over birth families as well as the support of a neoliberal agenda. While the government is granted a role, the real work clearly belongs to the churches and should not be *outsourced*. James 1.27 is shorthand to identify the command of orphan care. While the biblical text calls on Christians to care for orphans *and widows,* only children are mentioned here: Government is to protect children; churches are to embrace children. Churches are also to embrace families that embrace children, but unmistakably this refers to adoptive and foster families, not birth families. Identifying the government role as that of protecting children calls to mind child protective services, which often removes children from birth families. Consider how this passage would read differently if instead the government was granted the vital role of *supporting families.*

Framing adoption as foundational to the mission of the church and, even more, as an imitation of the gospel glorifies adoption over any other kind of orphan care, prioritizes adoption into evangelical families over family preservation, and dismisses the birth mother from consideration. Furthermore, adoption as an observable parallel to atonement theology promotes adoption of nonwhites by American white evangelicals in order to make adoption and the church visible to the world. In all this, adoptive parents are ultimately privileged in their behavior and interests because their actions parallel the deity's: They are elevated as the ones who offer salvation. The result is a narrative that reinforces adoption and the church as the solution to a very complex social situation.

The Doctrine of Adoption and the Neoliberal Agenda

There is an idealized view of adoption as a win-win situation in which couples who want children provide a family for children who need one. The children are *lucky* and *chosen*; the adoptive parents are commended for *saving* a child. The birth mothers are grudgingly commended for *making a loving choice*. The practice of adoption is more complex than the idealized narrative and happens for a myriad of often interconnected reasons, ranging from social to economic factors. Whether it is a domestic or transnational adoption, rarely does adoption involve a true orphan—a child with no living parents—and more rarely does it involve a child without any extended family (Graf; UNICEF). Most often, the child moves from a marginalized or disenfranchised family to parents who are middle class or wealthy and white. Given the complexities surrounding adoption, the ethical issues, and the psychological difficulties that sometimes affect the children and birth families, adoption is a debated practice.[15] Clearly, given the economic factors that often lead to the relinquishment of a child, welfare provisions provided by the US federal or state government—in the form of such things as food stamps, affordable housing, childcare subsidies, or medical care—contribute to family preservation. Similar economic policies and state support would also increase the possibility of family preservation in countries that are large sending nations for international adoption.[16] One might think the family values often promoted by evangelical Christians in America would be in line with such economic policy. The political reality is not the case. In the evangelical Christian narrative, the solution is adoption: The *fatherless family* needs a father. The theological narrative behind the evangelical orphan care movement supports the removal of the

---

15. Pound Pup Legacy is a voice within the adoption community dedicated to discussing problems in adoption and foster care.

16. See Laura Briggs's discussion of socioeconomic factors in transracial and transnational adoptions in *Somebody's Children*.

child from the birth family, glorifies adoption, and ultimately lends support to the neoliberal ideal that minimizes state support for impoverished single mothers while seeking private solutions for children in need.

The movement appropriates the Bible to reshape a complex problem of women and children into a dramatic and preordained act of salvation on the part of the adoptive parents. The theological context ultimately centers the needs, wants, and perspectives of the adoptive parents. The child is the object of their wants and *salvific* actions, and he or she is to be grateful to the adoptive parents as Christians are to be to their God. The birth mother is kept backstage, having been written out of the production.

With the adoptive parents firmly identified with God, ethical concerns associated with adoption and foster care are effectively dismissed. Coercion, deception, and a system that prioritizes adoptive or foster families over birth families are all acceptable risks of evangelism. In the case of international adoption, this *Gospel-centered* adoption takes advantage of Western privilege to victimize women in developing nations as a form of Christian neocolonialism. In domestic adoption and foster care, God's *heart for adoption* allows the desires of wealthy, privileged members of society to take precedence over the needs and wishes of vulnerable women and their attempts at family preservation. The Bible and culture intersect to contribute to the vulnerability of certain women while promoting the interests of others, namely white evangelical Christian women. While clearly benefitting these women over others, the theology of the evangelical orphan care movement is a theology of patriarchy that fundamentally privileges God the Father.

Works Cited

ABBA Fund. www.abbafund.org.

Adoptive Families Circle. www.adoptivefamiliescircle.com/blogs/.

America World Adoption. "One Orphan." www.awaa.org/one-orphan.

The Bible. The New Oxford Annotated Version: New Revised Standard Version, 4th ed., Oxford University Press, 2010.

Briggs, Laura. *Somebody's Children: The Politics of Transracial and Transnational Adoption.* Duke University Press, 2012.

Christian Alliance for Orphans. "About Us." cafo.org/about/.

———. "Core Principles." cafo.org/about/core-principles/.

Cooper, Melinda. *Life as Surplus: Biotechnology and Capitalism in the Neoliberal Era.* University of Washington Press, 2008.

Cruver, Dan. "Adoption of the Prodigals." *Reclaiming Adoption: Missional Living through the Rediscovery of Abba Father,* Cruciform Press, 2011, pp. 7–18.

Dillon International. "Our Mission." www.dillonadopt.com.

Ephesians 3:20 Foundation. "Do You Qualify for a Grant?" www.eph320foundation.org/.

Graf, E. J. "The Lie We Love." *Foreign Policy,* 6 Oct 2009, foreignpolicy.com/2009/10/06/the-lie-we-love/.

Hatmaker, Jen. "Jen Hatmaker—Examining Adoption Ethics: Part One." 14 May 2013, jenhatmaker.com/blog/2013/05/14/examining-adoption-ethics-part-one.

HCCH. "Adoption Section." www.hcch.net/en/instruments/conventions/specialized-sections/intercountry-adoption. Accessed 15 Dec. 2017.

Joyce, Kathryn. *Child Catchers: Rescue, Trafficking, and the New Gospel of Adoption.* Public Affairs, 2014.

Medefind, Jedd. "Orphan Sunday 2016 Blew Us Away!" *Christian Alliance for Orphans,* 22 Nov. 2016, cafo.org/2016/11/21/orphan-sunday-2016-blew-us-away/.

Merida, Tony, and Rick Morton. *Orphanology: Awakening to Gospel-Centered Adoption and Orphan Care.* New Hope Publishers, 2011.

Miller, Adam. "Panel: Adoption Part of the Great Commission." *Baptist Press,* 9 July 2012, www.bpnews.net/38228/panel-adoption-part-of-the-great-commission.

Moore, Russell. *Adopted for Life: The Priority of Adoption for Christian Families and Churches.* Crossway, 2015.

Orphan's Ransom. "Welcome to Orphan's Ransom." orphansransom.blogspot.com/.

Piper, John. "Adoption: The Heart of the Gospel." *Reclaiming Adoption: Missional Living through the Rediscovery of Abba Father,* edited by Dan Cruver, Cruciform Press, 2011, pp. 95–107.

Pound Pup Legacy. "About Us." poundpuplegacy.org/about.

The Schuster Institute for Investigative Journalism. "Fraud and Corruption in International Adoptions," www.brandeis.edu/investigate/adoption/index.html.

Show Hope. "Our Story." showhope.org/about-us/our-story/.

Shull, Shay. "Party of Five." *Mix and Match Mama,* 27 June 2016, misandmatchmama.com/2013/08/party-of-five/.

Solinger, Rickie. *Beggars and Choosers: How the Politics of Choice Shapes Adoption, Abortion, and Welfare in the United States.* Macmillan, 2001.

UNICEF. "Orphans." 15 June 2015, www.unicef.org/media.

Weber, Jason. "One Question from a Pastor Changed Things for Hundreds in Foster Care." *Christian Alliance for Orphans,* 11 Aug. 2017, cafo.org/2016/08/05/one-question-pastor-changed-things-hundreds-foster-care/.

Wright, Dawn, and Jason Wright. "Our Family Story." *Wright Family USA—Are These Kids All Yours?,* arethesekidsallyours.blogspot.com/p/blog-page.html.

CHAPTER 3

White Futures

Reproduction and Labor in Neoliberal Times

HEATHER MOONEY

UNTIL 2016, Mexico was among the "rising stars" in destination commercial gestational surrogacy.[1] Following the 2014 bankruptcy of Planet Hospital, a California-based hospital that connected domestic clients with international providers (Lewin), international surrogacy programs developed to capture the burgeoning market. Catering largely to same-sex couples, Mexico-based clinics deployed a niche marketing strategy around *all families*. Like other international surrogacy destinations, Mexico was appealing to intended US parents given the lower cost (about one-third of US costs), availability of English-speaking staff, broker-client relationships that mediate across industries and match intended parents with contracted surrogates and oocyte vendors, Western medical and birthing practices, and vague philanthropic gestures of helping women in poverty. While these themes are present in commercial surrogacy discourse globally, Mexico was unique in its representations of and advertising to lesbian and gay parents, its close proximity to the US, and its connection with US partner clinics (streamlining transportation of sperm, zygotes, and/or surrogates across borders). As online magazine *Gays with Kids* concisely described: "Mexico is the rising star in affordable surro-

---

1. Commercial gestational surrogacy describes a procedure wherein a fertilized egg is implanted in a contracted laborer for the gestational period. With the increasing accessibility of assisted reproductive technologies, commercial surrogacy has skyrocketed in popularity across the globe.

gacy for gay men who are priced out of the US market. Mexico's advantage is the proximity to the US, its affordable medical and legal processes, as well as arrangements with Californian IVF [in vitro fertilization] clinics to create and implant embryos." In January 2016, however, laws in Mexico changed to prevent international surrogacy, which catalyzed hybrid clinics: California- and Mexico-based facilities that move Mexican surrogates and embryos across the US border to comply with new laws (The Fertility Institutes). Currently, in Tabasco—the state most popular with reproductive tourists—only heterosexual couples, who are Mexican citizens, are allowed to participate in surrogacy (Care Surrogacy Center Mexico).

Seventy-three percent of medical tourists research destinations and hospitals online (Stolley and Watson 188), making clinic websites an important site for analysis. From November 2014 through March 2015, I monitored seven websites to analyze transnational commercial surrogacy markets: CARE Surrogacy Mexico, Surrogacy Cancun, IVF in Mexico, Sensible Surrogacy, IP Conceptions, Surrogacy Beyond Borders, and New Life Mexico. These websites provide information through a series of tabs running across the tops of their pages, mostly on clinic services, legalities regarding contracts, FAQs, and so on. They boast prenatal interventions, such as sperm sorting to screen for genetic diseases, gender selection, and sperm washing (for intended parents with HIV or hepatitis). Some of the companies, such as New Life, are composed of global networks with "clinics and fertility centers . . . in various parts of the world," such as China, Georgia, Kenya, South Africa, India, Poland, Ukraine, and Mexico. Despite different clinic locales, the websites are strikingly uniform and showcase photos of smiling white babies and families. While the window into Mexico's destination surrogacy market was brief, this case study explores evolving assemblages of race and reproduction at the US/Mexico border.

To understand emerging forms of racialization, it is imperative to analyze the diffuse roles technology plays in producing bodies, reproduction, populations, and imagined futures. Enabled by new technologies, the outgrowth of international surrogacy journeys for the relatively elite is one obvious site through which individuals build, stylize, manage, and imagine family and the symbolic future. US anti-immigration discourse, often coalescing around the US/Mexico border, also provides a pertinent site to understand how race is produced through sociopolitical rhetoric, ideological anxieties about future-potentials, policing, and surveillance technologies. While different, surrogacy and anti-immigration discourses share key elements—technological advancements, economic relationships restructured by neoliberal policies, and the accompanying visualization and management of (reproductive) futures—and, importantly, they both symbolically and literally employ Latinx's bodies and (embodied) labor. These commonalities, explored in this chapter, undergird both industries and further entrench and extend patterns of racialization.

This essay begins by situating commercial surrogacy in Mexico against the backdrop of neoliberal policies and ideologies that impact raced and gendered labor formations in the global (bio)economy. Next, I explore emerging and competing framings of Latinx fertility in the commercial surrogacy market and in the mainstream anti-immigration discourse that exists in the US. This chapter focuses exclusively on US discourse and intended parents. This limited focus is because the surveilled border, (gendered) anti-immigrant rhetoric, and America's emphasis on *anchor babies* yields a unique site for understanding emerging forms of racialization in the contemporary US. By connecting these elements, specifically the construction and production of families and the projection of (threatening or hopeful) futures, we can explore how technology—as a constellation of sites, techniques, discourses, materials, and apparatuses—is employed and deployed in emerging forms of racialization. Following, I focus on how inclusive commercial surrogacy programs, like the pre-2016 clinics in Mexico that advertised explicitly beyond the heteronormative family structure, constructed *all families* through latent iterations of whiteness, futurity, techno-science, and consumption.

Finally, this analysis examines competing, future-oriented assemblages of racialization, where techno-scientific productions of hopeful or threatening futurity vis-à-vis family and fertility racialize bodies and populations, enabled and obscured by neoliberal market formations. Again, surrogacy and anti-immigration discourses are analyzed side by side, as both are saturated with future-oriented projections, which racialize through emerging technologies and biopolitically manage, surveil, and construct reproduction. In surrogacy markets and anti-immigration discourse, new visions of bodies (affect, movement, parts) made possible by technology (heat sensors, digital eyes, drones, macroscopic images of cells) extend patterns of racialization beyond morphology while paradoxically signifying on the future through projections of (raced) reproduction as threatening or hopeful. Though camouflaged by the intersecting neoliberal discourses of volunteerism, choice, and commerce, a clearer vision of a raced future emerges when looking across different formations of racialized labor and transnational flows of bodies, body parts, and capital.

Neoliberalism, Race, Gender, and Labor

Contemporary commercial gestational surrogacy is undergirded by neoliberal economic policies encouraging privatization, retrenchment of welfare states, lowered taxation, reduced state involvement in the economy, and opening of international borders for unfettered movement of capital, labor, and goods. Neoliberal labor practices continue to crumple existing regulations on employment, wages, worker rights, and labor conditions, making labor increasingly deleterious to employees and these effects largely invisible to consumers. These practices are coupled with future-facing, self-improving neoliberal subjectivities, anchored to the narrative of agency, free choice, individualism, and self-sufficiency, which in turn serve to obscure the socioeconomic systems that effectively constrain choice.

Commercial gestational surrogacy and other forms of embodied/affective labor have been identified as *stratified labor*—that is, as Colen describes, how "physical and social reproduction tasks are accomplished differentially according to inequalities that are based on hierarchies of class, race, ethnicity, gender, place in a global economy" (Twine 3). Neoliberalism exacerbates preexisting racialized and feminized labor formations, inviting women to work in positions of precarity that are associated with stratified labor more broadly. Currently, commercial surrogacy follows an existing neoliberal road map in which corporations invite low-cost, subcontracted surrogates to enter the global (bio)economy, promising a win-win for both consumers and laborers.

Predating neoliberal policies and amplified by their implementation, migrant labor within and across borders is notably gendered and raced. When studying women's migratory patterns, Ehrenreich and Hochschild note, "as women have become an ever greater proportion of migrant workers, receiving countries reflect a dramatic influx of foreign-born domestics. In the [US], African-American women, who accounted for 60 percent of domestics in the 1940s, have been largely replaced by Latinas, many of them recent migrants from Mexico and Central America" (6). In addition to care work, the overrepresentation of women of color in unskilled and semiskilled factory labor abroad and care labor in the US is well documented. In garment production—infamous for dangerous conditions—the workforce is also disproportionately female (about 70 percent) and young (Women in Informal Employment: Globalizing and Organizing). According to a 2013 report by the Center for American Progress, wages in Mexico (one of the top five countries in garment exportation to the US) declined between 2001 and 2011 by an average of 14.6 percent. Regardless of the task, these trends in labor are marked by hallmarks of neoliberal policies: lower pay; the gendered divide of the service economy; and the informalization and flexibility of labor made possible by subcontracting, precarious job security, and hours dictated by the contracting company (Monnier).

The implementation of neoliberal economic policies not only structures labor formations but also carries raced and gendered stereotypes. "It has been pointed out that the ideal global factory worker is a young woman, often a teenager, who is seen by the employer as having 'nimble fingers,' 'good hand-eye coordination,' and the 'ability to patiently accept a repetitive task.' . . . In the view of the West, women in the Global South are also seen as dependent, submissive, repressed and controllable—characteristics that make them particularly desirable for exploitive labor practices" (Bonacich et al. 350). Likewise, the assumption that women are designed for care labor—or that commercial gestational surrogates are inherently altruistic, fertile, and kind—reveal how labor is constructed vis-à-vis race and gender. Straddling neoliberal labor formations—from factory labor to domestic work to reproductive labor—"the construction of the 'Third World female worker' in . . . the global division of labor is shaped by both race and gender oppression" (Bonacich et al. 350), which legitimizes stratification through concrete policies as well as supposedly natural characteristics.

Neoliberalism and Surrogacy in Mexico

Neoliberal policies have extended wage and labor stratification, signifying and (re)producing racialized and gendered systems in the global bioeconomy, which is manifest in Mexico's commercial surrogacy market. Previously, *altruistic* surrogacy was legally allowed in Mexico. In turn, contracts varied greatly, from obligations-oriented to rights-oriented (including the right of the woman to have a say over the contracted pregnancy). Surrogate laborers at times were required to stay in dormitories for the gestational period, though some gestated the pregnancy in their homes (Field). As clinic websites and existing research suggest, oocyte vendors can be sourced from anywhere in the world, and those vendors with white skin and features are more highly valued (Harrison; Schurr).

In Mexico's pre-2016 surrogacy market, women came from a variety of socioeconomic and education backgrounds and reported a variety of reasons for participation in the industry. However, the "common denominator [was] that . . . they [were] unemployed and in a tight financial situation" (Schurr and Perler 3). Recruited via Facebook or other means, the payment for their services ($11,000 to $19,000) represented about three to four times the minimum wage and the average household income in Mexico (Schurr and Perler 3). This was especially pertinent in Tabasco, where surrogacy was legal and the unemployment rate is highest in Mexico (Burnett). As a Mexican woman interviewed in *The Guardian* described, the monthly payments "tripled her previous income from working as a maid. 'I'm doing this for my children,' she said. 'It's a hard job, but it's better than prostitution, which is the only other thing round here that can earn you a bit more'" (Tuckman).

Most seeking surrogacy in Mexico pre-2016 were economically elite, white foreign nationals from Europe and the US (*güeros*), with white gay-identified men from the US as the primary clientele (Schurr 249). In Tabasco, where surrogacy briefly boomed, commercial surrogacy was made illegal due to claims of foreigner *abuse* of the system. However, others believe it is less about *abuse* of children and women and more about institutionalizing heterosexism against the majority same-sex couples seeking surrogacy in Mexico (Burnett).

While contested in their emergence and application, the confluence of new technologies and existing global neoliberal labor formations propelled commercial surrogacy in places such as Mexico, where existing forms of feminized and racialized labor are literally embodied in reproductive markets.

Framing Fertility

Although neoliberal policies structure the sociohistorical field of reproductive markets in Mexico, this section examines paradoxical framings of Latinx fertility. First, I analyze the construction and erasure of Latinx fertility in reproductive markets from the perspective of race, futurity, neoliberal discourse, and techno-science. Next, I examine the stereotypes of Latinx fertility in mainstream anti-immigration discourse. The purpose of this section is to examine how disparate frames of Latinx fertility reify and extend stratified labor formations.

Framing Fertility: Anti-Immigration Discourse

In mainstream US discourse, Latina women's bodies, reproduction, and fertility are often rendered through vitriolic anti-immigrant rhetoric. These anti-immigration discourses are notably raced and gendered, as they hinge on the supposed excess of Latinx reproduction. This pathologization of *excessive* Latinx bodies, families, and cultures is accompanied by a discourse of contagion, poisonous to the supposed American lifestyle. Latinxs are targeted within and across multiple social silos, including academics, popular culture, and politics, due to perceived threats posed by proximity and perceived *otherness*. Such vitriol is the result of racism and socioeconomic anxieties undergirded by flows of capital, representing a supposed threat to the economic stability of the US from its neighbor Mexico.

For instance, the terms *anchor baby* or *terror baby* (Cohen) linguistically highlight the anxieties about the reproductive capacity of noncitizens as inherently threatening. These terms displace the threat onto future-potential children as always already destructive to the hegemonic social order. The anchor baby is a sociopolitical symbol: It is racially coded and indicates future-directed anxieties around citizenship, reproduction, and belonging. Further, the anchor baby is tied to supposed malignant forms of (raced) reproduction, specifically related to projections of excessive Latinx fertility.

Indeed, "fears of immigrants' sexuality and their reproductive capacities are not new. Race, immigration, and fertility have formed a fearsome trinity for much of US history" (Chavez 71). The 1968 text *Population Bomb* posited that high population growth in places like Latin America would catalyze "environmental degradation, famines, pestilence, and wars between rich and poor." Alarmist news titles such as "White Americans to Become Minority by 2044 Thanks to Ageing Population while Hispanics Will Make up a Quarter of US Citizens" predict the exact "year when minorities will outnumber whites" (Pleasance). In mainstream US imaginaries, the future is constructed as threatening: *overpopulated* and *outnumbered* by *minorities*, hinging on the supposed *excess* of Latinx reproduction.

Raced and sexualized nation-space is also produced through fantasy sites, like the online game *Border Patrol* where users have "one simple objective [. . .] keep them out . . . at any cost!" Players are able to point and shoot at three stereotypical "border crossers," including a female figure with her children labeled "breeder" (Chavez). In 2014, the adult website PornHub launched an atrocious miniseries that depicted the rape of Mexican women and girls at the US/Mexico border by border patrol agents, before forcibly returning the women to Mexico (O'Neil). In these sociopolitical fantasy spaces, Latinx women are imagined as threats vis-à-vis reproductive excess and policed for their imagined or physical proximity to the US nation. They are punished for their perceived transgression sexually or using symbols of their reproduction; users are invited to affirm violent US masculinity by disciplining so-called illegals along raced, gendered, and (hetero)sexualized lines. While these practices are not inherently tied to surrogacy and those who partake, they are part of a broader (neo)liberal landscape where nation, reproduction, gender, and race are produced through a constellation of diffuse sites and practices.

In its myriad social forms, this rhetoric has had concrete effects in the US, where in the 1960s through today, "concerns about overpopulation, . . . increasing Mexican immigration, rising welfare roles [sic], and the alleged costs of delivering the children of undocumented immigrant women in US hospitals influenced the identification of Mexican-origin women, who were believed to have many children, as a group needing to be sterilized in the Southwest" (Gutiérrez and Fuentes 90). While women in general experience gendered pressures of reproduction, women of color disproportionately experience the reach of reproductive racism, including symbolic/discursive violence of "controlling images" (Collins 69), sexual violence, forced sterilizations, hysterectomies given without informed consent or under duress, aggressive marketing of experimental and questionable contraceptives, and invasive legislation in the US and internationally. In the face of such violence, women of color have overwhelmingly organized against white supremacist systems, launching covert and overt campaigns to resist myriad forms of reproductive oppression (Silliman et al.). In addition, while reproductive racism continues in diverse forms, there are mobilizations against it, such as the recent implementation and then cessation of enforced separation of migrant children from their families at the US/Mexico border (Gonzalez). While this does not guarantee migrants and their families safe entry, it does indicate some normative limitations on reproductive racism that emerge in US discourse. Given this confluence of forces, the biopolitics of race and reproduction in the context of neoliberalism is at once contested and clear.

Sterilization and reproductive control haunt surrogacy landscapes in Mexico. For example, in the pre-2016 Mexico-based commercial surrogacy market, one group of prospective parents to whom surrogacy was directly advertised was HIV-positive couples. While developing (bio)technologies that offer new and exciting options to HIV-positive individuals seeking biologically related children, this marketing trend ran in contrast to data on sterilization—including of HIV-positive women—in Mexico and Latin America more broadly. During a four-country study in 2014 (focusing on El Salvador, Honduras, Mexico, and Nicaragua), researchers found that one-quarter of the 285 women in the study living with HIV reported pressure from healthcare providers to undergo sterilization. While HIV diagnosis and pregnancy and children strongly predicted medical pressure to sterilize, young women and women without children also experienced pressure to sterilize from doctors. Indeed,

> women who had a pregnancy in which health care providers knew they were living with HIV—who were either diagnosed with HIV during prenatal care or had a pregnancy after the diagnosis—were almost 800% more likely to experience pressure to sterilize. . . . In addition, we found that only slightly more than half of the women who participated in the study were told that there exists an intervention—a regimen of AIDS-fighting antiretroviral drugs—that can reduce the probability of HIV mother-to-child transmission by 98%–99%. (Feldscher)

Using sperm washing, economically advantaged HIV-positive parents can reduce the possibility of HIV transmission from parent to child. Alternatively, Mexican women of childbearing age continue to face a real possibility of experiencing pressure to sterilize due to their HIV-positive status. The contradiction is clear: US HIV-positive couples were invited to reproduce biologically related families through Mexico-based commercial surrogacy, whereas some Mexican women are excluded from accessing such techno-scientific interventions or from reproducing altogether. Further, women with more children were more likely to experience this pressure, violently enacting the containment of excessive fertility. This form of neo-eugenics (Pande 104) reflects the differential policing of bodies in the global (bio)economy, which manifests along racially and economically stratified lines. In contrast to mainstream discourse, Latina women's pivotal role in assisting (white) reproduction is valorized through emphasis on "shared values," family-oriented "dreams," and medical innovations on surrogacy websites.

Framing Fertility: Surrogacy Websites

As Cooper and Waldby, Pande, and Deomampo have shown, the construction and marketing of commercial gestational surrogates' fertility often focuses on the rhetorical camouflaging of commerce using gift narratives, a common practice in reproductive markets. Clinics often framed surrogacy using altruistic motivations (especially where legal codes require it), which obscures the social and economic conditions that inform the decision to labor as a surrogate. New Life Mexico noted, "We thoroughly screen our intended parents, surrogates and egg donors to ensure that all parties share the same values and commitment" (New Life Egg Donors). Surrogacy Cancun reported, "Our surrogates are treated with the greatest of care and attention, in line with the incredibly selfless act they are performing."

Pre-2016 Mexico-based surrogacy websites also included frequent references to tourism, as multinational fertility corporations aligned themselves with Mexico's burgeoning health tourism industry. Mexico is highly ranked in terms of international tourist destinations, with medical tourism a booming segment of the tourist industry in Mexico (Oxford Business Group). Overall, tourism constitutes about 9 percent of Mexico's GDP (United States–Mexico Chamber of Commerce). According to the Medical Tourism Association, "almost 12 million international visitors arrived in Mexico in 2013, 6.5 million of the visitors were from the US." Patients Beyond Borders describes, "The lion's share of medical travelers to Mexico patients are regional—from Texas,

Nevada, Arizona and Southern California seeking easy access to affordable dental care and cosmetic surgery. However, patients from Canada and the UK are also drawn to the region due to the lack of waiting times from overburdened public healthcare systems and the lure of the warm Caribbean waters."

In Mexico, medical tourism locations were strategically located in tourist areas. For instance, Surrogacy Cancun states,

> Cancun is extremely friendly to tourists as direct flights arrive daily from the US, Canada, the UK, Russia, and other countries. . . . An additional benefit to starting your surrogacy journey in Cancun is the sheer number of tourism opportunities that also exist. From the incredible beaches, to the amazing Mayan temples like Chitzen Itza and Tulum, to the ecotourism opportunities in places like Xel Ha, there is something for everyone. It will make your surrogacy journey to Cancun even more memorable.

"Surrogacy journeys" are situated within broader enterprises of experiential travel, replete with a "sheer number" of "opportunities" integral to the tourist/consumer experience. Surrogacy, and the (future) consumers therein, becomes folded into tourism and vice versa. Pre-2016 commercial surrogacy in Mexico mirrored existing patterns where economically elite and, often, white bodies moved unperturbed across borders, following sociohistorical flows of capital, labor, and biopower. Commercial gestational surrogacy in Mexico capitalized on existing industries, including the tourism industry.

Brokering strategies—wherein intended parents are connected with surrogates through a third party—were common to the industry. CARE answers "How Can We Build a Family?" by stating, "Gay male couples who are pursuing their dreams of building a family are able to use donated eggs with the help of a gestational surrogate. [CARE makes] the process for gay male couples as straightforward as possible, helping you not only select the proper surrogate mother but also providing meticulous legal guidance." This process facilitated client-to-clinic relations while framing and constructing the surrogate laborers as requiring surveillance and social control. Surrogacy Cancun's "Common Questions" page stated: "It is sometimes possible to meet the surrogate, but direct communication is not allowed during the process. If you wish to communicate with your surrogate . . . we can setup a video conference through our office." On the FAQ page of Surrogacy Beyond Borders, the query "Can I meet the surrogate?" was answered thus: "Yes, we can arrange for you to meet or Skype with your surrogate once there is a confirmation of pregnancy. All of our meetings or Skype calls are chaperoned by our Mexico manager as we do not want our clients to be put in position where they could potentially be leveraged for more money." Brokering strategies and paternalistic language, while common in Mexico-based and reproductive markets more generally, constructed gestational surrogate mothers through rhetorics of control.

Framing Fertility: All Families?

While gift narratives, racial coding, tourism advertising, and brokering models are common on international surrogacy websites, the focus of pre-2016 Mexico-based websites on *all families*—that is, LBTQ+, HIV positive, single, and other variations—was unique. This seemingly pluralist marketing strategy invites analysis of the neoliberal logics of choice that undergird assemblages of whiteness, futurity, and the constructions of family.

In the techno-scientific family-building market of commercial gestational surrogacy, the deployment of neoliberal choice-based rhetoric is clear. As Chen and Gill have both noted, "choice," "agency," and "freedom" are integral to neoliberal projects, signifying an agentic subject through consumption and individual desires. Similarly, neoliberal subjects are invited to actively invest in the future through techno-scientifically aided family production and consumption. Their agentic choices can be described as *entrepreneurial interventions* into the future—that is, choices made in the present in order to stylize the future (in terms of self, family, and community). In such interventions, futurity is produced and consumed in the process of family-building. Surrogacy websites appeal to future-oriented neoliberal subjectivities by evoking *hopes* and *dreams,* which can be materially actualized through consumption. Not only is a literal child produced through the surrogacy process, but subjects are also invited to construct symbolic futures through market participation. This serves the neoliberal function of agentic/subjectified production (of the child/future) and consumption (of the child/future).

Mexico-based surrogacy websites were consistent and unique in the pluralist emphasis on *all families,* a term used to market toward lesbian and gay couples, as well as single and HIV-positive couples, who have typically been economically, legally, or socially prevented from adopting children or undertaking surrogacy arrangements (American Civil Liberties Union). Every website examined included a "Gay Surrogacy" tab on their homepage or a "Surrogacy"/ "Intended Parents" tab that led to a "Gay Surrogacy" or "Gay Intended Parents" option. As the "Welcome" page of New Life Mexico stated: "[We are] dedicated to help local and international, single, married, straight, LGBT and HIV-Positive intended parents realize their dream of having a child." The home page of Surrogacy Cancun featured the image of two white men

FIGURE 3.1. Surrogacy Cancun advertisement
highlighting fertility tourism

FIGURE 3.2. Surrogacy Cancun advertisement
showing symbolic elements of family and futurism

embracing and smiling, with the caption "Global Leader in Same Sex Surrogacy" and "Gay Surrogacy With Savings up to 75%." IP Conceptions featured an up-close shot of a white man and infant, with white-text overlay: "Mexico offers surrogacy to ALL intended parents." Sensible Surrogacy opened with a white child swaddled in white blankets, underscored by "A complete family is within the reach of every loving couple."

All families were vividly described and visualized on the web pages. Figure 3.1 shows one advertisement for Surrogacy Cancun, which features a family nearly eclipsed by a looming, white, blue-eyed baby superimposed into the beach skyline.

Figure 3.2, also from Surrogacy Cancun, includes many symbolic elements of family and futurism, featuring two white men holding hands, walking on a sunny beach into their new lives. In this image, the lack of a transition (sunrise or sunset) suggests the shared and glorious infiniteness associated with the future.[2] The inclusive, family-oriented future—much like these ocean-side strolls—are bright, infinite, and promising. Under "Our Commitment to Gay Surrogacy!" Sensible Surrogacy stated,

> We believe all loving couples deserve the right to a complete family. In our contemporary culture, families come in all forms. . . . What defines a family is the bond between its members, not traditional stereotypes. We consider it our moral responsibility to assist all loving couples in the creation of complete families, regardless of gender. We are committed to finding affordable, legitimate, and secure solutions for same sex & single parents looking to fulfill their dreams.

The pluralist construction of *all families* was vividly illustrated on these websites. Families are a life-right, determined by "bonds" forged "between members" and "not traditional stereotypes." Borrowing from the logics of (neo)liberalism, families are an intentional choice, a "moral responsibility" and a "dream" to be "fulfilled." The "bond" between its members is made by techno-scientific intervention beyond the body, tied to the desire for biologically related offspring. While indicative of important strides made toward social acceptance of lesbian- and gay-identifying parents, paradoxes emerge.

---

2. The complete removal of darkness or nighttime in the frame not only hails futurity but also erases suggestions of (homo)sexuality. As latent and overt heterosexism and homophobia continue to manifest across the globe, this image desexualizes same-sex relationships by removing the suggestion of a gay couple together at night, while maintaining the positive associations with reproduction, family, and futurity.

Who constitutes *all families*? In this market, who was invited to (re)produce, and who—through material and rhetorical effects—did it repress? In neoliberal times, what does the present-day racialization of labor flows and families reveal about the racialization of the future? When considering the evocation of *all families,* the racial coding on these websites made the limitations of *all families* clear. In this instance, *all families,* while not necessarily heterosexual, were overwhelmingly white and relatively elite (Schurr 248). *All families* on these sites did not include the economically disadvantaged and those who labor to make *all families* a reality for consumers. When examined at these disparate sites, *all families* is a selectively used trope that represents a space of hope, dreams, and personal fulfillment through white family reproduction, amplified by neoliberal policies and the rhetoric of choice. In sharp contrast to the discourse of *all families* that threaded through Mexico-based commercial surrogacy markets, the social and political vitriol levied at Latina women shows how *all families* obscures how some families are denied reproductive freedom, and labor in the production of *all families.*

White Futures

This final section aims to illustrate how neoliberalism and techno-science are complicit in the racialization of the future through disparate constructions of fertility. First, the connections between futurity and fertility must be made. The future, never reachable but constructed in present time, is paradoxically experienced as a space of both promise and threat (Gregg and Seigworth 10). These dual possibilities demand contemporaneous action to maximize promise and alleviate threat. The "self-renewing menace potential" (Massumi 53) of the future describes how threats produced in the present are always juxtaposed by hope of what is to come. Circularly, there is need of immediate action to allay future-potential threat. This future paradox melds with neoliberal, capitalist logics through the constitutive discourses of choice and informed consumption, as perpetual investments are made into the future to create surplus value. Neoliberalism invites the mitigation of future anxieties through informed consumption and investments, which map onto existing patterns of stratification. Fertility, also related to future imaginaries and embedded in neoliberal logics, can be analyzed on individual and social levels as a part of the promise/threat paradox.

Second, the conflation of (racialized) fertility and offspring with certain visions of futurity is well documented, with the figural (white) Child a guiding specter of sociopolitical systems (Bliss 85; Edelman). As Edelman describes, the Child "terroristically holds us all in check and determines that political discourse conform to the logic of a narrative wherein history unfolds as the future envisioned for a Child who must never grow up" (11). Bliss and others critique this, pointing to how marginalized populations have been denied and controlled by reproductive futurism in white supremacist systems (86). This essay has already articulated how the symbolic construction of futurity and (raced) reproduction manifests on Mexico-based commercial surrogacy websites and in anti-immigration discourse. While both discourses employ Latinx fertility and reproduction, the resulting assemblages are quite different. On commercial surrogacy websites, Latinx fertility is tied with *promise* and *hope* in the production of white families. In anti-immigration discourse, Latinx fertility and reproduction imply the *threat* of (over)production of Latinx families. The promise/threat of futurity is rendered visible as a racialized phenomenon.

One must, therefore, examine how racialized futurity is produced at these disparate sites. In commercial surrogacy and anti-immigration discourses, techno-scientific surveillance is—in part—complicit in producing future imaginaries. Surveillance technologies, medical industries, and labor are all enmeshed in neoliberal policies of production and exchange. Technologies are also fundamental to the (bio)mediated production of race and racialization. Put differently, constructions of race are actually beyond physicality; they are an insidious series of institutional and sociopolitical effects that produce the precarity racialized bodies experience. Part of this production includes new ways of coding and representing the body *beyond* morphology. As Clough states, "Although the visibility of the body-as-organism still plays a part, the biomediated body allows the raced body to be apprehended as information" (220), through which racialization and social control newly manifest.

Both surrogacy and immigration share a preoccupation with surveillance over bodies, bodily affect, and body parts, qualifying and quantifying data about body composition, surfaces, and movement through informatic biomediation. Surveillance mechanisms—such as heat and motion sensors, digital eyes, drones at the border, or biomedical monitoring of a fertilized egg and the laborer that houses it—that "[apprehend] as information" (Clough 220) are complicit in racialization beyond physical morphology. The surface and movement of the body is re-visioned through techno-scientific surveillance, in turn reassembling and extending racialized productions of fertility and futurity along familiar lines.

Products of US border surveillance technology produce popular conceptions of an overflowing Mexican citizenry, (re)producing the larger anxiety of overpopulation. The US/Mexico border is monitored in border patrol

23/06/2007 05:04:46

FIGURE 3.3. "Secure Border Intel"

offices and by civilian groups like Secure Border Intelligence, who provide interactive maps allowing users to explore grainy footage collected by night cameras, heat sensors, live radio streams, and mobile drones. Most of these videos, like the one in figure 3.3, show slow and seemingly endless processions of people walking "north," while others depict the corralling and arrest of presumably immigrants by border patrol agents.

The border images produced by such surveillance invoke (future) threat vis-à-vis depictions of illicit movement, further circulating the affective logics of uncontrollable excess. Both explicitly and implicitly, these techno-mediated representations reference the supposedly excessive reproduction of Latina/xs, producing charged discourses around "swarms of illegal aliens crossing the US Border" (National News Channel), or the 2018 migrant caravan allegedly concealing terrorists who threaten US national security (Youseff and Caldwell; Epstein and Sink).

Techno-scientific border surveillance footage stands in stark contrast to the images of reproductive surveillance on commercial surrogacy websites. In contrast, surrogacy websites erase surrogate laborers and employ techno-scientific images to incite promise and hope. First, surrogate laborers are markedly absent from clinic websites. The "present absence" (Smith 9) of sur-

FIGURE 3.4. Mexico Surrogacy Law

rogates is telling, particularly since this absence is *whitened,* filled with images of white families and babies. Whiteness, of consuming families and future children, is prominently featured on web pages. When visible, pregnant bellies—as a stand-in for surrogate laborers—are often white or ambiguously raced.

Second, the surrogate's body and labor are often replaced with images of the IVF process, such as a macroscopic shot of a needle piercing an egg. These repeated images represent the fertilization of the intended parents' (commissioned) egg prior to its implantation in the surrogate mother. On the clinic websites, Latinx fertility is sanitized, contained, or erased, and the future child (signified by cells) is curated, protected, and coupled with rhetoric of pregnancy and labor as "selfless," "altruistic," and "kind." In the computer-generated, microscopic images of assisted reproduction, the single egg mid-IVF signifies the miracle of life *and* the miracle of science, while also showcasing the sanctity of white (future) life within it. These images are part of the broader assemblages of racialized reproduction and racialized futures, with one image of Latinx reproductive capacity signifying *the miracle* and the other *the contaminant.*

The (bio)technical visual field that extends and produces knowledges and future-potentials builds on existing forms of stratification and narratives, ultimately reifying the sociohistorical biopolitics of (raced) reproduction. On pre-2016 Mexico-based commercial surrogacy websites, Latina women's fertility was reconstructed through the discourse of future-promise rather than future-threat, a site of promise rather than a site of destruction via unrestrained population growth or inherent illegality. Conversely, the so-called illegal immigrant is placed under police surveillance with state-of-the-art technology to protect the US border and the white citizens and space. The projected risk/value to racialized neoliberal futurity is monitored and controlled accordingly, both with material impacts on Latina women's bodies and reproduction. Both forms of techno-scientific surveillance are invested in present-future *protection* and *hope*—one of the US nation-space and the other of the commissioned fetus (further symbolic of nation itself). One hope is created by containing threat, the other by producing a white future child. The visions of overflow and malignant excess versus contained and technologized moderation are attached to the same body, differently deployed in constructions of (white) futures.

Conclusion

This chapter has argued that techno-scientific surveillance present in pre-2016 Mexico-based commercial surrogacy websites and border monitoring serves to racialize the hopeful or threatening future by differently deployed visions of Latina/x women's fertility. Both Mexican commercial surrogacy websites and anti-immigration discourse are part of competing assemblages of Latina women's fertility. Looking across disparate socioeconomic formations, techniques of racialization, violence, exploitation, resistance, and constructions of life itself become more salient. These constitutive processes apprehend bodies and novel renderings thereof in neoliberal and biopolitical formations, racializing projections of futurity. These are intertwined with and grounded in existing and emerging labor structures, wherein the production and commodification of embodied labor is reified and reconstructed through new processes of racialization. Importantly, this follows a road map of racist, sexist, and colonial histories, which are magnified and camouflaged by neoliberal policies and ideologies that frame stratified production and consumption of future life as a *win-win*.

Works Cited

American Civil Liberties Union. "Overview of Lesbian and Gay Adoption and Foster Care." *American Civil Liberties Union,* 2016, www.aclu.org/fact-sheet/overview-lesbian-and-gay-parenting-adoption-and-foster-care.

Bliss, James. "Hope against Hope: Queer Negativity, Black Feminist Theorizing, and Reproduction Without Futurity." *Mosaic,* vol. 48, no. 1, 2015, pp. 83–98.

Bonacich, Edna et al. "The Racialization of Global Labor." *American Behavioral Scientists,* vol. 52, no. 3, 2008, pp. 342–55.

Burnett, Victoria. "As Mexican State Limits Surrogacy, Global System Is Further Strained." *The New York Times,* 2017, www.nytimes.com/2017/03/23/world/americas/as-mexican-state-limits-surrogacy-global-system-is-further-strained.html.

Care Surrogacy Center Mexico. 2015, www.surrogacymexico.com/.

Center for American Progress. "Global Wage Trends for Apparel Workers, 2001–2011." *Workers Rights Consortium,* 2013, pp. 1–5.

Chavez, Leo. *The Latino Threat: Constructing Immigrants, Citizens, and the Nation.* 2nd ed., Stanford University Press, 2013.

Chen, Eva. "Neoliberalism and Popular Women's Culture: Rethinking Choice, Freedom and Agency." *European Journal of Cultural Studies,* vol. 16, no. 4, 2013, pp. 440–52.

Clough, Patricia. "The Affective Turn: Political Economy, Biomedia, and Bodies." *The Affect Theory Reader,* edited by M. Gregg and G. J. Seigworth, Duke University Press, 2010, pp. 206–29.

Cohen, J. Richard. "Campaign to Rewrite the 14th Amendment Based on Fearmongering Politics, Not Facts." *Huffington Post,* 28 March 2011, www.huffingtonpost.com/j-richard-cohen/campaign-to-rewrite-14th-_b_841480.html.

Collins, Patricia Hill. *Black Sexual Politics: African Americans, Gender, and the New Racism.* Routledge, 2004.

Cooper, Melinda, and Catherine Waldby. *Clinical Labor: Tissue Donors and Research Subjects in the Global Bioeconomy.* Duke University Press, 2014.

Deomampo, Daisy. "Transnational Surrogacy in India: Interrogating Power and Women's Agency." *Frontiers,* vol. 34, no. 3, 2013, pp. 167–88.

Edelman, Lee. *No Future: Queer Theory and the Death Drive.* Duke University Press, 2004.

Ehrenreich, Barbara, and Arlie Hochschild, editors. *Global Woman: Nannies, Maids, and Sex Workers in the New Economy.* Holt Paperbacks, 2002.

Ehrlich, Paul and Anne. *The Population Bomb.* Ballantine Books, 1968.

Epstein, Jennifer, and Justin Sink. "President Trump Admits He Has 'No Proof' Terrorists Are in the Migrant Caravan." *Time,* 23 Oct. 2018, time.com/5432702/president-trump-admits-he-has-no-proof-terrorists-are-in-the-migrant-caravan/.

Feldscher, Karen. "Under Pressure: Latin American Women Face Forced Sterilization." *Harvard School of Public Health,* 2014, www.hsph.harvard.edu/news/features/latin-american-women-face-forced-sterilization/.

The Fertility Institutes. "IVF Programs." *Fertility Institutes,* 2015, https://www.fertility-docs.com/programs-and-services/ivf-procedures/in-vitro-fertilization-options.php.

Field, Martha A. "Compensated Surrogacy." *Washington Law Review,* 2014, vol. 89, pp. 1155–84.

Gays with Kids. "Gays with Kids—Changing Surrogacy Options for Gay Men around the Globe." *Gays with Kids,* 2015, gayswithkids.com/changing-surrogacy-options/.

Gill, Rosalind. "Postfeminist Media Culture: Elements of a Sensibility." *European Journal of Cultural Studies,* vol. 10, 2007, pp. 147–66.

Gonzalez, Antonio. "Surrogacy Legal Frame and Procedure in Tabasco." *Mexican Surrogacy Law,* 2013, mexicansurrogacylaw.blogspot.com/2013/09/mexican-surrogacy-law-explained.html.

Gregg, Melissa, and Gregory J. Seigworth, editors. *The Affect Theory Reader.* Duke University Press, 2010.

Gutiérrez, Elena R., and Liza Fuentes. "Population Control by Sterilization: The Cases of Puerto Rican and Mexican Origin Women in the United States." *Latino(a) Research Review,* vol. 7, no. 3, 2010, pp. 85–101.

Harrison, Laura. "The Woman or the Egg?" *Genders,* vol. 58, 2013, pp. 1–19.

IP Conceptions. 2015, www.ipconceptions.com/.

Lewin, Tamar. "A Surrogacy Agency That Delivered Heartache." *The New York Times,* 27 July 2014, www.nytimes.com/2014/07/28/us/surrogacy-agency-planet-hospital-delivered-heartache.html?_r=0.

Massumi, Brian. "The Future Birth of the Affective Fact: The Political Ontology of Threat." *The Affect Theory Reader,* edited by M. Gregg and G. J. Seigworth, Duke University Press, 2010, pp. 52–71.

Medical Tourism Association. "Research, Surveys, Statistics." *Medical Tourism Association,* 2015, www.medicaltourismassociation.com/en/research-and-surveys.html.

Monnier, Christina. "Gender and Globalization." *Global Sociology,* 2011, globalsociology.pbworks.com/w/page/14711179/Gender%20and%20Globalization.

National News Channel. "Photographer Captures Swarms of Illegal Aliens Crossing US Border." *YouTube,* 2014, www.youtube.com/watch?v=lwqTWj_tlNU.

New Life Egg Donors. "Surrogacy in Mexico Is Still an Option." *New Life Mexico,* 2017, www.newlifeeggdonors.com/fertility-blog/surrogacy-mexico-still-option/.

New Life Mexico. 2015, www.newlifemexico.net/.

O'Neil, Patrick. "'Border Patrol Sex' Is the Lowest of the Low in Online Porn." *The Daily Dot,* 4 Dec. 2014, www.dailydot.com/politics/border-patrol-porn-sexual-assault/.

Oxford Business Group. "Efforts underway to diversify Mexico's rapidly growing tourism sector." *Oxford Business Group,* 25 March 2018, https://oxfordbusinessgroup.com/overview/strong-performer-efforts-are-under-way-diversify-rapidly-growing-sector.

Oxford Business Group. "Investment in expanding Mexico's medical tourism segment." *Oxford Business Group,* 25 March 2018, https://oxfordbusinessgroup.com/analysis/feeling-better-already-investing-expanding-medical-tourism-segment.

Pande, Amrita. *Wombs in Labor: Transnational Commercial Surrogacy in India.* Columbia University Press, 2014.

Patients Beyond Borders. "Mexico." 2015, www.patientsbeyondborders.com/mexico.

Pleasance, Chris. "White Americans to Become Minority by 2044 Thanks to Ageing Population While Hispanics Will Make up a Quarter of U.S. Citizens." *Daily Mail Online,* 16 Dec. 2014, www.dailymail.co.uk/news/article-2875786/White-people-minority-2044-thanks-ageing-population-Hispanics-make-quarter-U-S-citizens.html.

Schurr, Carolin. "From Biopolitics to Bioeconomies." *Society and Space,* vol. 35, 2016, pp. 241–62.

Schurr, Carolin, and Laura Perler. "'Trafficked' into a Better Future? Why Mexico Needs to Regulate Its Surrogacy Industry (and Not Ban It)." *Open Democracy,* 17 Dec. 2015, www.opendemocracy.net/beyondslavery/carolin-schurr-laura-perler/trafficked-into-better-future-why-mexico-needs-to-regulate.

Secure Border Intelligence. "Secure Border Intel—Arizona." *Secure Border Intelligence,* 2015, http://secureborderintel.org/arizona.html

Silliman, Jael, et al. "Undivided Rights: Women of Color Organize for Justice." *Center for American Progress,* 1 Oct. 2004, www.americanprogress.org/issues/women/news/2004/10/01/1115/undivided-rights-women-of-color-organize-for-reproductive-justice/.

Smith, Andrea. *Conquest: Sexual Violence and American Indian Genocide.* South End Press, 2005.

Stolley, Kathy, and Stephanie Watson. *Medical Tourism: A Reference Handbook.* ABC-CLIO, 2012.

Surrogacy Beyond Borders. "Surrogacy in Mexico—Home." *Surrogacy Beyond Borders,* 2015, surrogacybeyondborders.com/.

Surrogacy Cancun. 2015, www.surrogacycancun.com/.

Tuckman, Jo. "Surrogacy Boom in Mexico Brings Tales of Missing Money and Stolen Eggs." *The Guardian,* 25 Sep. 2014, www.theguardian.com/world/2014/sep/25/tales-of-missing-money-stolen-eggs-surrogacy-mexico.

Twine, France Winddance. *Outsourcing the Womb: Race, Class, and Gestational Surrogacy in a Global Market.* Routledge, 2015.

United States–Mexico Chamber of Commerce. "Issue Paper 3: Tourism Development, Medical Tourism, and Safe and Secure Tourism in Mexico." Aug. 2011, www.usmcoc.org/papers-current/3-Tourism-Development-Medical-Tourism-and-Safe-and-Secure-Tourism-in-Mex-ico.pdf.

Visit Mexico. "Mexico—Health Tourism." *Visit Mexico,* 2012, www.visitmexico.com/en/health/medical-tourism. Accessed 29 Dec. 2015.

Women in Informal Employment: Globalizing and Organizing. "Case Studies: Garment Workers around the Globe." *WIEGO,* 2015, wiego.org/informal-economy/case-studies-garment-workers-around-globe.

Youseff, Nancy A., and Alicia A. Caldwell. "Trump to Deploy 5,200 Troops to Southern Border." *Wall Street Journal,* 30 Oct. 2018, www.wsj.com/articles/military-to-deploy-5-000-troops-to-southern-border-u-s-officials-say-1540820650.

CHAPTER 4

One Woman's Choice Is Another Woman's Disobedience

Seguro Popular and Threats to Midwifery in Mexico

ROSALYNN VEGA

In the Nahua region of Veracruz, Mexico, two birthing women arrive at the midwife's home in the black of night. Since women are not allowed to give birth with a midwife, they are acting subversively. Both women are high risk: one is a young first-time mother, and the other has greying temples. Since local guidelines mandate that the midwife refer these cases to the hospital, she tacitly accepts the threat of imprisonment for defying government strictures.

In a wealthy neighborhood in the city of Irapuato, Yasmin sways back and forth in a birth pool, breathing deeply, timing her movements to the rhythm of soft music. She is surrounded by loved ones and the familiarity of her living room. Two young professional midwives reassure her. This is her third day of labor, but traumatic memories of a prior cesarean impel her to proceed. Finally, the baby begins crowning and moments later he is swimming in the water. Yasmin brings him to the surface of the water and begins breastfeeding him. The new family basks in their extraordinary achievement.

THIS ESSAY'S argument unfolds within the context of disparate birth experiences for the indigenous recipients of Mexico's universal health insurance, on the one hand, and affluent Mexicans receiving privatized care, on the other. I analyze how the emergence of Seguro Popular has inadvertently rendered midwifery difficult to practice and inaccessible to women who do not purchase medical services in the private health sector. That is, by offering medicalized birth free of charge to Seguro Popular enrollees, the modest out-of-pocket fees that midwives charge prove *expensive* in comparison. Furthermore, most poor indigenous women are also recipients of Oportunidades conditional cash transfer stipends. The Oportunidades program provides a living stipend to poor mothers, conditioned on their continued obedience to government mandates, which include giving birth in a public hospital (where the likelihood of cesarean section is high). Under these circumstances, midwives are forced to choose between economic insolvency or selling their services in the private sphere to affluent Mexicans and reproductive travelers seeking humanized birth.

The humanized birth movement in Mexico is an outgrowth of alternative birth movements in Europe, Canada, and the US. *Humanized birth* is a broad term used to describe nonmedicalized birth and was used widely by my study subjects to encompass natural birth, water birth, home birth, and midwife-assisted birth. In general, these births include vaginal delivery, resist the use of synthetic hormones and anesthesia, renounce the repetitive assessment of cervical dilation, and encourage a loving and pleasant environment in which the mother's comfort is primary. Thus, from the perspective of humanized birth leaders, it is important that women eat, walk, and spend time with loved ones during the birthing process. A smaller subset of informants preferred the terms *chosen birth* and *respected birth,* thus emphasizing the importance of respecting women's individual choices during the birthing process, and asserting that certain medical interventions are acceptable if they were elected by the birthing mother.

While the humanized birth movement gained popularity in Mexico, the introduction of Seguro Popular discouraged midwifery practices among poor indigenous women. I argue that by dismantling the economic pathways by which most midwives earned their living, Seguro Popular, in fact, has contributed to a burgeoning reproductive tourism industry, oriented around the *humanization* of birth.

Methods

This essay is based on twenty-eight months of in-depth research across thirteen Mexican states, from October 2010 to November 2013. Following Wilson,[1]

---

1. Wilson combines case studies from a variety of modern markets in order to paint a multifaceted portrait of the global economy. Similarly, my ethnographic work was organized around a variety of ethnographic sites through which I provide a detailed and complex description of traditional Mexican midwifery as a site of inclusion and exclusion.

I found different vantage points through which recent shifts in birth practices and healthcare can be examined. This method has been used by both American and Mexican anthropologists and harks back to Marcus and Menéndez. Echoing the multi-sited work of Rayna Rapp on amniocentesis, I uncovered inequality by interviewing people with a broad array of positionalities vis-à-vis midwifery and humanized birth in Mexico. In my research, I compare the experiences of Mexican women at both ends of the socioeconomic spectrum, thus revealing the powerful effects of affluent Mexicans and reproductive travelers seeking demedicalized births on the practice of traditional midwifery in Mexico.

This type of comparative research required redefining my preconceived notion of an ethnographic field site. The field I identified was not a *site* per se, but rather a network of people. I began with professional midwives in San Miguel de Allende, Guanajuato. These midwives connected me to other professional midwives practicing in other states,[2] and as I traveled across Mexico for participant observation and in-depth interviews, I also gained access to the clientele of this extended group of professional midwives. Through my attendance at multiple humanized birth conferences, I recruited more couples and humanized birth attendants, including physicians and obstetric nurses, to my study. Simultaneously, I volunteered at nongovernmental organizations (NGOs), gaining access to training workshops for indigenous traditional midwives. Having befriended a few indigenous midwives, and while staying as a guest in their homes during repeat visits to their villages, I witnessed their interactions with indigenous women and the *traditional* midwifery care they provide. Finally, I observed medical professionals and maternity patients in both private and public hospital settings and solicited interviews with physicians and policy makers.

The Scripting of Seguro Popular

After intense structural readjustment between 1983 and 1995, Mexico introduced neoliberal health reforms involving serious cuts in social spending, the privatization of public assets, and the reduction of trade barriers, which resulted in decreased salaries and limited employment (Laurell). The belief was that structured pluralism and market forces would foster competition, thus producing higher quality care at lower cost. This logic shaped the reform

2. My multi-sited research includes the states of Guanajuato, Guerrero, Jalisco, the Federal District, San Luís Potosí, Veracruz, Chiapas, Oaxaca, Quintana Roo, Michoacán, Hidalgo, Querétaro, and Nuevo León.

of employment-based health insurance schemes in 1995 to 1997 and in 2007 and was also the guiding logic during the scripting of Seguro Popular in 2004 (113). Instead, Mexico experienced an increasing deficit in the health sector. Laurell explains that within this context, Seguro Popular was proposed, in spite of "its limited packet of services; lack of medical facilities, personnel, and equipment; and insufficient budget to guarantee what it promises, etc." (116; my translation).

Since 2004, Seguro Popular has expanded to include 55.6 million people. According to the World Bank, 72.32 percent of Mexico's poor were enrolled in Seguro Popular by 2012. The *right to health* entitles enrollees to receive all interventions listed in the Universal Catalogue of Health Services (CAUSES) free of charge. Seguro Popular offers basic medical services in the areas of internal medicine, general surgery, obstetrics and gynecology, and pediatrics. This Selective Primary Health Care (SPHC) strategy is based on the principle of cost-effectiveness; as a result, CAUSES excludes most treatments for chronic illness and all expensive interventions.

It is noteworthy that CAUSES does not include services for specific illnesses and diseases; rather, it is a catalogue of concrete interventions that can be reimbursed through Seguro Popular insurance. For example, instead of including cervical dysplasia, CAUSES includes pap smears for female enrollees; as a result, once the patient has been diagnosed with cervical cancer, she is not provided with financial assistance, and treatment must be paid out of pocket.

The interventions covered by Seguro Popular especially target pregnancy, birthing, and early infancy, whilst primary causes of death in Mexico (neurological and vascular diseases, cancer, heart attack, cirrhosis, nephritis, and severe injury) are excluded. Laurell found that Seguro Popular enrollees are overwhelmingly women (82.4 percent), of whom nearly all are of reproductive age (94.3 percent are between 15 and 44 years old). Given these statistics, it is unsurprising that 61.2 percent of hospital visits made by Seguro Popular insured are related to pregnancy and birth (77). Laurell notes that despite this emphasis on pregnancy and birth, there has not been a significant reduction in maternal mortality. She speculates that the uneven coverage of Seguro Popular across different states and the "diversion of funds transferred to Seguro Popular to different ends" are potential culprits (77).

While cost-cutting is an announced goal, ironically, costly cesarean sections are performed in public hospitals at more than three times the World Health Organization (WHO) recommended rate. This essay points to the contradictions between global health metrics such as WHO-recommended cesarean section rates and the unfolding of citizenship-based healthcare programs such as Seguro Popular. I contrast global health goals with the lived realities of Mexican women—specifically, their inability to choose the birthing process within the context of an emerging universal health insurance that mandates medicalized birth, which often results in cesarean section. In essence, I argue that neoliberalism severely threatens the future viability of traditional midwifery and poor and indigenous women's access to such care.

The Effects of Millennium Development Goals (MDGs) and Seguro Popular on Midwifery

In 1997, the Center for the Adolescents of San Miguel de Allende (CASA) established a professional midwifery school and maternity clinic in Guana-juato, the heart of Mexico, the first accredited professional midwifery school in Mexico. The CASA model has since been replicated in the states of Guer-rero and Oaxaca—states with extreme poverty, large indigenous populations, and high maternal mortality rates. All three schools aim to recruit and train young women from rural and indigenous backgrounds with the hope that they will return to their natal villages to practice midwifery and thus reduce maternal mortality in places marked by the absence of medical resources and infrastructure.

In the state of Chiapas, however, a professional midwifery undergradu-ate program with the same recruitment strategy has received serious accu-sations from indigenous medicine practitioners of propelling the demise of traditional midwifery techniques. In a recently circulated letter, the midwives, indigenous doctors, and health promoters of the Organization of Indigenous Doctors of the State of Chiapas (OMIECH) claimed that the professional midwifery program was threatening traditional birth. The letter defended the continued need for traditional indigenous medicine in the state of Chiapas and denounced premeditated "ethnocide of indigenous midwifery." OMIECH also challenged claims of "reducing the maternal mortality rate through the professionalization of midwifery" and critiqued how maternal mortality *met-rics* were deployed to reinforce the hegemony of biomedical ideology and the undoing of traditional midwifery.[3] They further pointed to how both the state and federal health sectors lack the financial and structural resources to employ professional midwifery graduates, thus contributing to the privatization of midwifery and the undermining of midwifery's core values.

---

3. See Adams.

Of the CASA midwifery students I tracked over the course of nearly four years, very few chose to practice in high-need contexts after graduation. Instead, they chose to make a living selling private sector services in cities, and a couple of entrepreneurial-minded graduates planned to pursue lucrative opportunities in the *destination birth* industry by opening a *casa de parto* (a natural birth center) on the beach in Baja California. In the past few years, more and more wealthy couples from around the world have begun traveling to Mexican beach destinations to have a natural birth while, in the words of one informant, "swimming with the dolphins." These births are referred to as *destination births,* thus signaling their political and economic similarities with *destination weddings.* These midwives observed the financial success of European counterparts and obstetricians practicing humanized birth in the Tulum, Playa de Carmen, and Puerto Vallarta areas.

Millennium Development Goals (MDGs) are eight international development goals established after the Millennium Summit of the United Nations (UN) in 2000. All 191 member states of the UN and more than twenty international organizations agreed to meet these goals by 2015. While MDGs 4 (reduce child mortality) and 5 (improve maternal health) provide the impetus for philanthropic organizations and international donors to support the professionalization of midwifery in Mexico, professional midwifery services often do not reach their target population (the poorest women with the least access to gynecological services due to insufficient infrastructure and racial discrimination). This population includes indigenous women and those living in rural locations, since they are more likely to experience barriers when accessing maternal health services and their children face a greater risk of child mortality. In practice, however, the appropriate pathways are not in place to administer midwifery services to those who need it the most. Through my capacity as board member or volunteer at three transnational Mexico-US NGOs, I experienced firsthand the pressures NGOs face when seeking funding. NGOs submit grant proposals to funding sources using the rhetoric of MDGs, but funding sources' expectations for the implementation of MDGs can be at odds with the lived realities and priorities of the people for whom the intervention is intended. The inadvertent result is the reinscription of georacial and socioeconomic health disparities in Mexico.

I witnessed one concrete example of this conflict in an NGO proposal for an education-based intervention on birth spacing. This proposal appealed to the funding source's interest in reducing natality with the hope that this would lead to achieving the MDGs of reducing child mortality and improving maternal health. However, the proposal was intended for indigenous women, who, as a community, have been suffering from violating and traumatizing experiences of forced sterilization for decades[4] and for whom reducing natality was not a desired goal. In this instance, the need of the NGO to stay financially afloat played a role in wanting to carry out a project that, if funded, would be in stark opposition to the priorities of many among the *target population*.

Over the course of my fieldwork, I observed the circumstances under which NGOs that trained professional midwives received funding from the Carlos Slim Foundation, the MacArthur Foundation, and the Kellogg's Corporation. Unfortunately, many of these efforts not only made limited inroads in reducing child mortality and improving maternal health; they often failed to meet the needs of the target population. My observations signal how MDGs can inadvertently reinscribe inequality when neoliberal logic is used to shift the emphasis from public healthcare for citizens to cost-effective interventions for needy recipients[5]. The unintended consequences of this shift in logic are also evident when NGO-facilitated interventions elevate the priorities of funders over those of the target population.

In this already fractured milieu, the emergence of Seguro Popular played an important role in rendering the practice of professional midwifery in high-need settings an unviable economic strategy for professional midwives. In summer 2011, CASA midwifery services were included within Seguro Popular, supposedly rendering them free to all insurance holders. In practice, however, mothers seeking services had to get a referral from their assigned government clinic in order to transfer to CASA. These referrals were virtually unobtainable since in Mexico, hospital-based providers encounter the economic stimulus of reimbursement through Seguro Popular. In other words, the government clinic furnishing the referral would relinquish the reimbursement from Seguro Popular for services rendered to the patient. In the absence of referrals, midwives have become the *expensive* option, thus reinforcing biomedical hegemony and driving midwifery services further into the consumer market. In fact, I did not witness a single midwife-assisted birth during the summer of 2011. The absence of opportunity left the professional midwifery students frustrated and anxious about their lack of training *as midwives*—the vast majority of their experience was accrued in the general hospital, where they complained of serving as medical assistants in highly medicalized births.

At the time of my volunteering and direct participant observation of CASA, Sagrario Villareal was director. At the end of summer 2011, she accepted a position within the Center for Gender Equity and Reproductive Health in Mexico City, where she created a pilot program that used secre-

---

4. See Hall; also, see Frías.
5. See my article "Racial I(nter)Dentification."

tary of health funding to create salaried positions for CASA graduates within government clinics and hospitals in the state of Guerrero. I joined her for a supervisory trip of these professional midwives in summer 2013. While this trip gave me a more nuanced perspective on the difficulties of developing the midwifery model within medicalized hospital settings where cesarean procedures are rampant, in the intervening time, I observed how both traditional and professional midwives were being undercut by Seguro Popular's obstetric services.[6]

Las parteras se vuelven caras (Midwives Become Expensive)

The emergence of Seguro Popular supposedly meant free prenatal and medicalized birth services for all insurance holders; in actuality, however, as I observed during my ethnographic research, indigenous women often faced racial discrimination in government hospitals. Furthermore, while the development of universal health insurance was formulated as a political strategy to reduce health inequality among Mexicans, it has, in fact, reentrenched health disparities in some settings—especially in indigenous zones where a significant number of individuals do not possess the necessary documentation to enroll in Seguro Popular and continue to be uninsured.[7] For many of the low-income families eligible to enroll in Seguro Popular, the economic costs of giving birth are perhaps the primary consideration when choosing a provider or attendant. Despite complaints of racism and unnecessary medicalization of birth, many low-income families decide to give birth in the hospitals where Seguro Popular is accepted rather than pay out of pocket for a traditional or professional midwife. For Mexico's underclass, the decision-making process is shaped by serious financial constraints, thus uncovering how the neoliberal notion of *free choice* is predicated on the assumption of economic privilege and individual purchasing power. That is, the contrast between the natural births of humanized birth participants and the (at times coercive) medicalized births of indigenous women in government hospitals highlights the limits of *free choice* and the conditions under which choice-making unfolds in unequal contexts.

The introduction of Seguro Popular has had dire consequences for the livelihoods of traditional and professional midwives alike. I interviewed a

---

6. Here I am not labeling different types of midwives using hierarchical terms. Rather, I am using the terms these midwives use for themselves.

7. See Laurell.

Swiss midwife, Emma, the wife of a Mayan man and mother of their Mayan-Swiss children. Emma explained that before the implementation of Seguro Popular, her clientele was composed of locals, but after the initiation of Seguro Popular, she served a wholly foreign clientele. She opined that the decrease in women seeking midwifery services has led to an increase in competition among midwives for clients, and that as a result, "las parteras son muy envidiosas" (the midwives are very jealous of each other). She also commented, "I feel that in the future, if something doesn't change very soon, the midwife will only be for rich people."

Just a short distance away from Emma's home, Doña Carmelita receives patients who are referred to her from the hospital for *la sobada*.[8] While physicians possess limited training in repositioning fetuses and, therefore, tend to deliver breech-positioned babies via cesarean section instead of attempting a vaginal delivery, Doña Carmelita has had tremendous success using Mayan techniques for external cephalic version (controlled hand movements to manipulate a fetus's position), thus preventing many cesareans. Unlike the doctors who refer patients to her, Doña Carmelita cannot always provide services totally free of charge to her clients. She said, "If they want my touch, I receive them. If not, they go with Seguro Popular because it's free."

Another traditional midwife, Doña Esmeralda, complained that Seguro Popular has taken away all her clients. Before universal health insurance was implemented, she charged 600 pesos per birth (about 50 USD at the time or 30 USD at today's exchange rate). She would charge less and sometimes nothing at all if the client were unable to pay. She told me that after the initiation of Seguro Popular, her fellow villagers were only willing to pay 50 pesos for a birth and 9 pesos for a *limpia*[9] (about 4 USD and 75 cents at the time).

Three CASA students traveled to Aquismón in San Luís Potosí and discovered that patients would only seek help from them if their services were free. One of them provided this exchange to me:

"Are you here attending patients?"
"Yes."
"Are you charging?"
"No."
"Okay."

Only then would patients divulge their reproductive health concerns.

---

8. A form of Mayan massage.
9. An indigenous ethnomedical technique that removes illness and bad luck from the body.

In Michoacán, professional midwives training at Mujeres Aliadas, a civil association aiming to provide reproductive services to Purepechan women, faced similar challenges. At the time of my fieldwork, these professional midwives were charging a base price of 2,000 pesos per birth (about 160 USD). They applied a sliding scale based on patients' ability to pay and instituted an installment payment plan. Even these adaptations were not enough to outweigh the allure of Seguro Popular's free services. As a result, the users of Mujeres Aliadas birthing services turned out to be to middle-class mestizos, rather than the indigenous poor. When I interviewed Belinda, the resident physician at Mujeres Aliadas, she insisted that while the economic incentive to give birth in a hospital where Seguro Popular is accepted has been integral to patients' decision to forgo midwifery services, these patients very much wish they had an equally affordable alternative to the overcrowding, racial discrimination, and ill-treatment that many experience in hospital settings.

Thus, the result of Mexico's neoliberal healthcare system has been increased financial pressures for midwives, which in turn has led to the unaffordability of midwifery practices for the underprivileged. In fact, with the rise of reproductive tourism and *destination births,* midwifery services are increasingly sold as a market-based consumer good for those with sufficient purchasing power.

Seguro Popular: A Neoliberal Strategy

Seguro Popular has been presented as a great healthcare success in international health forums. Many of its proponents compare it to the Universal Health System (SUS) in Brazil. Lina Berrio at the Center for Superior Research and Studies in Social Anthropology, however, argues that Brazil's SUS is better funded than Seguro Popular, and questions the success of SUS given overcrowding, limited access, and long wait times.[10] I would argue that while Seguro Popular has been labeled *universal insurance,* in actuality, it is only for those who are not enrolled in employment-based health insurance. Furthermore, it is implemented distinctly in each Mexican state due to Mexico's decentralized healthcare system. Although Seguro Popular is federal policy, health administration decisions are made at the state level, and Seguro Popular has not been structured to meet the particular needs of Mexicans in disparate contexts. Finally, while Seguro Popular is touted as a global health

---

10. Lina Berrio expressed these criticisms to me in an ethnographic interview.

success using a rhetoric of *universality*, it in fact delimits and restricts public health services.

Also troubling is the fact that Seguro Popular has played an important role in furthering the privatization of the Mexican healthcare system. For example, when the government pharmacy lacks medication or the government hospital is unable to offer a service due to a lack of equipment or personnel, patients are referred to private pharmacies and private hospitals. According to Laurell, the fact that only 6.5 percent of Seguro Popular funds nationwide are spent on medications suggests that the private pharmaceutical sector is being significantly bolstered by Seguro Popular reimbursements (99). Thus, the privatization of health services is not beneficial to people living in rural and indigenous zones. Laurell writes,

> The assumption that the delivery of private services stands in for the lack of human and physical resources in the public sector seems to obey ideological reasoning more than real evidence. Although there is an increase in the private clinics and hospitals, by definition their emergence follows profit interests, and it is unlikely that this expansion will occur in the poorest zones of the country where there is the greatest shortage. (119; my translation)

Laurell's observations—that the institution of Seguro Popular has fueled privatization, which in turn follows market logics, thus authoring the abandonment of those living in the poorest zones of the country—were confirmed in my observations of Seguro Popular's effect on midwifery. I agree with Laurell's criticism that the very conceptualization of Seguro Popular reflects neoliberal, US influence. Despite its veneer of responsibility for social welfare and services, Seguro Popular is, indeed, an extension of the neoliberal logic that espouses minimal government intervention, reduces the state's responsibility for the welfare of its citizens, and increases privatization.

I argue that the neoliberal framing of universal health *insurance* as opposed to universal health *care* turns patients into *consumers* instead of *citizens*.[11] Essentially, Seguro Popular is a financial strategy for provisioning basic, cost-effective, and mostly preventative services—universal health *care* access would be needed to secure the universal right to health for all Mexicans. This latter framing would provide healthcare services to Mexican citizens as a citizenship-based right, thus eliminating barriers to healthcare and reducing the degree of inequality in Mexico.

---

11. See my book *No Alternative*.

Intersectional Inequalities Penetrating Midwifery in Mexico

When analyzing the state of midwifery in Mexico, Rickie Solinger's assertion is invaluable: "It is crucial to consider the degree to which one woman's possession of reproductive choice may actually depend on or deepen another woman's reproductive vulnerability" (7). In Mexico, the *humanized birth* movement broadens the range of birth choices for women with socioeconomic and georacial privilege; however, this movement inadvertently usurps, fractures, and reinvents the *traditional* birthing practices of indigenous midwives while excluding them from profit streams.[12] Here, *traditional* is placed within quotation marks because commodified practices (such as massage techniques using a Mexican shawl, water birth, womb steaming, homeopathic remedies, placenta art, herbal beauty balms, etc.) are marketed as *indigenous,* but are quite distinct from the birthing practices of the indigenous informants in my study. During ethnographic research, I observed how indigenous women defy Oportunidades mandates to orchestrate covert home birth with a midwife who has a multigenerational inheritance of knowledge of herbal remedies, while also recruiting allopathic techniques in a way that is compatible with traditional medicine—for example, applying an IV as a postpartum blood tonic.

Couples practicing humanized birth in Mexico are often urban, middle or upper class, fair skinned, well traveled, and highly educated. During my interviews with them, many of the couples identified their *nivel cultural* (their cultural level; that is, the degree to which they are *cultured*) as what distinguishes them from the majority of Mexicans. What their account erases, of course, are multiple, contingent processes of intersectional racialization.[13] In this context, *race* does not strictly coincide with phenotype, but rather, refers to a social category resulting from a dialectic process of perception and performance of an individual's positionality in society—a calculus that includes *race* and class, and ultimately maps race onto class, and vice versa.

Meanwhile, indigenous Mexican women and their traditional midwives are excluded almost entirely from this community. When *indigeneity* is invoked among humanized birth proponents, the object is fetishized, separated from its cultural, socioeconomic, and geographical context, and repackaged for mass consumption—leading me to question if the only pathway to citizenship in our neoliberal age is through consumerism.[14] During this process of commodification, the practice of indigeneity comes to represent

12. See my article "Commodifying Indigeneity."
13. See Crenshaw; also, see De Genova.
14. See Comaroff and Comaroff; Chow; García Canclini; and Mazzarella.

going back to *nature* and *tradition* in a way that is appealing to those seeking humanized birth (examples of specific indigenous practices are *temascales*[15] and herbal remedies). While indigenous people are often excluded from the consumption processes that flatten and then commodify indigenous culture, there are a few exceptions. During my participant observation and in-depth interviews, I noted that a select few indigenous midwives—only several across the entire country—are routinely invited to attend international new midwifery conferences and forums. At these events, they perform their *indigeneity*, wearing indigenous costume even if this is not their everyday attire, thus buttressing the uncritical claim that new midwifery is a descendent of *traditional* midwifery, and that humanized birth means *going back to nature* and recognizing *our shared humanity*. These few indigenous midwives have become representatives of *traditional* midwifery at transnational conferences; however, when I observed perhaps the most well-known of these traditional midwives, I noticed that her practice of more popularized techniques and monolingualism in Spanish may cause indigenous women to consider her to be on the fringes of traditional midwifery.

Indigenous birthing women also receive midwifery care, but the traditional care they receive is not celebrated—instead, it must be corrected, rescripted, controlled, and surveilled. The majority of women living in rural, indigenous villages are recipients of conditional cash transfers through programs like Oportunidades (which has since been rebranded with the name Prospera). While Seguro Popular and Oportunidades operated independently, both reflect neoliberal logic and have been lauded by the World Bank.[16] Women's stipends are conditioned on their compliance with government mandates, including their children's continued attendance in school and their submission to vaccination programs, among other things. In the realm of reproduction, these women are mandated to attend five prenatal visits in the government clinic and give birth at the highly medicalized government hospital. Meanwhile, in many states, traditional indigenous midwives are ordered to forgo offering services as midwives and instead refer obstetric cases to the government hospital. These midwives are threatened with imprisonment for homicide if a woman dies in childbirth while under their care.

Professional midwives and international NGOs participate in this process under the guise of *capacitaciones* (training workshops) meant to reduce maternal mortality. According to some of my indigenous informants, those running the trainings teach hygiene, nutrition, and family planning strategies

---

15. Indigenous sweat lodges.
16. www.worldbank.org/en/results/2015/02/26/health-coverage-for-all-in-mexico and http://www.worldbank.org/en/news/feature/2014/11/19/un-modelo-de-mexico-para-el-mundo.

that convert traditional midwives into community health workers, *promoto-ras,* and hospital referralists. However, I came to realize through extensive interviews with those giving the trainings that the well-meaning involvement of professional midwives and NGO employees is bolstered by what Didier Fassin describes as "humanitarian reason." That is, those who approach encounters with *needy* populations from a position of privilege do so because they believe intervention is not only possible, but necessary. In line with Fassin I ask, what is lost when a rhetoric of compassion and suffering occurs in lieu of interests and justice, thus legitimizing actions by rendering them humanitarian? Oftentimes, humanitarian encounters presuppose a relation of inequality, inadvertently reentrench political asymmetry, and reveal domination in the upsurge of compassion.

Destination Birth

Can I tell you a joke?
The good girls from the village go to have
Cesarean in the state capital,
The good girls from the state capital go to have
Cesarean in the nation's capital,
The good girls of the country go to have
Cesarean in the United States,
And the good girls from the United States come to
Give birth in your birthing center
Here in the village.
(anonymous; my translation)

This poem, circulated by a professional midwife on social media, is written partially in jest, yet it provides striking insight into the traffic patterns of reproductive migrations in Mexico. The first part describes the experiences of women living in rural contexts: If they submit to bureaucratic structures, their pregnancies are likely to end in cesarean section in state hospitals. The next part of the poem refers to the "good girls from the state capital" who go to the nation's capital to have a cesarean. These women are actively turning away from midwifery and seeking out cesareans—for them, to be treated as surgical subjects is to be cared for as modern beings (Roberts 77).[17] The poem goes on to describe the "good girls of the country" going to have cesareans in

17. Also, see Ceclia Van Hollen's book *Birth at the Threshold: Childbirth and Modernity in South India.*

the United States. The last section of the poem is perhaps the most striking: the "good girls of the United States" come to the Mexican village to give birth in a birthing center.

My ethnographic research provides evidence for explaining each layer of this poem. During my fieldwork, I observed how supposedly *hyper-fertile* indigenous women were subject to what Morgan and Roberts describe as "reproductive governance" through conditional cash transfer programs mandating that they have medicalized births in overcrowded government hospitals (often in the state capital). I argue that these *bad mothers* are never fully able to achieve the status of "good girls from the village" even when they are obedient to government mandates because of overlapping race- and class-based discrimination that, as Colloredo-Mansfeld has observed, casts them as dirty, ignorant, and negligent.

When these women *choose* or submit to the medicalization of their birth, they can be denied or delayed treatment with dire consequences. I interviewed an obstetrician in Chiapas who admitted to me that when he scans the waiting room, he (un)consciously makes decisions of whom to call in for treatment based on a hierarchy of hygiene. That is, indigenous patients often lack ready access to clean bathing water and may bathe every few days. Meanwhile, their urban, nonindigenous counterparts possess the infrastructural capacity to bathe daily. This physician is more likely to choose someone who has bathed more recently, so he tends to treat nonindigenous patients before indigenous patients, causing indigenous patients to wait the longest.

In Veracruz, I witnessed a fraught encounter between an indigenous midwife and the director of the government hospital. The midwife had referred a birthing mother to the hospital, as she is instructed to do in *capacitaciones* (government-sponsored training workshops), but when her patient arrived at the hospital, the patient was ignored. The indigenous mother gave birth to a stillborn in the toilet and hemorrhaged on the floor. She was then harshly admonished by hospital staff for sullying the floor and was forced to clean up the blood.

Within the context of cash transfers, most indigenous women giving birth *choose* such hospital encounters rather than risk having their cash transfers reduced or halted. In conditions of extreme scarcity, they submit to a free medicalized birth instead of having to pay out of pocket for the midwifery techniques they might otherwise prefer. However, some indigenous women, like the birthing mother in the vignette with which I began this essay, resist government mandates and surreptitiously seek out local midwives. If found out, their subversive actions may cause them to be labeled *bad mothers,* and their actions may be punishable.

Through ethnographic examples like the one offered in the opening vignette to this chapter, I consider the evaluative work on the part of indigenous women to achieve what they consider to be better birth outcomes. My work documents what the anthropologist James Scott describes as "weapons of the weak"—that is, the decision-making processes of poor, rural, and indigenous women who either proactively seek out citizenship-based health services or subversively evade racial discrimination in biomedical settings by turning to covert midwifery services. Building upon Philippe Bourgois's work, I argue that these actions, based on logical responses to an unjust reality, are later used by dominant sectors of society to label indigenous women as *backward,* child-endangering, irresponsible mothers, and in dire need of humanitarian interventions. I suggest that while all Mexican women enjoy formal access to Seguro Popular health insurance, the racial discrimination experienced by many of my indigenous informants in hospitals and the conditionality of the Oportunidades stipends they receive are indicative of substantive differences in access to healthcare. While indigenous mothers are racialized as recipients of developmental aid, the next layer of mothers position themselves as consumers of privatized birthing methods.

During my ethnographic fieldwork, I noted how affluent Mexicans aspired to inclusion in the global elite through social whitening. This desire to achieve elite status through consumption practices linking them to consumers in the developed world was paired with strategic acquisition of American birthright citizenship for their children. The couples I interviewed were often multinationals and their logic of transnationality is in some ways similar to the "flexible citizenship" Aihwa Ong describes.

The final layer of my ethnographic observations departs slightly from the poem since I noted that reproductive travelers seeking *destination births* in Mexico were from the global North but were not exclusively American. Instead, this group also included women or couples from Canada, England, France, Holland, Spain, Chile, Argentina, and Brazil. I argue that the movement at times romanticizes the birth practices of indigenous women by casting them as lingering inhabitants of a vanishing past. Furthermore, I noted how fervor for traditional indigenous birth practices often overlapped with the desire for homogenized, New Age iterations of ethnomedicine. That is, some reproductive tourists sample freely from ethnomedical practices (acupuncture, Ayurveda, Amazonian shamanism and *ayahuasca,* etc.) without awareness of the local, political, and economic histories and current conditions of the people from whom they are sampling.

Conclusion

My comparative research reveals the class-based effects of Seguro Popular on the birthing experiences of women. For Mexico's underclass, Seguro Popular has rendered midwifery the more *expensive* option, and poorer families often turn to medicalized births solely based on cost, despite their preference for traditional midwifery care. On the other hand, the introduction of Seguro Popular impelled professional midwives to seek a living in the private sphere, and their services have become a source of increased status among affluent Mexicans.

My argument is certainly not that humanized birth practitioners are actively seeking to commodify indigenous birthing practices in a way that reentrenches social and economic inequality. Rather, I suggest that these mothers strive to achieve demedicalized births because they believe that this is what is best for their well-being and that of their child. I further suggest that their notion of a *good birth* is socially scripted and maintained. At the same time, however, my research signals how decision-making processes regarding how to achieve a *good birth* are structured by the socioeconomic constraints or freedoms that families face.

While the humanized birth movement in Mexico is motivated by well-intentioned commitments to women's reproductive freedom of choice, midwives have *no choice* but to sell their services to elite women and reproductive tourists since Seguro Popular prohibits the use of midwifery in many indigenous regions. While consumers from around the world are buying romanticized indigenous birth and other privatized medical services in Latin America, many impoverished, indigenous women are ignored and abused in hospitals. For these reasons, midwifery is an ideal lens for examining how neoliberalism is dismantling not only traditional midwifery but also poor and indigenous women's access to quality care.

Works Cited

Adams, Vincanne. *Metrics: What Counts in Global Health.* Duke University Press, 2016.

Bourgois, Philippe. *In Search of Respect: Selling Crack in El Barrio.* Cambridge University Press, 2003.

Chow, Rey. *The Protestant Ethnic and the Spirit of Capitalism.* Columbia University Press, 2002.

Colloredo-Mansfeld, Rudi. "'Dirty Indians': Radical Indigenas and the Political Economy of Social Difference in Modern Ecuador." *Bulletin of Latin American Research,* vol. 17, no. 2, 1998, pp. 185–205.

Comaroff, John L., and Jean Comaroff. *Ethnicity, Inc.* University of Chicago Press, 2009.

Crenshaw, Kimberlé Williams. "The Structural and Political Dimensions of Intersectional Oppression." *Intersectionality: A Foundations and Frontiers Reader,* edited by Patrick R. Granzka, Westview Press, 2014, pp. 16–21.

De Genova, Nicholas. *Working the Boundaries: Race, Space, and "Illegality" in Mexican Chicago.* Duke University Press, 2005.

Fassin, Didier. *Humanitarian Reason: A Moral History of the Present.* University of California Press, 2012.

Frías, Sonia M. *Forced Marriage and Sterilization without Women's Consent in Mexico: Prevalence and Factors Associated. Evidence from Two Recent Surveys.* National Autonomous University of Mexico, iussp.org/sites/default/files/event_call_for_papers/Gender-based%20violence%20-%20iussp.pdf.

García Canclini, Néstor. *Consumidores y ciudadanos: Conflictos multiculturales de la globalización.* Grijalbo, 2001.

Hall, Courtney. "Latin America's Indigenous Women." *Human Rights & Human Welfare,* pp. 39–50, www.du.edu/korbel/hrhw/researchdigest/minority/Indigenous.pdf.

Laurell, Asa Cristina. *Impacto del Seguro Popular en el sistema de salud.* CLACSO, 2013.

Marcus, George E. "Ethnography in/of the World System: The Emergence of Multi-Sited Ethnography." *Annual Review of Anthropology,* vol. 24, no. 1, 1995, 95–117.

Mazzarella, William. *Shoveling Smoke: Advertising and Globalization in Contemporary India.* Duke University Press, 2003.

Menéndez, Eduardo L. *De algunos alcoholismos y algunos saberes: Atención primaria y proceso de alcoholización.* CIESAS, 1996.

Morgan, Lynn, and Elizabeth F. S. Roberts. "Reproductive Governance in Latin America. *Anthropology and Medicine,* vol. 19, no. 2, 2012, pp. 241–54.

Ong, Aihwa. *Flexible Citizenship: The Cultural Logics of Transnationality.* Duke University Press, 1999.

Rapp, Rayna. *Testing Women, Testing the Fetus: The Social Impact of Amniocentesis in America.* Routledge, 2000.

Roberts, Elizabeth F. S. *God's Laboratory: Assisted Reproduction in the Andes.* University of California Press, 2012.

Scott, James. *Weapons of the Weak: Everyday Forms of Peasant Resistance.* Yale University Press, 1987.

Solinger, Rickie. *Beggars and Choosers: How the Politics of Choice Shapes Adoption, Abortion, and Welfare in the United States.* Hill and Wang, 2001.

Van Hollen, Cecilia. *Birth on the Threshold: Childbirth and Modernity in South India.* University of California Press, 2003.

Vega, Rosalynn Adeline. "Commodifying Indigeneity: How the Humanization of Birth Reinforces Racialized Inequality in Mexico." *Medical Anthropology Quarterly,* vol. 31, no. 4, 2016, pp. 499–518, doi:10.1111/maq.12343.

———. *No Alternative: Childbirth, Citizenship, and Indigenous Culture in Mexico.* University of Texas Press, 2018.

———. "Racial I(nter)Dentification: The Racialization of Maternal Health through the Oportunidades Program and in Government Clinics in México." *Salud Colectiva,* vol. 13, no. 3, 2017, pp. 489–505, doi:10.18294/sc.2017.1114.

Wilson, Ara. *The Intimate Economies of Bangkok: Tomboys, Tycoons, and Avon Ladies in the Global City.* University of California Press, 2004.

CHAPTER 5

The Work/Life Equation

Notes toward De-Privatizing the Maternal

ZARENA ASLAMI

LET ME just admit that, at the time of this writing, I have canceled class to be home with my sick daughter. My spouse is out of town with our son, who has cerebral palsy, to get a second opinion on his vision impairments. My daughter sleeps off a fever on the red cushy chair just a few feet from me at the dining room table, where I type toward a deadline. My son (I learn later) melts down on the floor of the examining room four states away. I will not tell you about all the moments that have gone into the writing of this essay, all the early mornings before the children wake, the writing in thirty-minute intervals, the mind-fraying efforts to block out distractions, and so on. Perhaps you will sense those moments in the cracks of this essay. (And perhaps, you will sense the intimate moments, too—like watching a movie with my daughter when she awoke, her small body pressed into my side, or reading to and snuggling with my son when he returned—in the spikes of emotion in this essay.) But I will tell you that years before the twins were born, I read journalist Lisa Belkin's much-discussed 2003 essay, "The Opt-Out Revolution," published in the *New York Times Magazine*. At the time, it angered me. Its lack of optimism seemed to choke the voices of the author and the women she interviewed, shutting down feminist futures at what felt like every turn. So, I clipped it, knowing that I was not yet done with it. And, indeed, it has had a spectral quality, haunting the good and bad moments I have had with my children, my partner, and my work. It was not yet done with me either, it seems.

You might remember it. Belkin's article galvanized early twenty-first-century US discourse about a powerful minority: white, educated, professional, heterosexual, married, working mothers. Belkin's piece was, of course, not alone. It was joined later by Anne-Marie Slaughter's 2012 "Why Women Still Can't Have It All," published in the *Atlantic;* Judith Warner's 2013 follow-up "The Opt-Out Generation Wants Back In," also published in the *New York Times Magazine;* and Sheryl Sandberg's much acclaimed 2013 book *Lean In: Women, Work, and the Will to Lead.* We might also consider in this collection the recent media breakout figure of Ivanka Trump, who, during her father's 2016 presidential campaign, championed his proposed family policies and proclaimed herself an advocate for working mothers, eventually publishing her glossy *Women Who Work: Rewriting the Rules for Success* (2017).

These essays and books vary in tone and argument, from the celebratory if conflicted claim that women were making the "feminist" choice to leave work and become stay-at-home moms (Belkin), to the criticism that women were being forced out by a masculinist workplace acting against its own economic self-interest (Slaughter), to a confidence—buoyed by the downplayed power to afford domestic staff and otherwise have extraordinary abilities and resources at hand—that it is possible to have it all (Sandberg; Trump). Trump in particular articulates an acutely ideological blend of rhetoric around freedom and choice with the disavowal of the structural inequality of income and wealth that skews grotesquely in her favor.

But Belkin's article, I contend, still stands out for the way it articulates anxiety around the problem of work/life balance. Belkin's is not an essay about how hard it is to juggle everything, accompanied by stock photos of women in tailored business suits and high heels, briefcase in one hand, baby in the other. It is a thoughtful essay about high-achieving women with degrees from prestigious institutions who quit their professional jobs to become full-time mothers and who consequently experienced profound relief and anguish. Over the ten-plus years since it came out, Belkin's essay has been the subject of many opinion pieces and major sociological studies, including Pamela Stone's *Opting Out?: Why Women Really Quit Careers and Head Home* (2007) and Bernie D. Jones's edited collection *Women Who Opt Out: The Debate over Working Mothers and Work-Family Balance* (2012). Data-driven, these works demonstrate just how much the image of high-powered mothers quitting their jobs to be stay-at-home moms, the drama that fuels Belkin's article, is a media construction and not a sociological reality. This media construction performs a range of powerful ideological functions, including buttressing the idea that there is a rise in neotraditional values and substituting a story of female empowerment and choice for a critique of the structural conditions that make working and raising children impossible.[1] Both Stone and the scholars in Jones's edited volume concur: Given the small number of such women, and their status as privileged and elite, these stories of "opting out" exploit anxieties and also eclipse the material conditions of working parents who have much less in the way of support.

These sociological studies have been critical in exploding the mythifying power of "opting out" and drawing attention to the inequalities still inherent in modern heterosexual relationships and to the withdrawal of public support under neoliberal practices. In this essay, I do not seek to counter such critiques, but complement them by considering how Belkin's essay sketches out the affective contours of a form of personhood we could call ideal neoliberal motherhood. By focusing on Belkin's representation of this highly privileged and visible population, I hope to show, first, how recent framings of work/life balance operate under the sign of neoliberal rationality. As Wendy Brown has argued, neoliberal rationality evokes a new ideal subject, one who calculates according to economic advantage and for whom the moral and the political are recalibrated as the profitable and that which accrues financial value to the individual. This is not classical liberalism's ideal individual. Imagined by seventeenth-century English political theorists like John Locke and eighteenth-century English novelists like Daniel Defoe, the ideal liberal individual is self-determining, self-regulating, self-disciplining, and presented with a divided social world: a public space, in which he can compete and pursue his economic interests, and a private space, in which he can experience feelings and be guided by moral principles. Rather, this is "bare life" reworked as human capital: endowed with will and responsible for its fate and, at the same time, exposed to the vagaries of capitalism and ultimately disposable.[2] As such, under neoliberalism, we could say that the slash between work and life in the worn-out phrase work/life balance does not actually suggest a seesaw-like fulcrum between two separate domains. Instead, the slash masks an equal sign that signifies the full-scale economization of all aspects and faculties of human life. As seen by US legislation from the 1970s forward, with the economization of life comes the privatization of public services and supports not only for low-income mothers but also for all members of society, who are now seen solely as moralized economic agents.[3] Citizenship is now measured by how little one takes from society and how much one takes on oneself, without consideration for the economic landscape or scope of available opportunities.

---

1. See Stone and Hernandez in Jones 51–52.

2. In *Homo Sacer,* Giorgio Agamben uses the term *bare life* to describe how present states and institutions conceive of human life in purely biological terms.

3. For more on US neoliberal policy, see Brown, *Undoing*; Harvey; Giles.

Among the articles that followed hers, Belkin's is unique for its exposure of the affective remainder in what we can think of as the work=life equation for privileged subjects: angst. It is tempting to dismiss the angst of these elite women, but I would like to explore what happens when we reframe that angst as the compelling excrescence of a system that oppresses women across the socioeconomic spectrum. Belkin's essay presents in raw and dramatic terms the stresses generated by the idea of work/life balance for a privileged class and struggles in spectacular ways to organize a constellation of contradictory affects around ideal neoliberal motherhood and its relation to *choice*. It exposes the epic endurance of patriarchy and its capacity to sustain this moment of advanced capitalism. It does so by revealing how the neoliberal fetishization of choice works by threatening to decimate privilege: One demonstrates one's superior character by exercising choice. In effect, the pressure placed upon choice extorts certain women into maintaining a status quo that proclaims freedom for them, but actually threatens them with becoming their abject other: she whose *bad* choices have rendered her precarious and bereft of choices. The contradiction is pretty glaring: All humans under neoliberalism are exercising choice. But for some, public options run out, whereas for others, resources remain. In the process, the media construction of the plight of the working mother reinforces the inextricability of privilege and abjection. Through it all, we can see how popular media's fixation on privileged women's choice to stay home, to work, or to do both presumes the fixity of an environment that was not designed for their freedom, but for someone else's.

Ideal Neoliberal Motherhood

By neoliberalism, I refer to what theorists such as Brown, David Harvey, and Nikolas Rose describe as a new phase of production, governance, and political rationality that emerged in the late 1970s and early 1980s in the US and Western Europe. At the level of policy in the US, neoliberalism is typically understood as the rejection of Keynesian welfare state economics, with its emphasis on the capacity of banks and governments to stabilize the economy, and the espousal of the Chicago School, with its emphasis on humans as rational economic actors and the benefits of an unfettered and free market. In the domain of domestic economy, neoliberalism is thus associated with free trade; deregulation; privatization of public services, including education and child support; environmental resource exploitation; and the ascendance of finance capital. Globally, as it emanates from developed to developing nations, neoliberal economic policy operates as the imperial control of, as Brown puts it, "every aspect of Third World existence, including political institutions and social formations" (*Edgework* 38).

However, Brown is interested not only in these manifestations but also in something abstract and totalizing, which, as it serves to legitimize the material realities of mothering in an age with decreased public support, is significant to our understanding of the lived experience of contemporary motherhood: "the *political rationality* that both organizes these policies and reaches beyond the market" (*Edgework* 38). For Brown, the *neo-* in neoliberalism refers not to present economic policies, which are in fact traditional (derived from classical liberalism, with its emphasis on free markets), but instead to applications of economic logic to *all* aspects of human life, including the political, the moral, and the spiritual, resulting in the complete gutting of liberal democracy in Western nations. Thus, neoliberalism celebrates the retreat of the liberal democratic state from many domains of human life, and, as Brown puts it, the "'economization' of political life and of other heretofore noneconomic spheres and activities" (*Undoing* 17). Befitting the age of finance capital, the economization of all aspects of life does not just entail amassing profit. Rather, it requires the enhancing of one's perceived value. Brown argues that neoliberalism establishes a fearful symmetry among governments, corporations, and individuals: "Both persons and states are construed on the model of the contemporary firm, both persons and states are expected to comport themselves in ways that maximize their capital value in the present and enhance their future value" (*Undoing* 22). All three entities must behave in ways that increase their value or, Brown argues, they risk losing legitimacy, credibility, or even existence.

Neoliberalism thus remaps the everyday, obliterating distinctions among different domains that classical liberalism had held as distinct. Love, religion, education, marriage, family, labor, business, citizenship—all are reconceived as structured by economic rationality. A previously striated life is now homogeneous. If Brown sounds somewhat nostalgic for good old-fashioned liberalism, I think she might be. What appears to emerge in Brown's argument is a wish for a division between the public and the private, precisely one that liberal feminists had critiqued for the ways the division was gendered, confining women to the private sphere and denying the politics of the personal. But the difference between their critiques of the public/private divide and Brown's critique of the public/private collapse is profound: For Brown, liberalism at least had the capacity to contain the wild forces of capitalism in the economic domain. In liberal rationality, economic logic was confined to the economic sphere and its appearance in the private realm was cause for condemnation. In contrast, within neoliberal culture, as Angela McRobbie points out, women are coached unironically to make sound *investments* in their dating life. For example, in *Lean In*, Sandberg advises the reader to choose a mate according to who will most support and enhance their *earning potential*.[4] In other words, neoliberal subjects must operate according to economic imperatives, which ensure their self-reliance, in order to be good at life.

Two key aspects of McRobbie's work on postfeminism and recent media images of maternity are especially helpful for our understanding of the present. First, she argues that postfeminism—the phenomenon in which the goals of feminism appear to be accepted, but are treated as having already been accomplished, rendering feminism passé and obsolete—assigns, as she puts it, the tropes of freedom and choice to young women. What does a woman get in exchange for participating in the active rejection of feminist politics? She is able to see herself as coherent and free of contradictions. She is also granted entry to the new sexual regime in which she is proclaimed to be an equal sexual being and allowed to have her pleasure in a politics- and conflict-free zone where her choices do not implicate her in uneven power relations ("Postfeminism and Popular Culture" 34). In this imagined space, to rely on government support is shameful. In the meantime, neoliberal feminism actively seeks to delegitimize the other set of demands upon which earlier feminism—particularly socialist feminism—argued that freedom, choice, and equality depend, such as state-funded childcare. Instead, neoliberal feminism celebrates outsourcing domestic labor to hired help. McRobbie argues that this move is part of a trend of shoring up family values, even extending it to lesbian and gay couples, while defunding public and municipal projects. Secondly, McRobbie draws attention to the style of "affluent, feminine maternity," which she refers to as "mediated maternity," that circulates in partisan political discourse, conservative newspapers, fashion magazines, news channels, and other popular media in the UK. These images hail female subjects into becoming economically responsible, as well as sexually attractive, agents. This ideal of maternity requires the subject to be self-reliant and uncritical of power relations in exchange for sexual capital. McRobbie argues that the ideal toward which women aspire is not political equality, but physical attractiveness: Women place their value in their ability to be sexier than other women. To maintain one's sexual capital, one cannot complain, criticize, or demand rights. These civic activities are forfeited in the new game women have entered. Moreover, this ideal is formed over and against imagined others: "This idea of active (i.e., *en route* to the gym), sexually confident motherhood . . . is also consistently

---

4. See McRobbie, "Feminism," for an incisive critique of Sandberg's *Lean In*, especially pp. 133–35.

pitched against an image of the abject, slovenly and benefit-dependent 'under-class' single mother, the UK equivalent of the US 'welfare queen'" ("Feminism" 120). The figure of the "middle-class, professional, wife and mother" in the UK, who is implicitly white, McRobbie argues, is also set against that of the Muslim woman, who is "assumed to be oppressed and subjected to various forms of domination and control" ("Feminism" 121–22). In the US context, we can extend McRobbie's critique to include the ways that white motherhood is also opposed to black and brown motherhood.

While McRobbie's analysis forcefully explains the new gender, class, and race politics in play within neoliberalism, it tends to foreclose on the ways that popular media might offer the raw material with which we can critique the emerging norms of this "maternal-feminine," or ideal neoliberal motherhood. Specifically, Belkin's interviewees do not talk about themselves as professional family managers. Rather, they see themselves as making a "graceful and convenient exit" from the exploitative demands of professional labor. Belkin tries hard to read their decision to be full-time mothers as a critique of the workplace. Rather than only argue that Belkin and her interviewees have simply internalized neoliberal ideology, I am interested in how her essay allows us to see privileged women return repeatedly to their choices to make their life coherent to themselves and to others. The author and her interviewees are consumed by the nature of their choices. These women's compulsive return to their choices and the angst that attends those returns points, I argue, to the extent to which they are not free, and exposes the contradiction in the neoliberal equation of choice with freedom. In other words, their anguished fixation on the process and consequences of choosing indexes precisely the way in which neoliberal political rationality has turned choice and its ideological corollary, freedom, on its head.

Belkin's article, along with other texts in the oeuvre on work/life balance, imagines, reinforces, and struggles with ideal neoliberal motherhood. It reveals how compliance with this form of personhood requires that the subject make a choice between two modes of self-denial: full-time work or full-time mothering and domestic management. Examining more extreme situations in contemporary novels, like those involving life and death, Jane Elliott has called the mode of action emerging from this kind of scenario *suffering agency*: "Not only is self-preservation a foundational value for the forms of liberal political theory on which neoliberalism draws, but also, in the inexorability of what is commonly called the 'self-preservation instinct,' we glimpse something of the imprisoning nature of suffering agency, the way in which choices made for oneself and according to one's own interests can still feel both imposed and appalling" (84). Belkin's essay exposes the fantasy bribe into which privileged female subjects enter in order to live with their decisions. By revealing that fantasy, I argue, her essay also establishes the grounds for critique.

Maternity as Escape Hatch

"The Opt-Out Revolution" takes the temperature of the post-9/11, pre-2008 national scene in the US. Belkin's essay is based upon interviews with women who earned degrees at Ivy League schools and subsequently entered into high-powered jobs in law, journalism, publishing, education, brand consulting, and advertising/marketing, only to leave them after having children. Stone refers to Belkin's iconic essay as the "apotheosis" of a quasi-feminist narrative that began to appear in late 1990s popular media, celebrating not women's equality, but rather their right to return to traditional roles, now coded as a sign of affluence: "Stay-at-home moms were suddenly fashionable, the 'latest status symbol' according to an article in the *Wall Street Journal*. Working mothers, on the other hand, were pronounced 'passé' by a more widely acknowledged arbiter of hipness, *New York Magazine*" (4). Belkin's article is infused with what we might call a feminist gothic tone. Around the women, it sets up a mysterious and unsettling atmosphere: Why did they leave their prestigious jobs for traditionally female roles as mothers and home managers, and what are the consequences of their decisions for feminism? Belkin consults experts, such as social scientists, an anthropologist, and a university president, along with surveys, to provide data in the effort to answer this question.

The article opens with an invitation to the reader to imagine the women as a visual spectacle: "The scene in this cozy Atlanta living room would—at first glance—warm an early feminist's heart. Gathered by the fireplace one evening, sipping wine and nibbling cheese, are the members of a book club, each of them a beneficiary of all that feminists of 30-odd years ago held dear." In addition to setting the women within a detailed scenario, one with specific class markings (wine and cheese, fireplace, book club), this opening asks the reader to identify as an "early feminist" and to assume the proper interpretative framework. It also interjects a foreboding phrase, "at first glance," letting us know that there is more to this scene than we might at first think and that it will *not* warm an early feminist's heart. Finally, the historical consciousness of the article announces itself, noting "early" as the 1970s and bypassing the first wave of feminism altogether. We are told then that the women have earned degrees from Princeton, Harvard, and Columbia: "They chose husbands who could keep up with them, not simply support them. They waited to have children because work was too exciting. They put on power suits and marched off to take on the world." As readers, we now anticipate a downfall with trepidation.

The next paragraph reveals what will defeat any feminist triumphalism implied by such a description: These women quit their jobs, for which they worked so hard, to stay home with their young children. One woman tells Belkin, "I don't want to be on the fast track leading to a partnership at a prestigious law firm. . . . Some people define that as success. I don't." Another woman asserts, "I don't want to be famous; I don't want to conquer the world; I don't want that kind of life." From there the article asserts, by way of contrast, a classically liberal narrative about feminism, one that measures individual success in terms of possession, which these women's retreat from the work-force betrays: "Women—specifically, educated professional women—were supposed to achieve like men. Once the barriers came down, once the playing field was leveled, they were supposed to march toward the future and take rightful ownership of the universe, or at the very least, ownership of their half." In Belkin's article, feminism is a meritocracy that transcends gender yet remains structured on traditional social hierarchies and the accumulation of wealth. This version of feminism does not seek to do away with a capital-ist elite, it just seeks to open the door to allow in elite women: "The women's movement was largely about grabbing a fair share of power—making equal money, standing at the helm in the macho realms of business and government and law. It was about running the world." While this might be a fair charac-terization of one strand of liberal feminism, it becomes clear that this elitist structure, at base patriarchal, only generates more problems for women when they are actually allowed to participate in it.

The women Belkin interviews frame their choices in stark terms: Either they choose to devote themselves to work and keep getting promoted or they choose maternity and domesticity. One of the women casts the latter as an "escape hatch" from the stresses of the double bind of the so-called work/life balance. When the choice is framed between being famous and conquering the world, on the one hand, and staying home with children and doing house-work, typically cast as unappreciated and uncompensated labor, on the other, you bet the second choice is going to need a major PR campaign. And, indeed, in this language of opting out, we can see the spectral outlines of a liberal divi-sion of the public and private: the public as the scene of stress, competition, and contest and the private as the scene of serenity, continuity, and concord. By bodily placing themselves back into the domestic sphere, the women imagine themselves to be resolving the contradictions of their present: escaping a brutal working life *and,* by performing a feminist choice, maintaining a sense of themselves as agents.

However, this impulse to frame their decision to leave as their choice sits uneasily in the article. While she consults the work of social scientists, who argue that "the workplace has failed women," Belkin wants to go beyond that: "But to talk to the women of the book club . . . is to sense that something more is happening here. It's not just that the workplace has failed women. It is also that women are rejecting the workplace." A question recurs in the essay: "Why don't women run the world?" The first time it appears, the narrator rejoins with, "Maybe it's because they don't want to." Elsewhere, Belkin asserts, "As these women look up at the 'top,' they are increasingly *deciding* that they don't *want* to do what it takes to get there. Women today *have the equal right to make the same bargain* that men have made for centuries—to take time from their family in pursuit of success. Instead, women are redefining success. And in doing so, they are redefining work" (my emphases). Here we have the language of decision-making, desire, entering into contracts, and consent, all terms that belong to an emancipatory liberal discourse that Brown would argue has been nullified by neoliberalism's economization of all spheres of life and that McRobbie would argue become merely tropes that place responsibility upon citizens stripped of public supports.

But Belkin strives to see this move as a critical rejection of the values of the workplace: "There is nothing wrong with money or power. But they come at a high price. And lately when women talk about success they use words like satisfaction, balance and sanity." But is rejection the same as critique? As Joan Scott writes, "The point of critique is not to tear down or destroy but, by bringing to light the limits and inconsistencies that have been studiously avoided, to open up new possibilities, new ways of thinking about what might be done to make things better" (7). Being a full-time professional or a stay-at-home mom is not revolutionary. The choice between the two actually appears like a remarkably old way of thinking, one that runs in the grooves of old private/public distinctions that, due to the razing of boundaries wrought by neoliberalism, no longer accurately describe society, and one that rests upon economic privilege.

Belkin struggles to find something redemptive in what otherwise reads as a description of the ruins of these women's ambitions. But to listen to what these women are saying is to notice that something structural is affecting them. They consistently go to the language of personal responsibility and choice, expressing an extreme individualism in a defensive, if self-defeating, act of survival:

"I wish it had been possible to be the kind of parent I want to be and continue with my legal career," [Brokaw] says, "but I wore myself out trying to do both jobs well."

"It's more accurate to say I was no longer willing to work as hard—commuting, navigating office politics, having my schedule be at the whim of the news, balancing all that with the needs of a family—for a prize I was learning I didn't really want" [Belkin herself].

"As often as not . . . a woman would have loved to maintain some version of a career, but that job wasn't cutting it anymore. Among women I know, quitting is driven as much from the job-dissatisfaction side as from the pull-to-motherhood side" (Amsbary). (Belkin)

From a commonsense perspective, the logic here is convincing: These women had desirable full-time jobs and then they chose motherhood. They are, as Belkin wants to assert, rejecting a workplace that does not allow for flexible hours, telecommuting, or working from home, that fosters power struggles and subjects employees to top-down management. However, at no point do Belkin or any of her interviewees think of the state with optimism. Belkin does not suggest that perhaps it is a failure of the state to regulate an economy that produces harsh working conditions. Over these women's lifetimes, the state has withdrawn public support and actively created living conditions and modes of suffering agency for all people, regardless of class, gender, sexuality, race, ability, and parenting status. Nor, to return to McRobbie's critique, does the possibility of state-provided quality childcare, which would allow these women to maintain their careers and their families in ways that support society, appear as an option to Belkin or her interviewees. While Belkin does claim that the professional workplace is "macho," she does not use the term patriarchal or heteronormative to get at the way that it evolved out of asymmetrical gender relations, taking for granted that its employees are male, heterosexual, and married and have wives who stay home, manage the household, and raise children. With domestic labor taken for granted, employers' expectations of what they can demand from their employees adjusts accordingly. When you liberate those partners from the domestic sphere and bring them into the workplace without restructuring it or expectations about how much of one's life will be devoted to work, it is bound to generate more problems, especially to those who have newly arrived. In other words, when you are late to the party, like Cinderella, you have to find someone else to do all those chores. In the real world, mice do not pick up the slack. Often immigrant working-class women of color do.

Belkin is careful to foreground that her interviewees have ample financial support and health insurance from their husbands. However, I would
like to suggest that the lack of state regulation of workplaces and state-
provided childcare connects this tiny if powerful demographic to working
mothers across the socioeconomic spectrum. Seeing these connections has
the potential, I argue, to undo a sense of self shaped by neoliberalism. In a
quote mentioned earlier, Belkin features a woman who claims to define success for herself, which sounds like a very hard project indeed. And another
interviewee explains, "I've had people tell me that it's women like me that
are ruining the workplace because it makes employers suspicious. . . . I don't
want to take on the mantle of all womanhood and fight a fight for some sister
who isn't really my sister because I don't even know her.'" This declaration of
hyperindividualism and disavowal of feminism makes even Belkin uncomfortable, and she resorts again, projecting away from herself, to the conceit
of the early feminist: "These are fighting words of a most retro sort, and,
no doubt, a 70's feminist peering in the window would be confused at best
and depressed at worst." However, Belkin persists in trying to find something
positive and empowering in their stories: "But unmapped roads are not, de
facto, dead ends. Is this a movement that failed, or one reborn? What does
this evolving spectrum of demands and choices tell us about women? And
what does it mean for the future?"

These highly educated women, Belkin writes, mostly plan to reenter the
workforce when their children are older. They tell themselves that this is a
temporary exit. As they explain their choices to Belkin and as she describes
them in the essay, their anxiety about their identity is tangible, free-floating,
and competitive: "Talk to any professional woman who made this choice, and
this is what she will say. She is not her mother or her grandmother. She has
made a temporary decision for just a few years, not a permanent decision
for the rest of her life. She has not lost her skills, just put them on hold." Belkin quotes Brokaw, who entreats her, "Don't make me look like some 1950's
Stepford wife." *The Stepford Wives* was not published until the 1970s, but this
conflation, along with Belkin's skipping over first-wave feminism, speaks to
ongoing generational anxieties. And, later, through another literary allusion,
Belkin refers to Sylvia Plath's semiautobiographical 1963 novel about a young,
educated woman struggling against the lack of choices available to her in the
1950s when she defends Brokaw to the reader: "Don't look at her as something
out of the 'The Bell Jar' either. She is not trapped. This is a choice." The 1950s
feminine mystique, a term famously coined by Betty Friedan to describe the
injunction for middle-class women to be happy as mothers, firmly ensconced

in the domestic sphere, appears as a specter to be banished, no matter how accurately it might describe the present.

By the end of the article, the question "Why don't women run the world?" reappears. At this point, one wonders if that question is framed in a way that guarantees a broken answer. It would seem that gender equity is to be solved by class and race inequity: Preserve the social class hierarchy, just allow women at the top and pay them enough to hire domestic staff to maintain their home and raise their children. But the answer has changed from the beginning of the article, when Belkin tentatively suggests, as quoted earlier, "Maybe it's because they don't want to." By the end of the essay, she allows the voice of one of her interviewees to answer that question ("Why don't women run the world?") and have the last word of the essay: "'In a way,' Amsbary says, 'we really do.'"

What has happened in between the essay's asking of this question? How do we get from the narrator's initial hypothesis that women perhaps do not want to run the world to the assertion, in the words of one of the interviewees, that they in fact are already running it? Straight out of the Anglo-American nineteenth century, this sentiment expresses the compensatory fantasy for white, middle-class women who were privatized into the domestic sphere and granted moral and symbolic power, but denied political and economic power. In this context, it is dressed up in the neoliberal rhetoric of choice. However, the quotation falls flat at the end of an otherwise deeply concerned reflection upon the meaning of this historical trend. Belkin allows her voice to drop out, handing it over to Amsbary. This rhetorical choice suggests that Belkin herself registers this assertion of self-empowerment ambivalently, leaving the article open for readers to make their own assessments. Or, in neoliberal terms, to choose their own meaning.

Belkin respects her interviewees and seeks to validate their self-perception as making choices. But once choice and consent have been colonized by neoliberal political rationality, we have to consider Belkin's and her interviewees' anxious assertion of themselves as agents differently. The women Belkin interviews were the achievers who took advantage of the 1970s feminist movement and felt that they could do anything. Their sense of self rests upon feeling like they have agency and choice and that they can control their lives. To think otherwise would lead to two subject positions equally devalued within neoliberal discourse: victim, who is seen as robbed of agency, helpless, and weak; or poor person, who is cast as lazy, responsible for their own degradation, and ultimately disposable. No wonder the women interviewed tell the reporter and themselves that full-time motherhood, with all of its newly produced glamour and moral validation, as well as actual satisfactions, was their choice. The women who quit fast-track jobs cast their decision to leave as choice rather than as being an overdetermined bid to save aspects of their lives for which they felt solely responsible. In other words, these women who "opted out" demonstrate that they felt like they had *no choice* other than to think of themselves as taking an option. To admit otherwise, and maintain their sense of self, would be unthinkable.

Others who have engaged this question do not provide ways outside of these problems. For example, Slaughter's essay, which boldly argued that under present conditions, women cannot have it all, is bound by economic logic, which places it squarely within neoliberal discourse. Slaughter argues that workplaces should accommodate families: "Ultimately, it is society that must change, coming to value choices to put family ahead of work just as much as those to put work ahead of family." Here, the agent of change is society, not the state, raising this question: In the past, what agency other than the state has made workplaces operate by equitable principles, such as eight-hour workdays, weekends, safe work environments, fair wages, and so on, rather than bottom-line financial ones? Moreover, and paradoxically, like Sandberg's *Lean In,* which encouraged working women to assert themselves professionally and not retreat from career advancement, Slaughter's article, while arguing for a workplace that is not structured solely on profits, validates capitalist structures and culture. The essay's solutions boil down to social and workplace changes that accept the neoliberal idea that work is life and evoke an economic discourse: "flexible working hours, investment intervals, and family-comes-first-management." The example Slaughter provides of her own "investment interval" is when she and her husband took their sabbaticals in Shanghai: "We thought of the move in part as 'putting money in the family bank,' taking advantage of the opportunity to spend a close year together in a foreign culture. But we were also investing in our children's ability to learn Mandarin and in our own knowledge of Asia." The economic discourse of "investment" exposes how the neoliberal formula "work=life" forms the ground of the argument. As in Belkin's essay, appealing to the state to establish these work policies or provide childcare is beyond the imaginable within neoliberal logic. What is imaginable is arguing for solutions that will increase the individual's worth as human capital.

Warner's follow-up to Belkin's essay, "The Opt-Out Generation Wants Back In," begins to shift the argument slightly. Warner emphasizes how difficult reentering the workforce is for women who "opted out." Ultimately, Warner's essay, like Slaughter's, argues for a changed workplace. However, it goes a little beyond, first by highlighting the difficulties of a work=life model for both fathers and mothers. A working father who expresses envy at his wife's quitting her job states, "There has to be something more than going to work for 50 years and dying." Warner's only solution-like paragraph comes next, and it too argues for a change in workplace policies, but for men and women: "To find time for that 'something more,' husbands would need to join with their wives in rejecting nighttime networking sessions and 7 a.m. meetings. They would have to convey to employers that work-life accommodations like flexible hours or job sharing aren't just for women and that part-time jobs need to provide proportional pay and benefits." Second, Warner acknowledges the economic realities of work: "At a time when fewer families than ever can afford to live on less than two full-time salaries, achieving work-life balance may well be less a gender issue than an economic one." Given its overall grim reporting and scarce solutions, Warner's come closest to pointing to, without naming, that bugbear of liberal and neoliberal ideology: state-provided public supports.

To Mother

In *Revolutionary Mothering*, Alexis Pauline Gumbs asks, "What would it mean to take the word 'mother' less as a gendered identity and more as a possible action, a technology of transformation that those people who do the most mothering labor are teaching us right now?" (22–23). This 2016 volume of essays about mothering by women of color, edited by Gumbs, China Martens, and Mai'a Williams, like Brown's and McRobbie's work, offers a critique of neoliberal privatization, but it does so by combining theory with stories. Throughout this collection, mothers marginalized by race, sexuality, marital status, ability, and income narrate their lives and love for their children. The multiple introductions of the book frame these testimonials as revolutionary acts since they express the writers' desire to survive and thrive in a society that exploits and devalues them. As Gumbs, Marten, and Williams explain in the beginning of this collection, "We write in solidarity with mothers who must send their child out into the world, knowing that the powers that be would prefer their child not exist anymore" (Gumbs et al. 3).

Reading stories from *Revolutionary Mothering* alongside those told in Belkin's article exposes the devastating distance between the marginalized and the elite. We can see how the angst of Belkin's privileged interviewees is driven by the anxiety to hold on to that privilege and by the threat of its loss, of descending into social and actual death. While in no way do I want to divert from the brutalities of a system that marginalizes women of color, I do want to make two simple points: first, that this system polices women on both ends of privilege, and second, that the solutions offered by Belkin, Slaughter, and even Warner to change the workplace only further entrench and maintain this system.

The work of Gumbs, Marten, and Williams and that of reproductive justice scholars critique what is strangling the voices in Belkin's essay: the neoliberal feminist fetishism of choice. In its place, they offer collectivity. As Kimala Price explains, "Frustrated by the individualist approach of the pro-choice framework, a growing movement created and led by women of color has emerged to broaden the scope of reproductive rights. Calling itself the reproductive justice movement, this coalition of women of color activists and their allies are using a human rights and social justice framework to redefine choice" (42). Here, we see an emphasis on public support, municipal projects, and the importance of the state in redistributing resources and creating a field of opportunity. As Jael M. Silliman, Marlene G. Fried, Loretta J. Ross, and Elena R. Gutiérrez explain in the second edition of their *Undivided Rights: Women of Color Organize for Reproductive Justice,* "Reproductive justice activists are working on initiatives to enable women to obtain the support they need to have and raise children. This includes campaigns to end shackling during prison births, to raise the minimum wage, to expand government funding for childcare, and other efforts to ensure the dignity and well being of women, children, and trans* people" (xiii). In this discourse, motherhood is intimately connected to all forms of social justice. These scholars' emphasis on collaboration moves beyond neoliberal individualization and toward a caring state.

These concerns expand beyond issues of gender, racial, and class inequities. For example, disability-studies scholars like Rosemarie Garland-Thomson remind us that disability is inherent to the human condition, marking our bodies' encounters with the world. She argues that we should conserve, rather than eliminate, disabilities for they show our evolution as individuals and as species. Mothering, too, conserves and nurtures. The women in Belkin's article live in a rarefied world of status and luxuries, but this world is also one where the practice of mothering works toward the reproduction of patriarchal and white supremacist institutions, rather than being unleashed toward the creative project of loving and supporting all human life. Flex time and telecommuting only reinforce these dehumanizing institutions. They do not do away with the stresses, anguish, and alienating contradictions of neoliberal motherhood or the brutalizing inequities of racism and capitalism. Only practicing motherhood as a "technology of transformation," as Gumbs puts it, has the potential to do that.

Perhaps that is what is so painful about our private experiences of mothering. I started with my story of working and mothering, activities that feel locked together in a never-ending battle. As an academic, I have the rare privilege of institutional support and work flexibility. I could cancel class to take care of my daughter. My spouse could take off from work to take our son to a specialist. These are not the experiences of most working parents by far. But even we did so with the terror of mounting work, missed deadlines, and fear of repercussions. I used that time at home to work on this chapter, while keeping one eye on my feverish daughter and often a hand on her forehead, because I felt like I had to be productive even while caring for my sick child. My spouse used vacation days to seek specialized medical care for our disabled child and not for needed rest from a demanding work schedule. We struggle alone to help our offspring, in strife with ourselves and our fellow humans. Belkin's essay clues us in to why this struggle will persist until all are free.[5]

Works Cited

Agamben, Giorgio. *Homo Sacer: Sovereign Power and Bare Life.* Stanford University Press, 1998.

Belkin, Lisa. "The Opt-Out Revolution." *New York Times Magazine,* 26 Oct. 2003, www.nytimes.com/2003/10/26/magazine/the-opt-out-revolution.html.

Brown, Wendy. *Edgework: Critical Essays on Knowledge and Politics.* Princeton University Press, 2005.

———. *Undoing the Demos: Neoliberalism's Stealth Revolution.* MIT Press, 2015.

Elliott, Jane. "Suffering Agency: Imagining Neoliberal Personhood in North America and Britain." *Social Text Special Issue: Genres of Neoliberalism,* vol. 31, no. 2, 2013, pp. 83–101.

Garland-Thomson, Rosemarie. "The Case for Conserving Disability." *Bioethical Inquiry,* vol. 9, 2012, pp. 339–55.

Giles, Melinda Vandenbeld. "Introduction: An Alternative Mother-Centred Economic Paradigm." *Mothering in the Age of Neoliberalism,* edited by Giles. Demeter Press, 2014, pp. 1–30.

Gumbs, Alexis Pauline. "M/other Ourselves: A Black Queer Feminist Genealogy for Radical Mothering." *Revolutionary Mothering: Love on the Front Lines,* edited by Alexis Pauline Gumbs et al., PM Press, 2016, pp. 19–31.

Gumbs, Alexis Pauline, et al. "On the Organization of This Book: Roots and Branches." *Revolutionary Mothering: Love on the Front Lines,* edited by Alexis Pauline Gumbs et al., PM Press, 2016, pp. 3–6.

5. I would like to thank Juliet Guzzetta, Ellen McCallum, Modhumita Roy, Judith Stoddart, Mary Thompson, and the anonymous reviewers for their insightful comments on this essay. A special thanks to Robin Silbergleid for starting this conversation with me so many years ago.

Harvey, David. *A Brief History of Neoliberalism.* Oxford University Press, 2005.

Jones, Bernie D., editor. *Women Who Opt Out: The Debate over Working Mothers and Work-Family Balance.* New York University Press, 2012. ProQuest Ebook Central, https://ebookcentral-proquest-com.proxy2.cl.msu.edu/lib/michstate-ebooks/detail.action?docID=865620.

McRobbie, Angela. "Feminism, the Family and the New 'Mediated' Maternalism." *New Formations: A Journal of Culture/Theory/Politics,* vol. 80–81, 2013, pp. 119–137.

———. "Postfeminism and Popular Culture: Bridget Jones and the New Gender Regime." *Interrogating Postfeminism: Gender and the Politics of Popular Culture,* edited by Yvonne Tasker and Diane Negra, Duke University Press, 2007, pp. 27–39.

Price, Kimala. "What Is Reproductive Justice? How Women of Color Activists Are Redefining the Pro-Choice Paradigm." *Meridians: Feminism, Race, Transnationalism,* vol. 10, no. 2, 2010, pp. 42–65.

Rose, Nikolas. *Powers of Freedom: Reframing Political Thought.* Cambridge University Press, 1999.

Sandberg, Sheryl. *Lean In: Women, Work, and the Will to Lead.* Alfred A. Knopf, 2013.

Scott, Joan Wallach. "Introduction: Feminism's Critical Edge." *Women's Studies on the Edge,* edited by Joan Wallach Scott, Duke University Press, 2008, pp. 1–13.

Silliman, Jael M., et al. Preface. *Undivided Rights: Women of Color Organize for Reproductive Justice,* by Jael M. Silliman et al, 2nd ed., Haymarket Books, 2016, pp. vii–xiv.

Slaughter, Anne-Marie. "Why Women Still Can't Have It All." *The Atlantic,* July/Aug. 2012, www.theatlantic.com/magazine/archive/2012/07/why-women-still-cant-have-it-all/309020/.

Stone, Pamela, and Lisa Ackerly Hernandez. "The Rhetoric and Reality of 'Opting Out': Toward a Better Understanding of Professional Women's Decisions to Head Home." *Women Who Opt Out: The Debate over Working Mothers and Work-Family Balance,* edited by Bernie D. Jones, New York University Press, 2012, pp. 33–56. ProQuest Ebook Central, https://ebookcentral-proquest-com.proxy2.cl.msu.edu/lib/michstate-ebooks/detail.action?docID=865620.

Stone, Pamela. *Opting Out?: Why Women Really Quit Careers and Head Home.* University of California Press, 2007.

Trump, Ivanka. *#WomenWhoWork.* ivankatrump.com/womenwhowork/.

Warner, Judith. "The Opt-Out Generation Wants Back In." *New York Times Magazine,* 7 Aug. 2013, www.nytimes.com/2013/08/11/magazine/the-opt-out-generation-wants-back-in.html?pagewanted=all.

CHAPTER 6

The Angel in the McMansion

Female Citizenship and Fetal Personhood in *Fast Times at Ridgemont High* and *Juno*

DIANA YORK BLAINE

WHILE *ROE V. WADE* (1973) granted limited but unheralded legal protections to women seeking abortion, the ensuing decades have brought continued tensions between those who defend women's right to bodily autonomy and the cultural demand that women obey the dictates of pronatalism. In light of this ongoing battle between pro- and antiabortion camps, two otherwise seemingly inconsequential films, and their disparate representations of unplanned teen pregnancy, take on profound significance. I will demonstrate in this essay that the collapse of civic discourse that occurred over the last thirty years, resulting in what I am calling the *publicized private sphere,* has directly impacted the concept of the female citizen, one inextricably tied to reproduction and the family even in nondomestic contexts. This sexual and racial marking of women's public self has been produced by, and escalated, the impact of neoliberalism in the political, economic, and cultural spheres. As a result, in the contemporary political climate, the successful woman embraces maternity not as her inescapable destiny, but as her personal choice. Any sense that social imperatives lie behind the mandate to procreate are handily elided by nostalgia and sentiment, illustrated by the celebration of the private acquisition of a teenager's baby by Vanessa Loring (Jennifer Garner), a white woman of privilege, at the end of *Juno* (2007, directed by Jason Reitman). The film's sacrilizing of Vanessa's motherhood, and the young Juno's (Ellen Page) refusal to terminate the pregnancy, directly opposes the handling of unplanned pregnancy in

Ridgemont High (1982, directed by Amy Heckerling), which places Stacy Hamilton (Jennifer Jason Leigh), the young pregnant woman, in a public sphere inhabited by all citizens regardless of race, sex, or ability—or maternal ambition. In that free space, Stacy's abortion is logically and legally attained (complicated only by the impregnating male's failure to provide his half of the costs and the promised transportation to the clinic). In *Juno*, no such public sphere exists; instead, Juno's and Vanessa's public existence becomes conflated with the domestic exercise of private, affective emotions, with consumer-oriented mothering the only imaginable destination for middle-class modern white women.

The Womb as Publicized Private Sphere

Such radical shifts in the cultural imaginary from the right to choose to mothering being the only right choice paralleled the rise of mediating technology permitting the fantasy that individuals—not developing organisms—exist in the womb. The more the fetus has been represented as an individual, the less women have agency to deny its right to exist. This emergence of the fetal self was made possible by ultrasound technology, an innovation that, as Rosalind Petchesky demonstrates, aided the invention of fetal personhood, a key factor in the diminution of public support for abortion. The concept of fetal personhood dovetails perfectly with neoliberal myths of discrete individual citizens capable of rational decision-making irrespective of their cultural contexts. At its most extreme, we now find people willing to pretend that the capacity to exert one's self-will exists even before birth. For example, in April 2017, tabloid newspaper the *Daily Mail* ran a headline that read "Remarkable Moment an Ultrasound Shows Twin Girls Sharing a Kiss in Mom's Womb" (Edwards). The accompanying image, created when the pregnant Carissa Gill and her boyfriend Randy visited Fetal Imaging in Pennsylvania, depicts what appears to be two creatures modeled out of clay, turning stubby features toward one another as if in anticipation of an amorous embrace. Above their heads, alongside the identifying information about patient's name, date, and so on, the facility has added "kissing twins" to the medical record. In spite of the fact that kissing is a learned behavior and these two not-yet-actual individuals are not actually giving each other a kiss, the decision to adorn this ultrasound file with a caption memorializing their domestic bliss conflates the public medicalization of pregnancy with the intimacy of the private sphere. Ms. Gill's womb has become a domestic space—a home—where affective relations may, and will, occur. Indeed, in this sense woman's job has become making intimate relationships possible for others, not just within her house as traditionally mandated, but now within her very body, one that has become a publicized private sphere.

Perhaps this fantasy about fetuses snuggling together in utero reflects our urgent need for comfort in the face of the increasing neoliberal dictum that individuals are entirely responsible for themselves, that the only support we can expect will come exclusively from this private sphere. Robert Putnam has documented a sharp decline in the existence of civic organizations over the last decades of the twentieth century, resulting in an eroding sense of belonging to a public sphere in which members share common goals. One of the factors contributing to the disappearance of these voluntary associations is women's increasing participation in the workforce, as free time for volunteering has been replaced by wage work. Perhaps coincidentally, perhaps not, this disappearance of community (Putnam) occurs alongside an overdetermining of mothering that has arisen over the last three decades, because the category of mother symbolizes love, care, and connectedness—human needs no longer conceived of as flowing through civic channels. Patricia Ventura argues that neoliberalism's "most significant compensation [for its deprivation is] the family" (12). Notably this heteronormative procreative family is both created by and set against what Putnam identifies as a telescoping public sphere. Since neoliberalism's ideology requires the existence of the symbolic nuclear family that can and will meet all human needs—even those previously provided by social organizations—women must produce babies. No babies, no families. But ironically, this supposed choice to mother, and the physical, financial, and psychological burdens it brings, also gets thrust entirely upon the female who reproduces. Logically, compelling women to carry fetuses to term might also require that we as a people are compelled to help support those offspring. But the dismantling of the welfare state under neoliberalism in the 1990s has in fact guaranteed the opposite: myriad births of children whose mothers lack the resources to support them and decreasing governmental resources to fill those needs, resulting in a rise in extreme poverty (Shaefer and Eden). One conservative solution to this dilemma: Discouraging reproduction unless in the context of financial and racial privilege by encouraging middle-class white maternity while continuing to make it difficult for poor women and women of color who seek to have and raise families (Ross).

This imperative for white reproduction includes a fetishizing of the pure potential signified by the privileged white pre-person. As a result, the literally ungovernable space of the womb increasingly becomes imagined as the domain of a rational individual. Under the neoliberal agenda, this "contemporary national and mass-cultural fixation on turning women into children and babies into persons through the media of photography and cinema" (Berlant 83–84) constructs the individual as in charge of its destiny before it is even able to draw breath on its own. As in the case presented in the *Daily Mail* of whether to kiss or not to kiss one's sibling, we increasingly pretend that the fetus makes choices before birth. Under this taxonomy, the self is defined as one who chooses well or poorly, and those choices account for the social and material conditions of the individual. This ascribing of agency to individuals, both pre- and postpartum, denies the reality that the social and material conditions of individuals in any way constrain the choices they can make.

This word, *choice,* reverberates within both pro- and antiabortion rhetoric. Because neoliberalism as an ideology has produced the myth of the discrete individual, a self independent of, and not reliant upon, state services, choices are viewed as being made free from structural and situational constraints. Women *choose* to get pregnant, an assertion that erases the reality of the ways that white supremacist, capitalist patriarchy regulates our lives. From the neoliberal perspective, the responsibility of that *choice* must be borne entirely by the woman, an argument that perversely leads to adamantly antiabortion arguments: Her choice to get pregnant condemns her to carry the fetus to term, to produce another being in order to satisfy the demands of strangers who oppose females having the choice not to mother. In other words, she has a choice as long as the choice is to submit to the exigencies of "populist biological determinism" (Phipps 113).

Perhaps the fundamentalist Christian opposition to abortion makes a kind of sense from that theological perspective, but reliance on choice rhetoric also proscribes the proabortion movement. For example, many of my female students assert that while they would not want to see abortion outlawed, they would never choose to have one themselves. Such tepid support evinced by a generation raised with access to safe and legal abortion fails to provide powerful resistance to antiabortion rhetoric and indeed parallels it in ways that have proved detrimental to the existence of a robust proabortion lobby. According to this postfeminist neoliberal logic, women should be able to choose abortion, but no one should make that choice. With the rise of the publicized private sphere, where woman's body becomes the recognized home of other citizens, abortion becomes unthinkable, even for many of those self-defined as pro-woman, feminist, and liberal.[1] Can an unthinkable choice truly be defined as an option?

---

1. Heather Latimer makes the related point that one can now be both pro-choice and embrace fetal personhood.

Those who do choose this unthinkable option for themselves avoid the increasingly privatized and intensive demands of maternity. Seen from the vantage point of the enlightened liberal subject, it would be logical for a female citizen to abort a fetus rather than undergo a wholesale usurpation of one's life, plans, finances, and body. Imagining such a life, one predicated on self-determination, presupposes a space for female citizens. To be a female and be a citizen suggests that people's sexual identities do not determine the exercise of their civil rights in the public sphere. It also means a good life without raising offspring would be attainable through meaningful work and participation in community. The movements for civil rights in the United States have struggled to create precisely this sort of public sphere, one habitable by all regardless of race, class, sex, sexual orientation, class, or ability.

Public Citizens with Private Lives in Ridgemont High

The film *Fast Times at Ridgemont High* depicts such a society, one in which everyone is ascribed the role of public citizen, regardless of his relative intellectual value or her sexual identity, and regardless of their private desires. The main storylines feature teenaged males and females, African American, white, and mixed ethnicities, working and middle class, navigating academics, jobs, relationships, and leisure time. Lisa Dresner notes that *Ridgemont High* emerges during a period in which the advances in civil rights of the 1960s and 1970s have yet to be stalled by the encroaching neoliberalism and neoconservatism of the Reagan administration (Dresner 174). In American movies from this cultural moment, she observes, "girls' sexual decision making is represented as intelligent, responsible, and important" (174). Indeed, in *Ridgemont High*, the decision by the teenaged protagonist Stacy to get an abortion reflects her sound thinking and capable maneuvering within limited circumstances. The only negative aspect of her terminating the pregnancy, according to this abortion-positive narrative, is the failure of the impregnating male, Mike Damone, to take Stacy to the clinic and provide his half of the expenses. His fiscal and personal irresponsibility highlights her own responsible handling of her situation, including not carrying a fetus to term that she cannot support financially and getting a last-minute ride from her brother Brad so that she may keep her appointment. While Stacy does not tell her brother where she is going, and he drops her off without asking, Brad is waiting for her upon her emergence from the clinic. He has figured out where she was going, and asks her if she is okay. She says she is, and, to her relief, he promises to keep her business private, then suggests they get something to eat. No negative repercussions accompany Stacy's exercise of her right to safe and legal abortion; in fact, rather than focusing on her lost opportunity to mother, the scene portrays a growing emotional intimacy between Stacy and Brad. Dresner calls it "one of the most positive, moving abortion scenes portrayed in film" (187). The film ends with Stacy back at work at the mall, initiating coy flirtations with the more thoughtful and sensitive boy from her high school, whom she has decided to date rather than to bed.

It might seem that this ending, placing Stacy squarely in the clutches of compulsory monogamy, lends a reactionary note to what otherwise might be seen as a tale of female liberation. Without downplaying too much the ramifications of this romantic finale, or suggesting the film is not generically conservative or racially and sexually stratified, I argue that the depiction of her as someone who can be sexually self-determining without condemnation by the narrative can be understood by considering the plot involving Spicoli, a character easily dismissed as meaningless. Spicoli, a hapless stoner-surfer of marked Italian ancestry, seems to provide only comic relief as he goes on a series of misadventures while refusing to capitulate to the demands of the rigid Mr. Hand, his US history teacher. Mr. Hand, infuriated at Spicoli's lackadaisical attitude from day one, attempts to control Spicoli, but the young man seems not only incapable of being the well-regulated student Hand desires but also to enjoy his own unkempt, unmanageable existence. Given their fundamentally different approaches to life and running battle of the wills, this relationship seems unsalvageable, as does Spicoli's grade in US history.

But in an amazing turn of events, Mr. Hand chooses to permit his young charge one last chance to pass by granting him a special class session. To do this, Hand comes unannounced to Spicoli's bedroom, a beer- and bong-filled den of iniquity whose walls are covered with salacious posters of white women in various states of undress, and while the teenager scrambles to hide his drug paraphernalia, the teacher declares his intention to hold Spicoli hostage, in effect, while lecturing to the horrified young man about American history. He justifies this encroachment on Spicoli's private time and space as payback for Spicoli's semester-long encroachment on the teacher's public sphere classroom. In return he generously offers Spicoli the chance to succeed as long as his pupil can articulate back to him the basic tenets of citizenship at the end of the night. They proceed to have a class session in that bong-filled bedroom, with Spicoli ultimately articulating the foundations of our democracy as follows: "So what Jefferson was saying was, 'Hey, you know, we left that England place because it was bogus. So if we don't get some cool rules ourselves, pronto, we'll just be bogus too. 'K?" "Very close Jeff," replies the pristine Mr. Hand, framed by naked centerfolds. He tells the young man he will "probably squeak by" in the course, and the grateful student reaches out his hand. "Aloha, Mr. Hand," he says with great affection. "Aloha, Spicoli." Following this moment of mutual recognition and respect, the adult exits the room, pausing to shake his head in disgust at the female nudes displayed by the door.

Because scholars and critics alike have tended to categorize the film as a "sex romp" (Johnson 62; Nowell 15 n.1), no research considers the crucial implications of this Hand/Spicoli relationship. I want to call attention to the significance of this young man's fictional entrance into citizenship, as reflected by Mr. Hand's grudging extension of, yes, his hand, which symbolizes a willingness to pull this unpromising young person up and into the public sphere. Mr. Hand's character produces and reproduces democracy, that modern political system achieved through long and bloody struggle, one that extends the franchise to all adults, regardless of ability or resources, providing they meet a few minimum requirements. Hand does not withhold the right of citizenship from Spicoli, nor does he demand that in return the youth renounce his hedonistic lifestyle, one marked by drug use, promiscuity, and lassitude.[2]

This idea of America as an anti-England, with its "cool rules," exists as a fantasized space into which those who are allowed to enter become autonomous agents, unmarked and unstigmatized by their personal characteristics. While the promise has yet to be completely realized—after all, Jefferson formulated this bracing idea of liberty while holding people in bondage himself—waves of activism have resulted in the enfranchising of non-Anglos, poor Eastern and Southern Europeans, the freed slave class, and, most recently, all women. When they arrived in significant numbers, Spicoli's working-class immigrant Italian ancestors deeply troubled the ruling-class whites (the Mr. Hands) of the late nineteenth and early twentieth centuries, and laws were passed to try to control their lives, but by the time of this film, Spicoli's ethnicity was no bar to full consideration as American citizen. And due in part to the Nineteenth Amendment to the Constitution giving women the right to vote, Stacy, the young white female with the unplanned pregnancy, can also be shown entering this autonomous public sphere as an anonymous citizen with the right to seek an abortion, the operation necessary for her maintenance of bodily integrity and legal independence. No protestors stand outside the clinic, no characters shame her for her actions, no stain remains when she goes forward with her public life, one that includes returning to work. The

2. When asked, "Why don't you get a job?" by his disgusted peer, the hardworking and responsible older brother of Stacy, Spicoli responds in amazement, "Why?"

fact that Spicoli and Stacy are both nonnormative, he by lacking drive and she by having a female body, makes more stark the film's approbation of them as people, in their own right, with rights. Both are straight and white and middle class, which undoubtedly enables them to avoid punitive measures meted out to those falling outside of the mythical norm, but the progressive aspects of their treatment in this narrative reveal a cultural moment poised to embrace all unruly bodies as citizens.

However, during this very historical period in which civil rights movements of the 1960s and 1970s are making true inroads into law and culture, a shift occurs that will result in the stalling of this progress, perhaps coming as a reaction to the visible changes they effected. In the 1980s, the era that saw the production of this film, Lauren Berlant argues a mutation occurred in the definition of the citizen, making private concerns public business:

> Now everywhere in the United States intimate things flash in people's faces: pornography, abortion, sexuality, and reproduction; marriage, personal morality, and family values. These issues do not arise as private concerns: they are key to debates about what "America" stands for, and are deemed vital to defining how citizens should act. In the process of collapsing the political and the personal into a world of public intimacy, a nation made for adult citizens has been replaced by one imagined for fetuses and children. (1)

Ridgemont High flashes many of those precise things in people's faces, including pornography, sexuality, and abortion. In the film's imaginary world, Spicoli's personal space filled with *Penthouse* magazine, drugs, and alcohol and Stacy's private desire to seek out sexual relations with men to whom she was attracted did not prevent either one of them from being coded as individuals, emerging adults, entitled to live under those "cool rules" of the public sphere that Jefferson et al. devised for just such purposes. Their sexuality, while transgressive according to conservative Christian *family values,* was depicted as their own business in the film, and no bar to them getting accorded full entrance into citizenship. Spicoli's love of centerfolds clearly transgressed the feminist sexual politics of the era, yet their containment in his bedroom also marked desire as something private. He was no more outed or excluded from citizenship for his embrace of pornography than Stacy was for her abortion. These are treated as private decisions made by private citizens. But with the rise of the religious right, this balance between the public and the private, in effect a boundary permitting the concept of adulthood at all, collapses into Berlant's world of "public intimacy." As a result, "something strange" happens to citizenship (Berlant 1).

The Publicized Private Sphere in *Juno*

Nowhere is this "something strange" more perfectly represented than in the unplanned pregnancy narrative of *Juno*. The parallels with *Ridgemont High* are obvious: Both feature self-determining intelligent young white women who actively seek out sex with men; neither woman uses birth control; both women become pregnant. There the similarities end, reflecting drastic political and cultural changes that have occurred in the intervening twenty-five years, specifically the deepening of the backlash against civil rights–era progress that began with the Reagan administration and has culminated with the election of Donald Trump, a businessman who made it clear from the outset of his candidacy that he supports only heteronormative white male social structures. *Juno* is a film beloved by young women that falls neatly in line with the contemporary conservative political climate. The hysteria surrounding abortion in the film, and the overwrought sentimentalizing of the fetus, set the stage for the ideal neoliberal, neoconservative *happy* ending: the placement of a working-class woman's white baby in a white home with a materially acquisitive and anxious white mother who betrays no objectionable political opinions and conflates caregiving with the consumption of commodities.

Like Stacy, the teen in *Ridgemont High*, Juno acts on her own behalf with a self-determination that the narrative codes as admirable. At the outset of the film, we are introduced to a self-possessed character, rational and cool, contemplating the actions that have occasioned the need for a pregnancy test, which she fails—or passes, depending on how you look at it. In spite of being young, unmarried, and pregnant, Juno almost never betrays any sense of distress. Audiences are meant to admire this flattened affect, as she wisecracks like the dame in a 1940s Hollywood screwball comedy, flip and hip and modern.[3] That the character quickly dismisses the logical option of aborting the fetus has garnered attention from voices on both sides of the political spectrum, and much scholarship considers the ramifications of this plot point. Feminist academics note that *Juno*, like other films about unplanned pregnancy released in the same year, represents the potentially traumatic situation as one of light-hearted happy endings for all, thus asserting a pronatalist stance on maternity that reflects a "neoliberal demand for increased consumption," celebrating "young, American-born women who demonstrate their privilege as consumers and their modern female subjectivity through choosing to reproduce" (Thoma 412, 409).

---

3. See Tarancón for coverage of the critical and cultural reception of the film.

My contribution to this already rich conversation centers on the significance of the publicized private sphere in the narrative, that no separation exists, or is even imaginable, between the political citizen and personal moral choices.[4] Because the fictive Juno acts with such seeming self-determination, the film naturalizes the coercive ideological constraints regulating the behavior of girls and women both in the cinematic and the real world. Only those privileged enough to purchase products and people are validated, and yet audiences do not register this ideological thrust, as the sentimental mystification of birth softens the concomitant sadistic treatment of those characters unable or unwilling to cosign the mandate to participate in capitalism's new definition of citizenship.

At key points, the film uses this sleight of hand to mask its conservative trajectory, through maneuvers hidden in plain sight. For example, when the independent Juno decides not to abort the fetus, she claims not to want a "wholesome" adoptive couple, opting for something "edgier" instead. Yet upon seeing the ad featuring heteronormative Vanessa and Mark, beautiful, white, rich, and straight, she immediately selects them for no other reason than they are picture-perfect. No reflection whatever occurs about the ramifications of handing her child over to what the screenwriter herself terms "antiseptic yuppies," and thus the dis-ease that Juno represents as a working-class woman becomes healed—the pathogens get eliminated and a fantasy of life without contaminants in the married couples' Glacial Valley Estates home reigns supreme. In the final scene Vanessa, adoptive mother par excellence, the perfect white woman, played by the perfectly white Jennifer Garner, poses in bed with perfect hair, dressed in perfect white, in a white bed, with white sheets, in a room with white walls, staring dreamily at her new white baby, swaddled, of course, in white. The audience is meant to enjoy and admire this scene of privileged maternal and material bliss.

That this character was an object of contempt for most of the film demands consideration. How—and why—does the superficial, materialistic, pathetic woman become this Angel in the McMansion? Tarancón notes that the "sympathies of the audience are made to shift" toward this "neurotic and superficial yuppie" (461) but does not consider the ideological ramifications of the shift, nor the illogic of it, from either a filmic or political perspective. I argue two significant reasons for this shift exist: First, by shrilly insisting upon the Glories of Motherhood that can only be elaborated in fantasies like this film, *Juno* sanitizes messy chaotic realities like pregnancy, birth, death, the body,

---

4. For additional readings of the film besides those cited in the body of my chapter, see Willis; Oliver; Clarke; Troutman.

desire, and female subjectivity. Second, while these glories reflect the Victorian Cult of True Womanhood, in which a woman's place is in the separate, domestic sphere, away from the realm of politics, the film must also sanitize the more recent neoliberal elimination of social services, requiring the pretense of plenty for all, and free choice for all, regardless of race, class, sex, or ability. In this way, such films "combine uncertainty about options for women with 'an idealized essentialized femininity that symbolically evades and transcends institutional and social problem spots'" (Thoma 410). *Juno* allows us to turn away from practical concerns like access to resources, instead indulging in postfeminist fantasies of abundance.

Because the good life under neoliberalism must adhere to strict norms of consumption, the film naturalizes both the purchasing of objects and the spaces in which they are proffered. When Juno first meets the privileged prospective parents, she is bowled over by the plenty that their picture-perfect home contains. Although there is no baby, Vanessa already has stockpiled vast stores of consumer goods generated for the billion-dollar infant market. Husband Mark disdainfully refers to these purchases as stemming from her "mall madness," presented as gendered psychosis immanent in the female. Up until this point her character is clearly selfish, isolated, and materialistic—she always gets what she wants and now she wants a baby "so bad"—but this negative depiction takes a sharp turn toward validation of her presumptive maternal instincts when Juno happens upon her at, unsurprisingly, the mall. This scene emphasizes that despite her sterile home environment, her literal sterility, her mindless privilege, and her emasculating of her partner, Vanessa's individual ability to "have" a child makes her a good choice of mother. As the scene begins, we see Juno, the pregnant teen, surreptitiously watching Vanessa play with children in a space designed for this activity. (We are not meant to consider the significance of the fact that American children play at the mall rather than outdoors, but given the film's strenuous promotion of material privilege and consumption as the meaning of the good life, it bears mentioning.)

Because the adoptive father has had second thoughts, Juno was struggling with how to proceed until this scene at the mall when she realizes that with or without a husband, Vanessa is a *natural* mother. After watching Vanessa romp with a young girl, the two lead characters bump into each other on the elevator. Vanessa asks to touch Juno's stomach in the hopes of feeling a kick from the fetus, and then dispiritedly says, "It's not moving for me." It seems this character will be doomed to a barren existence, with no one to shop for, as even the child is rejecting her in utero, but then Vanessa drops to a squat position and speaks to Juno's swollen abdomen: "Hi baby, it's me Vanessa. I can't wait to meet you. Can you hear me baby? Sweet angel?" Upon hearing her voice, the baby kicks, and Vanessa beams with joy. "Magical," she says. From the perspective of the conservative right, this is indeed a magical moment, for it validates the belief that women are magically meant to mother, and it does so in the marketplace, which is no longer a public space, but an extension of the private home, a domesticated space for women to fill with objects they buy and burnish. At the mall, cavorting with the children of strangers, Vanessa wants to own a baby of her own to shop for and to teach how to shop. She represents the postfeminist "neoliberal global marketplace demanding new forms of consumption, labor, and citizenship" (Thoma 410).

Given the film's glorification of spending and acquiring, the narrative's utter silence on Vanessa's source of income loudly reverberates. She presumably has a great professional career, but we are never told what she does. As a postfeminist promise to the girls in the audience that political and cultural constraints against their full participation in the workforce have been eliminated, *Juno* makes concrete the fantasy that exciting, glamorous options are on the horizon.[5] What those options are is not, and cannot, be addressed, for it might pollute the pretty picture. Does she work for the military-industrial complex? How does her income affect those of the worldwide working-class? And, glaringly, who will be taking care of this baby once she springs from that white maternal bed and bustles off to work? Impoverished women, especially women of color, that is who. These laborers enabling privileged white mothers do not themselves enjoy the protections and stability of US citizenship, nor are their relationships with their children encouraged, validated, or celebrated (Parreñas). In fact, as of this writing, migrants of all stripes find themselves under increasingly hostile surveillance and regulation. But because she will hand over her domestic work to invisible others paid from her own pocket, Vanessa can fulfill a neoliberal fantasy, that of the ability to raise children with no need, use, or desire for any social services whatever. As long as she is straight, white, and rich, no one need concern herself with the material realities of other women's lives. All caring should be directed only toward one's own offspring.

---

5. Postfeminism is defined as the cultural movement that "works in part to incorporate, assume, or naturalize aspects of feminism; crucially, it also works to commodify feminism via the figure of woman as empowered consumer. Thus, postfeminist culture emphasizes educational and professional opportunities for women and girls; freedom of choice with respect to work, domesticity, and parenting; and physical and particularly sexual empowerment. Assuming full economic freedom for women, postfeminist culture also (even insistently) enacts the possibility that women might choose to retreat from the public world of work. . . . As this suggests, postfeminism is white and middle class by default, anchored in consumption as a strategy (and leisure as a site) for the production of the self" (Tasker and Negra 2).

The two characters who do express resistance to the otherwise unchallenged mystification of childbirth in the film are soundly trashed for so doing: Mark Loring (Jason Bateman) and the unnamed ultrasound technician (Kaaren de Silva). Mark, Vanessa's husband, ultimately rejects the plan to adopt, telling Juno that he is leaving his wife and moving to the city. While the film suggests his feelings for the young woman help spur this shift, his reversal also makes sense in the context of the story since it was Vanessa, not Mark, who wanted a baby from the minute they got married. He says he is not interested in being a parent, which seems a fine thing to know about oneself. His decision might even be coded as the responsible thing to do—that is, to come forward before the adoption occurs so that Vanessa is not left with being a single parent. Also, as a musician now reduced to writing advertising jingles, Mark's rejection of their status-obsessed corporate life could be viewed as a life-affirming alternative to the capitalist mandate that all meaning derives from consumption of goods. He wants to drop out of this regulated, sterile, commercial world. "She hates it when I sit around and watch movies and don't 'contribute,'" he tells Juno with a dismay Spicoli would understand, but there is no space in the film to consider these alternative desires as reasonable. In fact, it is the ostensibly bohemian Juno herself who delivers the punishing neoliberal judgment on Mark's resistance to being regulated: "Your shirt is stupid. Grow up."

The problem with this mandate to "grow up" stems from the decreasing possibility of being any kind of citizen except one devoted to conservative values. Berlant describes this type of citizenship as requiring adults to "'forget' or render as impractical, naïve, or childish their utopian political identifications in order to be politically happy and economically functional" (29). It is hard to imagine Spicoli from *Ridgemont High* as an adult in this highly regulated capitalist space welcoming only one kind of citizen, the apolitical compliant consumer. Mark represents precisely the dilemma of choice in such a culture, as his character must submit fully to the machine, churning out ads and shopping with his wife and baby, or, in resisting, become stigmatized as childish for wanting something more pleasurable, uncertain, and less sterile. As Vanessa's choice to adopt obscures the realities of those who toil to service women with reproductive privilege while being forced to separate from their own offspring, Mark's choice to move to a loft in the city obscures the situation of those who lack his character's resources and race, sex, and gender privilege. At the same time, the film does not validate his character's desire for something else besides the moribund sterility and sameness of suburbia, nor does the narrative allow space for imagining what that might be. Eliminating the problematic status of white masculinity by sending the husband away allows the narrative to hone in directly on its end goal: illuminating the pieta of white womanhood and baby.

That life in Glacial Valley Estates is a form of death was made clear early in the film as Juno and her father drove to Mark and Vanessa's home for the first time, passing one prefabricated home after another. The symbolism here is explicit: These funky working-class types have come to suburbia, where houses line up like tombstones, crypts for the wealthy, entombed by their possessions. Until this point, viewers are meant to identify with and admire Juno's nonconformity. She is fresh and funny, seemingly unselfconscious and lacking in shame. Her judgments on others seem deserving. We admire her longing for individual freedom and the lengths to which she is willing to go to get it. Thus, the comparison between her whimsical life and this mini-mansion cum Stepford wife tilts audience judgment initially onto Juno's side. First, the camera cuts to Vanessa's disembodied hand arranging everything perfectly in her perfect house—glass picture frames, diffuser. Magazines line up rigidly like in the doctor's offices that themselves reflect publicized private spheres, fake *living rooms* offering familiar sterility. The titles suggest intimate lives mediated by status: *Parents, Traditional Home, Family Circle, Country Living.* Mark tells Juno his wife "gave me my own room for all my stuff," and Juno teases him about this infantilization even as she also admires his collection of rock and roll accoutrement, and audience sympathy aligns with the two of them in disliking the punishing martinet Vanessa.

And yet the seeming condemnation of her sterile home and personality gets quickly elided by the magic of materialistic maternity. Initially crestfallen to discover that Juno had found them in the *Penny Saver,* perhaps because the working-class association of this advertising circular whiffs of unseemly labor rather than the fancy kind she does, Vanessa begins romanticizing pregnancy as "beautiful," but then, cautiously asks, "Are you looking for any other type of compensation?" The pregnant pause that follows reveals her concern that this young woman might be mercenary. Juno replies, "No, I don't want to sell the thing." Suddenly, peace descends, directing attention away from questions about how this exchange could or should fall outside of the capitalist economy that so clearly regulates every other aspect of the characters' lives. The answer, that as compensation for neoliberal privatization and alienation of human life, childbearing must be deemed special, meaning it cannot be monetized, reveals the romantic mythology at work here. Something mystical involving pregnancy and motherhood transcends the otherwise impersonal vagaries of commerce, and women find fruition in this economy rather than the capitalist one. "Have you ever felt like you were just born to do something?" Vanessa asks breathlessly, clearly referring to her own maternal drive.

"Yes," replies Juno's dad, "heating and air conditioning." The humor here softens the robust conflation of masculinity with productive work and femininity with the work of mothering. (Upon seeing Vanessa's Pilates machine in their living room, Juno's father asks, "What do you make with it?") But the fact that this natural-born-mother apparently cannot naturally birth children creates an opportunity for consumption, one this whole scene belies.

Also ignored are the race and class privilege that allow Vanessa, the wealthy white woman, to buy a baby, even after Mark, the cad, leaves her. As Kristen Hoerl and Casey Kelly have argued,

> Vanessa's choice to become a single mother, without becoming pregnant
> . . . reflects the consumer dynamic at work in the post-nuclear family. As
> a white, professional woman Vanessa exercises the range of choices at her
> disposal, to "have it all," so to speak "autonomy, career, and a child." (370)

Thus, *Juno* asks the audience to navigate two simultaneous value systems, one eschewing any thought of financial considerations, the other rejecting the idea that an impecunious life has any value. Only those females who have money are naturalized as mothers in the narrative, which is reflected in Juno's forthright acknowledgment that she is unprepared to raise a child, and in her stepmother's depiction as loving but crude. While Juno's character is valorized for making the right choice, a selfless sacrifice, sending the child off to the suburbs, paradoxically the ultrasound technician who dares to suggest that raising children requires resources is soundly humiliated. This scene at the clinic, breathtaking in its hypocrisy, misogyny, and illogic, reflects that same sleight of hand performed at key moments in the plot, allowing the audience to side both with the unconventional Juno and her unruly family *and* with the neoconservative and neoliberal mandates that nonconforming reproduction (that is, the reproductive *choices* of poor women and women of color, among others) be discouraged. It is worth looking carefully at the scene where Juno, her best friend, and her stepmother have gone in for an ultrasound. As the girls joke around, the technician looks on disapprovingly at their callow youth. When she finds out the baby will be adopted out, she murmurs, "Thank goodness for that." What has been a sentimental and comical scene swiftly pivots in tone as a sadistic attack on the woman is unleashed by Juno's insulted stepmother. The technician, pressed for an explanation, says, "I just see a lot of teenaged mothers come through here. It's obviously a poisonous environment to raise a baby in."

Given that the film rejects out of hand the idea that Juno herself should keep the baby, and that it ultimately sentimentalizes, mystifies, and celebrates the adoption of the baby by the privileged white consumer, this tech's observation would seem uncontroversial. Teenaged girls without resources cannot raise children as well as rich grown-ups; this is the ultimate message of the movie. But instead of letting this comment pass, or exploring the etiology of the "poison" to which she refers, the narrative has the stepmother, herself a working-class woman, viciously attack this female worker for daring to state the obvious. After the group protests that the adoptive parents could be much worse than Juno in raising the baby—how confusing is that, given the thrust of this plot?—the stepmother asks condescendingly, "What is your job title exactly?" She makes the point that this woman has stepped out of the bounds of her expertise by commenting on the fitness of teenage parents, which might be a valid observation under different circumstances, but instead audience members are forced to side with her and against this woman, granting Juno and her stepmother ethical status for in effect asserting that the right thing to do is to keep one's baby. Yet in the film the ethical thing to do is represented as giving it to someone in a privileged economic position.

This paradox (do not give it away / do not keep it) could be solved by abortion, as we have seen in *Ridgemont High*. McClennan and others have noted that instead, *Juno* the film and Juno the character reject the option of abortion with breathtaking speed and superficiality. Instead, the film scapegoats this ultrasound technician for pointing out the obvious, while simultaneously naturalizing babies being raised by their birth mothers as the best option. In this twist, we see a celebration of women's presumed individual rights, which, as Hoerl and Kelly have argued, is accomplished "without the corresponding structural critique of patriarchy and capitalism offered by feminists of the Second Wave" (370). In other words, instead of considering the material conditions that affect women's ability to choose to be mothers or to parent successfully, we, via the stepmother as mouthpiece for neoliberalism, turn on the worker and enjoy her degradation. Although the stepmother described herself modestly as a "nail tech" earlier in the scene, suddenly her character brings the full force of masculine dismissal of female waged-labor to bear, while the audience and the girls cheer her on. "Bren, you're a dick," says Juno. "LOVE it!!!" No female solidarity is possible in such a narrative. We have only individuals vying for dominance, absent any context about what structural forces proscribe all of their lives. The *choice* to mother is reserved only for women with access to wealth who choose to do so, and this becomes an excuse to deny social services to poor women (Hoerl and Kelly 377), an ambiguity wholly unexplored in this scene, which instead pits working women against one another.

Unlike *Ridgemont High,* which depicts young people getting socialized in school to become citizens, and operating as young adults in a public sphere unencumbered by their private sexual behaviors, in *Juno* all private activities such as pregnancy have become publicized, and no sense of a public sphere absent one's private choices appears to exist. In *Ridgemont High,* all the adults are teachers. In *Juno,* almost all the adults are parents—the only exception being a brief glimpse of a teacher engaged in a juvenile flirtation with Juno's best friend. Authority figures like Mr. Hand seem to have disappeared in this cultural moment, and in their place appear childish spokespeople for the reactionary right. "All children want to be borned," bawls Su-Chin, Juno's classmate and abortion protestor in the clinic parking lot. Unlike Stacy, Juno cannot make a private decision to seek an abortion, as this exercise of her civil rights has become public property. This publicization of the private sphere, reflected in the anti-choice rhetoric of the protestor, accompanies a privatization of the public sphere, as the bored and untrained clinic worker reveals intimate personal details of her sex life to the disgusted Juno. Ultimately washed of any political import, Juno's decision to reject abortion is coded in the film as an entirely individual decision, reflecting personality clashes with the worker and those other patients in the waiting room. She flees in disgust after their inaudible finger tapping and gum chewing become an unbearable cacophony. Indeed, abortion is only represented to suggest the full arsenal of choices supposedly available to liberated First World girls.

The silent star of this drama is of course the fetus itself, always already positioned as future citizen-consumer. The baby who waves to Vanessa from the womb has begun the inexorable command of her time and resources, representing the unlimited potential of the autonomous male, unbound by the female container/crypt. In this fantasy, we need not acknowledge the inevitable erasure of personhood that mortality guarantees. The unaborted fetus, neoliberal subject extraordinaire, waves from his cockpit, ready for launch into—what exactly goes blissfully unexplored for the happily-ever-after ending such movies generically require. Not only does the film leave us with a dewy white woman in bed with designer sheets and her newly acquired baby, but we also see Juno and her boyfriend Bleeker warbling away to each other as she asserts their undying future love for each other. No longer a resistant female, compliant Juno joins the conga line of normative ingénues. Her father has even promised her a return to the birthing room at the hospital someday "on her own terms." In this way films can promise us what embodiment cannot: permanence, stability, manageability. Such promises can only be made by ruthlessly editing out contradictory and nonnormative instances and by reproducing heterosexual romance, whiteness, and material privilege. The power dynamics underlying such warm and fuzzy plotlines—the oppression and marginalization of real bodies and environments required to produce a nostalgic fantasy of materialistic nirvana for select groups—emerge only upon close considerations of the fault lines in these compensatory narratives that assume "universal access to citizenship and consumer culture" (Thoma 411). The fetal rights manifested in *Juno* reflect a fantasy of coherence, belied by the lived reality of women's lives in a world of telescoping resources and concern for us as people.

Works Cited

Berlant, Lauren. *The Queen of American Goes to Washington: Essays on Sex and Citizenship.* Duke University Press, 1997.

Clarke, Kyra. "Becoming Pregnant: Disrupting Expectations of Girlhood in Juno." *Feminist Media Studies,* vol. 15, no. 2, 2015, pp. 257–70.

Dresner, Lisa. "Love's Labor's Lost?: Early 1980s Representations of Girls' Sexual Decision Making in Fast Times at Ridgemont High and Little Darling." *Virgin Territory: Representing Sexual Inexperience in Film,* edited by Tamar McDonald, Wayne State Press, 2010, pp. 174–200.

Edwards, Valerie. "Remarkable Moment an Ultrasound Shows Twin Girls Sharing a Kiss in Mom's Womb." *Daily Mail,* 10 Apr. 2017, www.dailymail.co.uk/news/article-4399244/Couple-witness-identical-twins-kissing-ultrasound.html.

Fast Times at Ridgemont High. Amy Heckerling, dir. USA Universal Pictures, 1982.

Hoerl, Kristen, and Casey Ryan Kelly. "The Post-Nuclear Family and the Depoliticization of Unplanned Pregnancy in Knocked Up, Juno, and Waitress." *Communication and Critical/Cultural Studies,* vol. 7, no. 4, 2010, 360–80.

Johnson, Brian. "Fear and Self-Loving: Masturbation in Teen Movie Comedies." *Film International,* vol. 13, no. 4, 2015, pp. 60–71.

Juno. Jason Reitman dir. USA Fox, Searchlight Pictures, 2007.

Latimer, Heather. "Popular Culture and Reproductive Politics: Juno, Knocked Up, and the Enduring Legacy of The Handmaid's Tale." *Feminist Theory,* vol. 10 no. 2, 2009, pp. 211–26.

McClennan, Rachael. "Cautionary Whales?: Adolescence and Genre in Juno and Push." *Mosaic: A Journal for the Interdisciplinary Study of Literature,* vol. 46, no. 2, 2013, pp. 105–21.

Nowell, Richard. "'For Girls': Hollywood, the Date-Movie Market, and Early-1980s Teen Sex Comedies." *Post Script: Essays in Film and the Humanities,* vol. 34, no. 1, Fall 2014, pp. 3–19.

Oliver, Kelly. *Knock Me Up, Knock Me Down: Images of Pregnancy in the Hollywood Film.* Columbia University Press, 2012.

Parreñas, Rhacel. *Servants of Globalization: Migration and Domestic Work.* Stanford University Press, 2015.

Petchesky, Rosalind. "Fetal Images: The Power of Visual Culture in the Politics of Reproduction." *Feminist Studies,* vol. 13, no. 2, Summer 1987, pp. 263–92.

Phipps, Alison. *The Politics of the Body: Gender in a Neoliberal and Neoconservative Age.* Polity Press, 2014.

Putnam, David. *Bowling Alone: The Collapse and Revival of American Community.* Simon and Schuster, 2000.

Ross, Loretta. "African-American Women and Abortion." *Abortion Wars: A Half Century of Struggle* 1950–2000, edited by Rickie Solinger, University of California Press, 1998, pp. 161–207.

Shaefer, H. Luke, and Kathryn Eden. "Rising Extreme Poverty in the United States and the Response of Federal Means-Tested Transfer Programs." *Social Service Review,* vol. 87, no. 2, June 2013, pp. 250–68.

Tarancón, Juan Antonio. "Juno: A Practical Case Study of Teens, Film, and Cultural Studies." *Cultural Studies,* vol. 26, no. 4, 2012, 442–68.

Tasker, Yvonne, and Diane Negra, editors. *Interrogating Postfeminism: Gender and the Politics of Culture.* Duke University Press, 2007.

Thoma, Pamela. "Buying Up Baby." *Feminist Media Studies,* vol. 9, no. 4, 2009, pp. 409–25.

Troutman, Stephanie. "The Cautionary Whale, Viking, Vessel, Planet or Saint?: Adolescence and Maternal Configuration in Juno and Beyond." *Counterpoints,* vol. 392, 2011, pp. 246–60.

Ventura, Patricia. *Neoliberal Culture: Living with American Neoliberalism.* Ashgate Press, 2012.

Willis, Jessica. "Sexual Subjectivity: A Semiotic Analysis of Girlhood, Sex, and Sexuality in the Film Juno." *Sexuality and Culture,* vol. 12, no. 4, 2008, pp. 240–56.

CHAPTER 7

"Masters of Their Own Destiny"
Women's Rights and Forced Sterilizations in Peru

JULIETA CHAPARRO-BUITRAGO

ON DECEMBER 19, 1997, the Peruvian newspaper *El Comercio* featured the story of Magna Morales Canduelas, a woman from Tocache, a town in the Amazon region, who was sterilized and subsequently died earlier that month at the local hospital. Days before her passing, Rita, one of the obstetricians, had visited Magna in her home to convince her to get the procedure. The first time she visited Magna's house, Magna's daughter remembers, she hid away. Rita was persistent, however, and the next day she managed to take Magna to the health center. Rita had recruited another woman, Bernardina Alba, who recounted that Magna was not entirely convinced about the sterilization. Repeatedly, she told the provider that her husband didn't agree with the procedure. "It doesn't matter, the obstetrician said, you get it today and you will be back home for cooking dinner. Your husband will never find out" Alba

I would like to express my gratitude to the scholars and institutions that contributed to this chapter. I was a visiting researcher in 2016 at IDEHPUC—Instituto de Democracia y Derechos Humanos—at Pontificia Universidad Catolica in Lima, where the first draft of this chapter was written. Special thanks to Iris Jave, Mario Cepeda Caceres, and Diego Uchuypoma for receiving me and for their support during my year there. Special thanks to professors Jane Anderson and Thomas Leatherman for their endless support, to professor Betsy Hartmann for her generous feedback and encouraging words, and to professor Laura Briggs for her fabulous comments on this piece and for pushing my thinking about family planning development in Peru. My research has received the generous support of the Social Science Research Council and The Wenner Gren Foundation.

remembered. In the end, Magna accepted. After all, as Mrs. Alba commented: "When you have nothing and they offer you food and clothes for your children, they manipulate you." The women got the surgery in the afternoon, and next morning they were back home.

When Rita visited Magna in her house for a follow-up, Magna told the nurse she was not feeling well; her feet were cold, she had difficulty urinating, and had nausea and diarrhea. Rita offered some painkillers but never came back to check on her. Magna's health deteriorated quickly to the point that she couldn't eat or get out of bed. The next day her husband rushed her to the hospital because the abdominal pain and headache had worsened, and she was unable to walk. When they arrived, the doctor refused her entrance to the ER. Magna was admitted after the president and members of the local Mother's Club showed up and argued with him. Magna's husband had to pay out of pocket for chloromycetin (a broad-spectrum antibiotic), serum, and painkillers for his wife's treatment.

Magna passed away only a few days after she was hospitalized. According to the doctor, she had several cardiac arrests, and they couldn't revive her. The institution refused to perform an autopsy, and when her husband pushed for it, the hospital director replied: "Why do we need to get it done if we already know what caused her death?" Local authorities decided not to open an investigation for Mrs. Morales's case, but one of her neighbors filed a complaint at the ombudsman's office, providing documentation, including a tape of the testimony of the doctor in charge, who assured him Mrs. Morales died of meningitis.

Magna's case is emblematic of the violations and abuses that thousands of Peruvian women experienced when they were sterilized under the auspices of the Reproductive Health and Family Planning Program 1996–2000 (RHFPP). These abuses took place under a program that had a progressive rhetoric of reproductive health and women's empowerment. The goal of this essay is to understand how a presumably *progressive* social policy that sought to expand women's reproductive health services ended up being the platform for sterilizing thousands of women in Peru without their consent.

Some commentators have noted that this program was rooted in population control principles and was part of a broader poverty reduction strategy (Ballon; Boesten, "Revisiting" and "Free Choice"; Ewig, "Hijacking"; Mooney). Peru was facing a dramatic economic downturn as a result of a stagnant economy, high inflation rates, and a bloody internal armed conflict. However, I find their analysis incomplete as they fail to explore the operation of the rhetoric of empowerment and autonomy for understanding the cases of forced sterilization. In *Governed through Choice: Autonomy, Technology, and the Politics of Reproduction,* political scientist Jennifer Denbow discusses the importance of analyzing the reproductive rights discourse for its underlying logic rather than assuming it has been merely manipulated for restricting women's reproductive lives. Her work leads to some provocative questions for reflecting on the Peruvian case: How did a program with progressive rhetoric give way to the large-scale sterilization of low-income, peasant, and indigenous women in Peru? How does the discourse of responsible parenthood and choice facilitate state interference in women's lives?

When we bring an intersectional lens to examine the notions of empowerment and autonomy foregrounded in the program, the issue of who can be considered an autonomous subject becomes apparent. I argue in this essay that gendered racism in Peru creates the conditions for indigenous and peasant women to be portrayed as irresponsible mothers unable to appropriately control their reproductive lives, turning them into the targets of coerced sterilizations. Building on Loretta Ross and Rickie Solinger's work on reproductive justice, I argue that the rhetoric of empowerment does not apply homogeneously to all women precisely because the intersections of race, class, and gender constitute the vulnerability of some women who are deemed as making *bad* choices about their reproductive lives—in this case, having children while poor.

In what follows, I begin with a historical overview of the implementation of the Reproductive Health and Family Planning Program and the controversy that emerged in the media around it. Next, I explore the novelty and limits of this program, particularly the use of empowerment and citizenship as solutions to poverty. I use Alberto Fujimori's speech at the World Conference on Women in Beijing to illustrate this point. Then, I analyze the program's rhetoric to underscore how two notions—responsible parenthood and choice— were fundamental to the coercive sterilization campaign that took place under the program. I introduce an intersectional approach to complicate the reproductive rights agenda and show how racialized gendered constructions about indigenous and peasant women, which depict them as unable to regulate their reproductive lives, turn them into the target of forced sterilizations.

A "Women Friendly" Government

In 1991, former Peruvian president Alberto Fujimori declared the 1990s the decade of family planning, and birth control–related activities intensified during his second presidential term (1995–2000). In his presidential address in 1995, he announced the creation of the new Reproductive Health and Family Planning Program that would guarantee low-income families access to affordable contraceptives and women the control of their reproductive lives. The RHFPP was introduced as a progressive program that sought to guarantee women's reproductive health at all stages of their lives. Having a fulfilling reproductive life, according to the program, would improve people's quality of life, increase equity, and contribute to a balanced relationship between society and the environment. The program described reproductive health as a fundamental human, social, and political right, which would guarantee one's autonomy, self-governance, and the exercise of women's citizenship. The language of the policy conveyed the idea that men and women as citizens were the new subjects of reproductive rights—yet the program placed at the center the notion of responsible parenthood as the standard of proper reproductive behavior.

Ideas about women's empowerment and women's rights had a significant presence in Fujimori's second presidential term. In 1997, for instance, a quota law was introduced to increase women's participation in Peruvian political life. Feminist scholar Cecilia Blondet observes that women elected for Congress went from 9 percent in 1995 to 25 percent in 2000 (*Mujeres y Política*), eight women became heads of ministries, and women regidoras (municipal representatives) reached 24.8 percent in 1998 (*Encanto del Dictador*). Congress approved important legislation for preventing domestic violence and sexual assault. In 1996, the government also created three public offices devoted to the expansion of women's rights: Promudeh (the Ministry of Women's Development and Human Capital); the Women's Rights Division at the ombudsman's office; and the Congress's Commission on Women. Additionally, Fujimori participated in the Fourth World Conference on Women in Beijing in 1995, where he delivered a speech ratifying his government's commitment to expanding family planning services as a platform for guaranteeing women's control over their bodies. He sent a persuasive message to Peruvians and the rest of the world: The expansion of women's rights stood as evidence of the democratic spirit of his government,[1] revealing the centrality of women's issues and liberation to liberal-democratic systems (Mahmood 2005).

---

1. Political scientist Christine Ewig suggests that Fujimori's speech at the Beijing Conference helped ease criticism after the self-coup in 1992 and allowed his government to access financial support from international agencies, such as USAID, that had withdrawn funding after he dissolved Congress ("Hijacking"). In fact, gender mainstreaming policies, like the Reproductive Health and Family Planning Program, served to cover up what critics said was Fujimori's authoritarian, violent, and corrupt regime (Boesten, "Revisiting") by conveying the idea of stability, order, and good governance (Blondet, *Encanto del Dictador*).

A Controversial Program

The excitement about the RHFPP was short-lived. News about coercive sterilizations began to appear in newspapers as early as 1996. Members of the clergy, healthcare professionals, and politicians critical of Fujimori's administration condemned the program for its potential abusive nature. Most of these critics considered it an attack on individual liberties and opposed to bioethical principles. Luis Bambaren, president of the Episcopal Conference of the city of Chimbote, denounced the classism of the program, arguing that it violated the dignity and freedom of poor people. In an interview with the newspaper *La Republica* on July 13, 1996, he criticized the use of public resources to sterilize women, rather than investing them in the expansion of social services for the poor. In another newspaper article published in *La Republica* on July 1, 1996, the president of the Medical Association of Peru, Franciso Sanchez Moreno, suggested that the government used incentives to pressure women with less socioeconomic power to accept the sterilizations. "Amidst poverty," Sanchez Moreno argued, "it is foreseeable that women would choose to get the procedure in exchange for some economic compensation." He condemned the use of bonuses for violating women's right to make free and informed decisions about their reproductive lives. News articles denouncing abuses and coercive sterilizations in different parts of the country continued to appear in the media in 1997, attesting to the nationwide scope of the program. Magna's case and other women's testimonies of coercive sterilizations across Peru were first featured in national media in December 1997, and they opened the door to an official investigation by the women's rights division at the ombudsman's office.

Simultaneously, the Latin American and Caribbean Committee for the Defense of Women's Rights (CLADEM), a feminist umbrella organization, was also documenting the abuses after they heard of coercive sterilizations during a field visit to Huancabamba, a province in the Coastal Department of Piura. Feminist lawyer Giulia Tamayo, in charge of the investigation, stumbled upon documents at the local healthcare center containing information on tubal ligation quotas for the province of Huancabamba for 1996, as well as a list of procedures done up to September that year, and dates and places for upcoming *campañas* (fairs) (CLADEM, *Nada*).

The ombudsman's office and CLADEM carried out separate investigations, yet arrived at similar findings. They found that healthcare centers had sterilization quotas and that personnel *captaba* (caught) patients to fulfill the numbers. Providers used incentives, such as food, clothes, and small amounts of cash, in exchange for women's compliance. The government also used stimuli for providers to fulfill sterilization quotas, through sanction or promotions on the fulfillment of quotas, and rewards to healthcare centers with the highest numbers of sterilizations. Healthcare centers across the country planned and executed massive *tubal ligation fairs* where providers performed sterilizations and vasectomies in unsanitary conditions, and without providing information on other contraceptive methods.

Coerced sterilizations were concentrated in rural communities populated by indigenous and peasant women, as well as in low-income neighborhoods in cities such as Lima. Women in these areas received family planning services from the government, making them more vulnerable to coerced and unconsented sterilizations in health centers run by the Ministry of Health. Statistical projections find that women who were more likely to be sterilized during the campaign were younger, with considerably less education, and more likely to live in rural areas in the Amazon or the Andean region (Byker and Gutierrez). Indigenous women with one or two children were more likely to be sterilized compared to nonindigenous women, revealing a class and ethnic bias in the sterilization campaign that targeted indigenous women living in poverty (Rendon 2017). The ombudsman office's first report, from 1998, found eight cases; the second, from 2000, found 157; and the last one, from 2002, documented more than 200,000 cases of low-income, peasant, and indigenous women who were sterilized in the span of the four years, many of whom were bribed, deceived by healthcare providers, and in some cases forcibly sterilized in health centers.

If the main goal of the RHFPP was the expansion of women's reproductive health, how do we account for the abuses committed under its auspices? Different authors have suggested that poverty reduction was one of the primary purposes behind the program (Ballon; Boesten, "Revisiting" and "Free Choice"; Coe; Ewig, "Hijacking"; Mooney). The government believed that reducing birth rates and restructuring family size would empower women and improve the economic conditions of their families and the country at large. Equating lowering birth rates with poverty reduction is an old idea, one that had gained popularity after World War II, when population growth—often associated with nonwhite and Third World populations—started to become a social problem that needed attention and intervention for the dangers it posed to the world (Connelly; Gutierrez). Demographers, historian Matthew Connelly suggests, reformulated the demographic transition theory to make the reduction of birth rates a necessary condition for the modernization process and economic development. Population control policies then were used to solve Third World countries' so-called development *problems,* such as recurrent famines and political and economic instability (Hartmann). Peru followed this formula for alleviating the high poverty rates that plagued the country during the 1980s and 1990s.

Poverty reduction, however, is not the only explanation behind coerced sterilizations of indigenous, peasant, and low-income women in Peru. I am interested in how the language of women's empowerment and autonomy could be used as a discourse of control, calling into question the idea that Fujimori's government merely used the language of rights and feminism to cover up what has been described as a corrupt and abusive regime, as feminist scholar Jelke Boesten ("Revisiting") and political scientist Christina Ewig ("Hijacking Feminism") have suggested. We could indeed think that feminist agendas were manipulated to advance economic goals; however, this explanation has two significant shortcomings. It means not uncovering the influence of neoliberal principles in this program that brought together the promise of empowerment for women, a new modern feminist subjectivity, and the idea of citizenship as the solution to poverty (Grewal). Additionally, not exploring the program's rhetoric leaves us oblivious to how the presumably benign language of women's empowerment, choice, and responsible parenthood serve the purpose of controlling indigenous and peasant women's lives.

Family Planning Meets Reproductive Health

The terrifying novelty of the RHFPP was its selective appropriation of the reproductive health concerns that emerged from the UN-sponsored International Conferences on Population and Development[2] (ICPD) and the Fourth Conference of Women in Beijing, which challenged neo-Malthusian views of population control and economic development. These conferences offered a comprehensive model for reproductive rights programs, including "full antenatal and obstetric care, infertility treatment, breastfeeding, prevention and treatment of gynaecological cancers, HIV and other STDs, as well as a wide range of family planning methods and counseling" (Petchesky 154). Ignoring the comprehensive model, however, the RHFPP focused on fertility rates, population growth, and economic development as pathways to women's empowerment and reproductive autonomy.

---

2. The conference brought together women's health activists, both from the developed countries and the South, to influence the discussion about population control (Rao and Sexton). Their goal was to bring together population policies and women's reproductive rights, and they were backed by the population policy establishment (the World Bank, the Population Council, and other international NGOs) (Rao and Sexton). These groups crafted the "Cairo Consensus" that gave life to the ICPD's Programme of Action, which would regulate population policies across the world, and which was signed by some 179 countries (Rao and Sexton).

Even though the RHFPP included an expanded agenda of reproductive rights and maternal and infant health, fertility rates were still the primary target. The goals of the program were to expand the use of modern contraceptives in order to reduce overall fertility rates—from 3.2 children per woman in 1995 to 2.5 children in 2000—and to reduce maternal mortality rates to fewer than 100 deaths per hundred thousand live births. The RHFPP maintained an approach to fertility and economic development built around the idea of overpopulation and the need to lower fertility rates to improve the country's economic problems. This program reinforced a historical belief that the incidence of poverty among rural women is explained by high fertility rates. It tied development goals to population dynamics while embracing the language of women's rights and reproductive health.

Jelke Boesten (Prologo) and Anna-Brit Coe argue that a shift from demographic goals to a discourse of rights transforms public policies to "enhance women's and men's capacity to exercise their rights and address their reproductive health concerns, including but not limited to their need for contraceptives" (Coe 56). The Peruvian case, however, shows that the introduction of the language of reproductive rights and health did not automatically displace concerns with overpopulation and poverty. This is partly inherent to the Programme of Action of the ICPD, which retained the same model of capitalist economic development as the foundation for reproductive rights agendas (Petchesky). Even though it "enshrine[d] an almost-feminist vision of reproductive rights and gender equity" (Petchesky 152), the program failed to address the devastating effects of privatization and structural adjustment policies in the lives of women and lacked enforcement and accountability mechanisms to dismantle population control principles (Petchesky). Additionally, this program retained population management goals because the Peruvian National Population Act of 1985, which gave shape to family planning activities, had as its primary goal the regulation of population growth, and the RHFPP was expected to fulfill this objective.

Despite these shortcomings, the appealing innovation of the RHFPP was the introduction of women's empowerment and citizenship as a new solution to poverty, a framework that has become mainstream in contemporary family planning agendas. Within this new framework, women's autonomy and decision-making are the solutions to high fertility rates, access to contraceptives, and poverty. Empowerment rhetoric has been useful for feminists and progressive politics, but it has also become a means of governance within neoliberal projects (Sharma). When empowerment rhetoric gets entangled with neoliberalism, it becomes a tool for governing poor people through the cultivation of a sense of self-care and self-improvement (Sharma) that aids a neoliberal agenda.

Empowering Women, Managing Poverty

In his speech at the Fourth World Conference on Women held by the United Nations in 1995, Fujimori focused on women's empowerment and their role in the economic and social recovery of a country that was ravaged by poverty and violence. He began his speech with what is still the most common figuration of poverty in Peru: a woman from rural areas "carrying a baby wrapped in a blanket on her back, surrounded by an additional three or four more children. Even more unbelievably, she often carries one more human being in her womb. Many of these women are single mothers, estranged from their spouses or the sole support of their families" (Fujimori, *Speech*). This image contrasted with the description of women in grassroots organizations who, according to Fujimori, played a central role in fighting poverty and terrorism. They joined *rondas campesinas* (peasant patrols), community-organized security forces in rural areas that fought against guerrilla organizations, he contended. Women also had an important role in mitigating the effects of the economic collapse, as they courageously "created unique mechanisms to solve the problems of hunger and unemployment by promoting popular kitchens, 'glass of milk committees,' *Wawa Wasi* [day care centers], creating close-knitted solidarity networks which benefited entire communities" (Fujimori, *Speech*). The contrast between a poor woman, a passive recipient of society's contempt, and an active and empowered one who can bring about significant changes to society indicated a new approach to citizenship in this program. It presupposed an active member of society, capable of self-improvement. Women's empowerment, Fujimori noted, was a good reason to "invest in women as the most profitable way to reduce poverty and improve [Peru's] social conditions" (*Speech*).

Fujimori spoke in detail about the Reproductive Health and Family Planning Program as a key program in his poverty reduction scheme. It would provide extensive information and reproductive health services to women who could access—with full autonomy and freedom—the tools necessary to make autonomous and rational decisions about their lives. This program, Fujimori suggested, reflected the desires of poor women to control their fertility and reduce the number of pregnancies, but it was received with hostility by the Peruvian Catholic Church, who accused his government of "trying to kill poor people or mutilate them" (Fujimori, *Speech*) after Congress legalized voluntary vasectomies and tubal ligations in 1995. He described the Catholic Church's position as intransigent, an ultraconservative force trying to keep women confined to their restrictive ideas about family planning. By contrast, he claimed, his government was a vanguard force willing to bring forward the changes needed to empower women. Modern family planning methods would be available to women, men, and families of all social classes. As autonomous and responsible parents, they would use them or opt for another solution according to their personal or family beliefs, he concluded.

The exaltation of women in Fujimori's speech was a pivotal strategy to deal with the impacts of social adjustment (Rousseau 35). *Empowerment,* a term inherited from the repertoire of nongovernmental organizations (NGOs) as well as feminists and women's organizations, portrayed women as active subjects who could acquire the necessary skills and capabilities to escape poverty by their individual efforts (Molyneux; Sharma). The RHFPP built on this principle to convey the idea that women could be educated to make appropriate decisions about their fertility, family structure, and parenting. Empowerment was not simply a palliative to poverty; it would produce long-term changes in the way women managed their fertility to become responsible parents. Women were not merely recipients of welfare benefits, but empowered citizens capable of determining their own needs and setting the priorities for social programs that would pave their way out of poverty (Molyneux).

The impulse to transform women's behavior through empowerment fit the behavioralist approach that characterizes certain family programs, as Corinna Unger shows. Rational-choice theory as well as behavioralism, which gained relevance during the mid-twentieth century, were influential in family planning policies in various parts of the world, including the US, India, and Pakistan. In the global South, family planning involved strategies to modify people's reproductive behaviors through the provision of information that would lead to a decrease of population growth. High fertility rates became a sign of backwardness, the result of traditional and old-fashioned institutions that represented obstacles to individual decision-making. The assumption was that women, when presented with information about contraceptives, birth spacing, and desired family size (nuclear), would adopt family planning practices and transform their reproductive behavior: "'Fate would give way to control,' this was the hope of many demographers and family planning pundits who saw in dismantling traditional marriage structures, the possibility for individuals to make 'rational choice-based family planning'" (Unger 71). People would be able to decide who and when to marry, and their fertility would no longer be "a rather uncontrolled, fateful concomitant of the expression of sexual desires," but would become "dependent on a conscious decision to have children" (Unger 67).

Empowerment rhetoric suited the behavioralist aspect of family planning and amplified its liberal language of responsibility and autonomy. The RHFPP drew on the overlap between neoliberal empowerment rhetoric and the liberal language from family planning programs to promise autonomy, free decision-making, and liberation from oppressive institutions such as the Catholic Church, which did not want to recognize women as "the masters of their own destiny"—one of Fujimori's favorite catchphrases. If women changed their behavior through available information and resources, they would be able not only to control their reproduction but to liberate themselves, to become new subjects of rights, and to be recognized as citizens.

(Ir)responsible Parents

One of the central goals of Fujimori's program was to lower the fertility rate from 3.5 to 2.5 by the year 2000. The program disaggregated fecundity rates by socioeconomic groups and showed that non-poor women had on average two children and that the average almost doubled for poor women (3.9) and tripled for women living under extreme poverty (6.9). Despite the wide variation in fecundity rates, the program suggested a clear tendency among all women to limit childbirth regardless of their socioeconomic status. Presumably, all women aimed to have 2.4 children. Non-poor women's reproductive behavior was used as the referent for desired fecundity and, most importantly, for setting up the program's goals.[3] This referent lies at the heart of Peru's sterilization program that targeted women who deviated from this expected reproductive behavior.

Here is where two central notions of the program—choice and responsible parenthood—need to be scrutinized to complicate the interpretation that legislators disingenuously used concepts like autonomy, choice, and

---

3. One could argue that the population replacement rate guided the program's goal regarding fertility reduction, and was not necessarily a class-coded expectation. However, as Guzman argues, the urban and highly educated sectors of the population exhibited lower fertility rates compared to the rest of the population, particularly the peasantry and low-income families. The "diversity in reproductive behavior may be found in the markedly elitist character of Latin American societies and the social, economic, and cultural marginalization of the great mass of the population, especially the peasantry" (Guzman xxvi). In the 1960s, the idea of a smaller family, characterized by the nuclear, bourgeois family, "took a root among an increasing portion of the population, leading to the desire and later the practice of birth control" (xxvii).

rights in their efforts to control women's lives (Denbow). Jennifer Denbow calls into question this premise and examines how the notion of autonomy as self-governance can be used to restrict women's reproductive decisions. An autonomous individual is self-reflective and capable of making decisions that comply with existing social norms and power relations. According to Denbow, the notion of autonomy as proper self-management "allows for the appearance of respect for women's rights and self-determination, while justifying increased surveillance and management of women's bodies and reproductive decisions" (3). Women get the possibility to choose and make decisions about their reproductive lives; however, it is ultimately the state—in the form of experts—that decides if they are making the right choices and whether or not to intervene to steer their behavior toward expected goals (Denbow).

In the Peruvian case, the concepts of responsible parenthood and choice presupposed the notion of autonomy as described by Denbow. The notion of responsible parenthood,[4] according to Raul Necochea López, has its roots in a Catholic-inspired family planning program from the mid-1960s to the mid-1970s that responded to the rapid demographic growth that Peru experienced during the second half of the twentieth century. This family planning program combined the provision of contraceptive pills and sex education to train working class and poor families to become responsible parents (Necochea López). The program was not a platform for women's empowerment, the author notes, because fertility control was not understood as a woman's right. The program was instead a way to promote Catholic values among future parents in charge of providing children with spiritual formation, material support, and education. The National Population Act of 1985 officially included a notion of responsible parenthood that transformed it from a Catholic value into a fundamental right of every couple to freely and responsibly decide the number and spacing of their children, along with the obligation to educate them and to adequately meet their basic needs (MIMDES 11).

Being a responsible parent meant making the appropriate decisions about one's reproductive life, such as having a certain number of children and using modern contraceptive methods to align one's behavior with normative ideas about family structure and sexual behavior. As explained above, women were expected to limit their fertility and comply with the program's goals of achiev-

---

4. The notion of responsible parenthood figured in other Latin American family planning programs, such as Mexico. As Elyse Singer notes, the idea of responsibility first appeared in the 1970s, when fears about population explosion were the engine of family planning campaigns that the Mexican government designed to curb population growth. Responsibility was understood as the adoption of modern contraceptives to reduce family size and control the spacing of births. This same language appeared in the abortion bill that legalized this practice in Mexico City in 2007.

ing a heterosexual, nuclear family of two children per household as an expression of their reproductive autonomy. At the interface between state authority and individual self-governance, the concept of autonomy gains relevance as autonomous subjects are those who are deemed capable of governing themselves (Denbow).

As feminist scholars have noted, the expansion of the idea of choice can result in increased regulation of bodies and sexualities (Brown and Halley; Denbow; Menon; Ross and Solinger). Such was the case in Peru, where the RHFPP increased the regulation of women's reproduction by taking a coercive turn. What happens when certain groups of women, like indigenous and peasant women, are perceived as being unable to self-govern? What do race and gender have to do with ideas about self-governing?

Nikolas Rose describes governance as the "conduct of conduct," including "all endeavors to shape, guide, direct the conduct of others" (3). Through governance, individuals are educated to tame their passions and keep their instincts under control—in sum, to govern themselves (Rose). Contemporary practices of governance presuppose the freedom of individuals to act and to adjust themselves to norms of socially accepted behavior. Governance, then, is an intervention in one's behavior and actions; nonetheless, coercive forms of governance have not been abandoned, nor have they disappeared. As Rose notes, groups such as ethnic minorities, inhabitants of inner cities, and mothers on welfare "are defined, demarcated and delineated such that they can be the legitimate targets of such negative [coercive] practices of control" (10). Even in these instances, the use of coercion is configured through the grammar of freedom as its justification. We see this logic operating in the program that used the language of women's empowerment and responsible parenthood to forcibly control peasant and indigenous Peruvian women's reproduction.

The fact that peasant and indigenous women were disproportionately targeted by this program calls for a scrutiny of the notion of autonomy foregrounded in the RHFPP. Who are the women that can make good use of the information given to them to make decisions about their reproductive lives and futures? Who can make these decisions "with full autonomy and freedom," as Fujimori claimed (*Mensaje*)? As described in the previous pages, the program suggested that all women could use the contraceptive method of their choice to control their fertility and to make decisions about family size. However, the implementation of the program took a more coercive expression targeting mainly peasant, indigenous, and low-income women for non-consented sterilizations. Building on reproductive justice scholarship (Ross and Solinger), it is possible to understand the coercive expression of the RHFPP once we analyze the operation of a rights discourse along class categories that racialize gender identities. A reproductive rights agenda builds on the premise of guaranteeing women's autonomy over their bodies, but racialized gendered images that depict indigenous and peasant women as excessive breeders and negligent mothers turn them into the targets of coerced sterilizations.

The issue of coercion illustrates how the rights discourse can certainly empower women who conform to expected reproductive behavior, but this discourse is neither gender nor racially neutral. The intersections of class, race, and gender delineate the contours of the sterilization program in Peru. As Jennifer Denbow notes, societies often see marginalized social groups as incapable of governing themselves, and bestowing autonomy on women and other—often racialized—minority groups is conditional on their adherence to dominant social norms. The violation of these norms often results in forms of exclusion, marginalization, or even violence. The behavioralist impulse of the RHFPP program expected women to curb their reproductive behavior, and that meant limiting the number of births by using contraceptive methods. However, indigenous and peasant women were perceived as incapable of appropriately doing so. Their alleged ignorance about birth control methods and inability to properly use them legitimized coercive measures to force women to comply with the expected reproductive behavior.

Although one could argue that the program never used racial categories to describe its target population or the goals to be achieved, one of its important effects was the racialization of gender differences. Earlier, I described the most prevalent figuration of poverty in Peru: an indigenous woman surrounded by children. In Peru, race, gender, and class overlap as poor sectors of the population tend to be mainly composed of racialized groups, and indigenous women in particular. "Women are more Indian," Marisol de la Cadena writes, to describe how within a peasant community in Cusco women's subordination is constructed in ethnic terms. I extrapolate this argument to Peruvian society at large to show how racialized gender constructions present indigenous women as bad and irresponsible mothers. It explains why women were disproportionately affected by the sterilization program as this racialized and class configuration had a gendering effect, placing women as its primary target. The assumption was that peasant and indigenous women would not conform to the expected models of responsible parenthood, and therefore, the government must intervene in their reproductive lives. The cure for poverty, then, was made to hinge on women's choice to limit their fertility. If women, out of ignorance, from irrationality, or against their *best interests,* were understood to be refusing that choice, coercion and violence in the name of women's freedom seemed rational, almost imperative. The non-self-reliant, non-self-regulatory subject is the one that was forcibly controlled.

Final Thoughts

In this chapter, I have provided a different interpretation of the role of the RHFPP in the sterilization of women in Peru. It is part of a broader landscape of gendered racism that has subjected peasant and indigenous women in Peru to various forms of violence, including sexual violence in the context of the armed conflict and later, the sterilization program. They have been the targets of these different forms of violence because of their racialized class position within Peruvian society. A careful reading of the program reveals that the seemingly neutral terminology of *choice* and *responsible parenthood*—within a context of racialized and gendered inequalities—created the conditions for the outrageous mass sterilization of women. The RHFPP exposes the control of poor women's reproduction as part of a broader project of realigning the democratic system and bringing into line women's reproductive capacities with an envisioned economic future, a neoliberal horizon of self-management, rational reproduction, and proper parenthood.

I do not argue that all family planning programs that use this rhetoric lead to sterilization practices; instead, I show how the sociopolitical context in which this program was implemented created the conditions for this abuse to take place in the name of economic development, poverty reduction, and democratization. It is also important to note that abusive practices in reproductive healthcare provision in Peru had already been documented in the report *Silencio y Complicidad: Violencia Contra las Mujeres en los Servicios de Salud Publicos en el Peru*. Giulia Tamayo, a feminist lawyer in charge of the investigation, identified the Peruvian government as responsible for violence and other types of abuses committed against poor, indigenous, and peasant women who sought reproductive care. The intensification of reproductive care activities in Peru after the second half of the 1990s gave way to new modalities of coercion and discrimination. The government implemented the RHFPP without modifying healthcare providers' often negative perceptions of women and their subordinated status within their healthcare system (CLADEM and CRLP). The RHFPP exacerbated these conditions and placed women as the targets of coercive sterilizations.

Works Cited

Ballon, Alejandra, editor. *Memorias del caso peruano de esterilizacion forzada*. Biblioteca Nacional del Peru, 2014.

Blondet, Cecilia. *El encanto del dictador: Mujeres y politica en la decada de Fujimori*. IEP, 2002.

———. *Las mujeres y la politica en la decada de Fujimori*. Documento de trabajo No. 109. IEP, 1999.

Boesten, Jelke. "Free Choice or Poverty Alleviation? Population Politics in Peru under Alberto Fujimori." *European Review of Latin American and Caribbean Studies,* no. 82, 2007, pp. 3–20.

———. Prólogo. *Memorias del caso peruano de esterilizacion forzada,* edited by Alejandra Ballon, Biblioteca Nacional del Peru, 2014, pp. 21–26.

———. "Revisiting 'Democracy in the Country and at Home' in Peru." *Democratization,* vol. 17, no. 2, 2010, pp. 307–25.

Brown, Wendy, and Janet Halley, editors. *Left Legalism/Left Critique.* Duke University Press, 2002.

Byker, Tanya, and Italo Guitierrez. *Evaluation of Female Sterilization Campaign in Peru: An Application of Propensity Score Reweighting Methods with Unobserved Participation Status.* Rand Corporation, 2015.

CLADEM. *Nada Personal: Reporte de Derechos Humanos Sobre la Aplicación de la Anticoncepcion Quirurgica Voluntaria en el Peru 1996–1998.* CLADEM, 1999.

CLADEM and CRLP. *Silencio y Complicidad: Violencia Contra las Mujeres en los Servicios Publicos de Salud en el Peru.* CLADEM, 1998.

Coe, Anna Britt. "From Anti-Natalist to Ultra-Conservative: Restricting Reproductive Choice in Peru." *Reproductive Health Matters,* vol. 12, no. 24, 2004, pp. 56–69.

Connelly, Mathew. *Fatal Misconception: The Struggle to Control World Population.* Harvard University Press, 2008.

de la Cadena, Marisol. "Las Mujeres son mas indias: Etnicidad y Genero en una Comunidad del Cusco." *Revista Andina,* no. 1, 1991, pp. 7–29.

Denbow, Jennifer. *Governed through Choice: Autonomy, Technology, and the Politics of Reproduction.* New York University Press, 2015.

Diario la Republica. "Rechazan plan de esterilizacion que otorga premios e incentivos a promotores" July 2, 1996.

Ewig, Christina. "Hijacking Global Feminism: Feminists, the Catholic Church, and Family Planning Debacle in Peru." *Feminist Studies,* vol. 32, no. 3, 2006, pp. 632–59.

Fujimori, Alberto. *Mensaje del Presidente del Peru ingeniero Alberto Fujimori ante el Congreso de la Republica,* 28 July 1995, www4.congreso.gob.pe/museo/mensajes/Mensaje-1990-2.pdf.

———. *Speech Fourth World Conference on Women, Beijing.* 15 Sept. 1995, www.un.org/esa/gopher-data/conf/fwcw/conf/gov/950915131946.txt.

Grewal, Inderpal. *Transnational America: Feminisms, Diasporas, Neoliberalism.* Duke University Press, 2005.

Gutierrez, Elena R. *Fertile Matters: The Politics of Mexican-Origin Women's Reproduction.* The University of Texas Press, 2008.

Guzman, Jose Miguel, et al., editors. *The Fertility Transition in Latin America.* Oxford University Press, 1996.

Hartmann, Betsy. *Reproductive Rights and Wrongs: The Global Politics of Population Control.* South End Press, 1995.

Mahmood, Saba. *The Politics of Piety: The Islamic Revival and the Feminist Subject.* Princeton University Press, 2005.

Menon, Nivedita. *Recovering Subversion: Feminist Politics beyond the Law.* University of Illinois Press, 2006.

MIMDES. *Poblacion y Desarrollo: Compendio de Normas.* Direccion General de Inversion Social, Oficina de Poblacion (Ministerio de la Mujer y Desarrollo Social), 2004.

Ministerio de Salud. *Programa de salud reproductiva y planificación familiar 1996–2000*. Dirección General de Salud de las Personas, 1996.

Molyneux, Maxine. "The 'Neoliberal Turn' and the New Social Policy in Latin America: How Neoliberal, How New?" *Development and Change,* vol. 39, no. 5, 2008, pp. 775–97.

Mooney, Jadwiga E. Pieper. "Re-visiting Histories of Modernization, Progress, and (Unequal) Citizenship Rights: Coerced Sterilization in Peru and in the United States." *History Compass,* vol. 8/9, 2006, pp. 1036–54.

Necochea López, Raul. "Priests and Pills: Catholic Family Planning in Peru, 1967–1976." *Latin American Research Review,* vol. 43, no. 2, 2008, pp. 34–56.

Petchesky, Rosalind. "From Population Control to Reproductive Rights: Feminist Faulty Line." *Reproductive Health Matters,* vol. 3, no. 6, 1995, pp. 151–62.

Rao, Mohan, and Sarah Sexton. "Introduction: Population, Health, and Gender in Neo-Liberal Times." *Markets and Malthus: Population, Gender, and Health in Neo-Liberal Times,* edited by Mohan Rao and Sarah Sexton, Sage, 1995, pp. 1–30.

Rendon, Silvio. "Política de esterilizaciones con información incompleta: Perú, 1995–2000." 2017. Slideshow.

Rose, Nikolas. *Powers of Freedom: Re-Framing Political Thought.* Cambridge University Press, 1999.

Ross, Loretta, and Rickie Solinger. *Reproductive Justice: An Introduction.* University California Press, 2017.

Rousseau, Stephanie. *Women's Citizenship in Peru: The Paradoxes of Neopopulism in Latin America.* Palgrave MacMillan, 2009.

Sharma, Aradhana. *Logics of Empowerment: Development, Gender, and Governance in Neoliberal India.* University of Minnesota Press, 2008.

Singer, Elyse Ona. "From Reproductive Rights to Responsibilization: Fashioning Liberal Subjects in Mexico City's New Public Sector Abortion Program." *Medical Anthropology Quarterly,* 2017, pp. 1–19.

Unger, Corinna. "Family Planning—A Rational Choice? The Influence of Systems Approaches, Behavioralism, and Rational Choice Thinking on Mid-Twentieth-Century Family Planning Programs." *A World of Populations: Transnational Perspectives on Demography in the Twentieth Century,* edited by Corinna Unger and Hartmann Heinrich, Berghahn Books, 2014, pp. 58–82.

CHAPTER 8

It's All Biopolitics

A Feminist Response to the Disability Rights Critique of Prenatal Testing

KAREN WEINGARTEN

OCCASIONALLY A VIRUS dominates a season, and in the summer of 2016, as news reports documented the rise of infected babies born with microcephaly, Zika, a virus previously unknown outside the world of epidemiology, played that role. Zika, which is primarily transmitted through mosquitos, captured the media's attention, and soon the South American governments most impacted by the virus were making impossible recommendations: Remain celibate until the virus has passed! Avoid pregnancy! Postpone marriage! Stay indoors for six months! Anxiety about the Zika virus drew attention to *how* we talk about pregnancy, and particularly how women's reproductive lives are so deeply entwined with fears about disability.

In Florida, where mosquitos with the virus were discovered fairly late in summer, news reports documented women who stayed indoors or covered themselves head-to-toe with mosquito repellent on the rare occasion they ventured outside (Rabin). The World Health Organization issued a recommendation in June 2016 telling people to delay pregnancy if they lived in or had traveled to a country affected by the Zika epidemic (Sun). There was talk that Brazil might liberalize its strict antiabortion laws (Romero), and the pope even suggested that women infected with Zika could use contraceptives to

I'd like to thank my writing group, Sarah Blackwood, Lauren Klein, and Kyla Schuller, for their comments on earlier versions of this essay. The editors of this collection, Modhumita Roy and Mary Thompson, also provided invaluable insight.

avoid pregnancy (Bailey). This wasn't the first time a virus had such a potentially important role in shaping social policy. In the 1960s, the measles epidemic in the US played a similar role in changing abortion law (Garsd). The
measles virus, like Zika, usually causes only minor illnesses in most adults and
even children; however, fetuses infected with the measles are often born blind,
deaf, and developmentally disabled. Leslie Reagan documents how this discovery contributed to the movement that would legalize abortion in the US,
first on a state-by-state basis and ultimately nationally in *Roe v. Wade*. Reagan
argues that it was in part this fear of disability that led Americans to accept
abortion as a viable option that should be legal (2–4). Now almost seventy
years later, Zika is similarly drawing attention to how intersected women's
reproductive lives are with fears about disability.

In the months before Zika made news, abortion and disability were
entwined through an entirely different discourse. In March of 2016, then Indiana governor Mike Pence signed a law forbidding abortion in cases where
a fetus was diagnosed with a disability (Cox). A federal judge subsequently
overturned the law two months later (Kelly). However, as of the writing of
this essay, North Dakota still has a similar law in effect, and other states have
tried—but so far failed—to follow suit (Balmert). In these cases, antiabortion activists and lobbyists are borrowing from the language of disability
rights, and even claiming—in some cases—that their goal is not antiabortion
but pro-disability and pro-child.[1] To support their position, they cite studies showing that in the majority of cases, women choose to have an abortion
when their fetuses test positive for Down syndrome. These laws, we're told,
are meant both to protect those with Down syndrome today and to prevent
future discrimination against people with disabilities.[2] It is an argument that
has circulated among disability studies scholars and disability rights activists
for at least four decades (Fine and Asch 19–20).

The anxiety about Zika's effects on fetuses and the antiabortion laws that
attempt to curtail access to abortion in cases when a fetus has been diagnosed with a potential disability are rooted in the ways in which disability
is marginalized, ostracized, and even feared in American society. What kind

---

1. See, for example, the statement made by Mike Fichter, president and CEO of Indiana
Right to Life. In applauding then Indiana governor Mike Pence for signing a law that bans abortions on the basis of gender, race, or disability, he stated, "By signing the dignity for the unborn
bill, Gov. Pence has again signified his commitment to protecting life. We are pleased that our
state values life no matter an individual's potential disability, gender or race" (Indiana Right to
Life).

2. A study published in 2012 suggested that between 50 percent and 85 percent of women
aborted fetuses with a prenatal diagnosis of Down syndrome. The authors also suggest that this
rate seems to be decreasing. See Natoli et al.

of life will my child with microcephaly live? a woman pregnant with a fetus diagnosed with the condition might wonder. Will my child be able to live independently? Will she have a full life? A happy life? In a country that has increasingly moved away from the welfare state toward a neoliberal state that privileges self-reliance, autonomy, and financial independence, it is no wonder that any condition that limits the ability to achieve these fantastical states of being creates alarm.

Yet the critique of that fear is so clear and so necessary: As disability activists and scholars have argued since before the passage of the Americans with Disabilities Act in 1990, disability is as much a constructed category as race, gender, and sexuality, and that construction is tied to normalizing discourses and built environments that attempt to hierarchize, ostracize, and circumscribe our bodies. As awareness about disability has entered the public sphere, it has joined race and gender, sexual identity and sexuality as an identity marker. This recognition and protection is inarguably a positive step. However, problematically, it's also precisely this logic that antiabortionists have latched onto in their arguments that abortion should not be allowed when a fetus has been diagnosed with a possible disability. The antiabortion argument claims that if disability is a protected category, then aborting a fetus because it has been diagnosed with a genetic mutation or potential impairment is both eugenic and discriminatory against the child to come and all those currently living with that disability. It is this line of thinking, one that is shared by both antiabortion activists looking to overturn abortion laws and some disability scholars and activists, that this essay will question. I want to carefully examine the underlying argument that calls the abortion of a fetus with a potential disability eugenic or morally wrong for the ways in which it places the responsibility of population building on women's shoulders and for the ways in which it intentionally—or unintentionally, in many cases—constructs the fetus as already a child. Finally, I also want to take up Alison Piepmeier's challenge that feminists invested in reproductive justice, or the understanding that access to abortion and contraception is always entwined with other social and political issues, also need to address its intersection with disability rights and recognition ("Inadequacy" 161). This essay is a feminist response to that call.

Is Prenatal Testing Eugenic?

I'm particularly interested in how—and whether—the belief in reproductive justice can coexist with the critique that women's choice to abort fetuses with potential disabilities is a new form of eugenics. This argument has recently become especially relevant as new forms of prenatal testing have emerged that allow women to know earlier than ever whether their fetus has a genetic mutation; perhaps even more significantly, these tests are much less invasive than earlier forms of prenatal testing that carried the risk of miscarriage.[3] I borrow my definition of *eugenics* from Wendy Kline's historical tracing of the word. While Kline overlooks how fears about disability shaped eugenic policy, she does trace the development of eugenics to the drive to control women's reproductive lives. As she explains, "Reproductive decisions would then be based not on individual desire but on racial duty" (2). In other words, eugenicists believed that reproduction should be managed on the level of the population primarily through legally enforced sterilizations and educational programs encouraging *fit* women to reproduce. Through both these means, women were portrayed as "responsible not only for racial progress but also for racial destruction" (3). The future of humanity was placed on their shoulders.

After Hitler's horrific experiments in Europe's concentration camps, the word *eugenics* would perhaps have been archived as a relic of this history, a description of practices that no longer have traction in contemporary scientific circles. However, more recently, *eugenics*—sometimes termed *neo-eugenics*—has become a key word for disability studies scholars and activists disturbed particularly by advances in prenatal genetic testing.[4] In *Extraordinary Bodies*, Garland-Thomson's 1997 groundbreaking book about physical disability in American culture and literature, she briefly notes in her opening chapter that prenatal testing might create a future that attempts to eliminate disability. More recently, in 2012, she expanded this idea in the *Journal of Bioethical Inquiry* to argue for conserving disability as an enriching and essential component of human culture, and to state that any attempt to eliminate it not only engages in new forms of eugenics but also impoverishes the human experience. Garland-Thomson isn't the first or only disability studies scholar to make this claim.[5] Ruth Hubbard and Elijah Wald connect the long history of eugenics in Europe and the US to current forms of genetic testing, and particularly prenatal testing that results in abortions, calling these procedures "the new eugenics" (22–38). In a talk at Columbia University, Alison

---

3. I'm referring to free cell DNA testing, which can locate fetal cells in the mother's blood and test for mutations that cause Down syndrome and other trisomies, as well as some chromosomal duplications and deletions.

4. It is, in fact, a key word in the recently published *Keywords in Disability Studies (Adams et al.)*.

5. Sharon Snyder and David Mitchell also argue for understanding current discrimination against people with disabilities as a new (or continuing) form of eugenics in *Cultural Locations of Disability*. However, their work doesn't address the case of prenatal testing and selective abortion. Whether they make a convincing case for using the concept of eugenics to describe the pathologizing of people living with disabilities is a topic for another time.

Piepmeier argued that choosing to abort a fetus with a potential disability discovered through prenatal testing not only limits human diversity but is a form of eugenics.[6] All four critics share the same underlying suspicion of pre-natal testing, but they also make explicit their commitment to reproductive justice and access to abortion (sometimes this is framed as a pro-choice argu-ment and sometimes it is more explicitly critical of the admittedly problematic framework of choice).

However, there are arguments against viewing prenatal testing as eugenic, and my argument here builds on those. Nikolas Rose, known for his analyses of contemporary scientific technologies and biopower, argues that describ-ing prenatal genetic testing as eugenics is a misnomer. According to Rose, prenatal testing—and other forms of genetic testing labeled as preventative medicine—is "individualized, voluntary, informed, ethical, and preventative" and organized around the "pursuit of health" (55). Even as Rose is aware that these tests work to "eliminate differences coded as defects" (55), he insists that they cannot be called eugenic because, as he explains, eugenics is concerned foremost with state action—that is, with persuading the state to set laws and policies that shape the population in order to form a nation-state with an identity determined by the governing body. Furthermore, he points out that genetic testing (and, it follows, abortion of a fetus with potential disabilities) is never compulsory but voluntary: "Seldom, if ever, are the actions or judg-ments of any of the actors in these practices shaped by the arguments that the nation is somehow weakened geopolitically by the presence of 'diseased stock' within the population" (69). In other words, prenatal testing for him can't be a form of eugenics because its justifying rhetoric and any abortions that might follow are personal, are individualized, and don't echo early-twentieth-century claims about national consequences of reproducing *badly*.

I'm going to turn now to examining one of these personal accounts that evokes the tensions between what it means to value disability and to still choose to abort a fetus diagnosed with a genetic mutation in order to show how limiting it is to simply label such a decision eugenic. Emily Rapp's 2013 memoir *Still Point of the Turning World,* about her son, his disability, and hers, eloquently explores the pain of receiving a fatal diagnosis for her child that could have been discovered prenatally. Rapp's son Ronan was diagnosed with Tay-Sachs at nine months old after Rapp and her husband had some concern about missed milestones, which they thought might be due to his eyesight. Therefore, it was an ophthalmologist who gave them the heartbreaking news

6. This talk was filmed as part of a series, "Evaluation, Value, and Evidence: Parenting, Narrative, and Our Genetic Future," organized by Rachel Adams and presented at Columbia University's Heyman Center for the Humanities.

that Ronan had a genetic mutation that has no treatment and no cure. Rapp
had been tested for the Tay-Sachs gene, even though she was of neither Ashke-
nazi nor French Canadian descent, but because she carried a rare form of the
mutation, the screenings didn't flag her as a carrier. And because her husband,
who was Jewish, did carry the more common Tay-Sachs mutation, their child
had a 25 percent chance of inheriting both copies of his parents' Tay-Sachs
mutations and dying in early childhood, which is what happened.[7]

Rapp recognizes the unusual conditions that led her son to die prematurely,
but her memoir is in part a narrative that wants to undo the distorted logic of
luck—that it was *unlucky* that she had an unusual and undetectable Tay-Sachs
mutation, that it was *unlucky* she had a child with another Tay-Sachs carrier,
and that it was *unlucky* that their first child fell into the 25 percent category of
inheriting both his parents' mutations. Narratives of luck, the memoir so beau-
tifully explains, are about illusions of control and learning about how little control we ultimately have over the bodies into which we're born. This is one of the
subjects she explores in prose that is as poignant as it is philosophic and intellectual. As Rapp describes in her memoir, Tay-Sachs was not her first encounter with disability; Rapp was also born with a physical disability that shaped
much of her childhood and adult life, and she readily admits her own desires
to try to control the narrative around her own body so that her identity was
not defined through her disability. Much of her writing engages with disability
discourses through a feminist understanding of how bodies are constructed,
controlled, and represented. Rapp's astute understanding of disability, and her
ability to write about it so movingly, is in fact one of the reasons disability
studies scholar Rosemarie Garland-Thomson draws on her memoir to argue
that all forms of disability, even Tay-Sachs, are worth conserving. Even more
significantly, Garland-Thomson argues that the prenatal genetic testing used to
eliminate conditions like Tay-Sachs are a form of eugenics in part because they
work to eliminate a core experience that makes us human: suffering. Garland-
Thomson explains that "suffering expands our imagination about what we can
endure," and she cites Rapp's memoir because "her careful balancing of suffering's costs with the benefits of the 'blissful' love Ronan begets" is an example of
what she terms a *counter-eugenic* logic. Garland-Thomson argues that prenatal

7. Disability scholar Marsha Saxton, quoting the epidemiologist Abby Lippman, notes
that Tay-Sachs serves as a problematic model for rationalizing prenatal testing because it's both
rare and extreme in its effects. Saxton and Lippman are right that Tay-Sachs is an example
on the margins, especially in comparison to more common and less disabling conditions like
Down Syndrome. However, extreme examples have the ability to expose the limits of arguments
and their full repercussions, especially in this case for women's reproductive bodies. Which
disabilities, for example, should be deemed acceptable for prenatal testing and who should be
demarcating these lines of acceptability?

genetic testing—and presumably the selective abortions that follow—would strip us of complex emotions, however painful, and thus make the world a less diverse, more eugenic place. While Garland-Thomson acknowledges that the term *eugenics* is a "controversial and complicated" word to use, she nonetheless evokes it to refer to the practice of eliminating "the human traits and ways of being in the world that we probably understand as disability" (340 n.1). Her definition elides the historical underpinning of eugenics as an explicit nation-building project in both the US, where thousands of women of color and women deemed *imbecilic* were forcefully sterilized in the name of national good, *and* in the brutal history of Nazi Germany.

While Rapp's memoir doesn't address abortion, she did write on the topic a year before Ronan's death in the online journal *Slate*. There she argued, in response to conservative politician Rick Santorum's antiabortion critiques of prenatal testing, that if she had known Ronan had Tay-Sachs when she was still pregnant, she would have had an abortion. As she explains, "I love Ronan, and I believe it would have been an act of love to abort him, knowing that his life would be primarily one of intense suffering, knowing that his neurologically devastated brain made true quality of life—relationships, thoughts, pleasant physical experiences—impossible" ("I Would Have"). Rapp, in this argument, is balancing her deep love of Ronan with the suffering he endured, but unlike Garland-Thomson, she decides that some forms of suffering cannot be justified by the love or experience gained. Yet Garland-Thomson, while acknowledging in the same essay that she knows Rapp would have had an abortion had she received Ronan's diagnosis prenatally, dismisses Rapp's understanding of her own experience to present it as an example of "counter-eugenics." While critics regularly undermine writers' assessments of their own work, what's significant about Garland-Thomson's argument is that by discounting Rapp's belief that aborting a fetus with a potentially significant disability would have been a compassionate decision, she implies that had Rapp made that decision, she would have been engaging in eugenics.

What are the implications of calling the abortion of a fetus with Tay-Sachs eugenic? For that matter, what are the implications of accusing *any* woman who chooses to have an abortion because of the results of her prenatal genetic tests of engaging in eugenic practices? Rapp states in unequivocal terms that in an ideal world, her son would never have been born. Yet nowhere does Rapp argue that all fetuses with Tay-Sachs should be aborted or that her son challenges the reproductive decrees of the state. On the other hand, Garland-Thomson's argument about Rapp's experience attempts to situate disability as a form of biodiversity and make larger claims about population building. Rapp's writing about her son, however, never tries to find any good in his suffering. His suffering, she lets us know explicitly, is bad: heartbreaking, painful, unbearable. Rapp is not looking to optimize her experience or her understanding of her son's illness; rather, as she tells us, her memoir is about writing as a means of survival, and it is about learning to let go of illusions of control.

Because the word *eugenics* is strongly associated with the elimination of certain bodies, it has the means to powerfully convey the ways in which people with disabilities have been ostracized, disenfranchised, and physically harmed. At the same time, calling prenatal testing *eugenic* has the potential to shame women who have turned to these tests for whatever reason. It builds on the shame that already surrounds abortion in the US. It doesn't fully take into account the lived pain of Rapp's son Ronan or the emotional suffering of his parents, and it doesn't acknowledge the economic repercussions of having a severely disabled child with a limited life-span. Yet I would be remiss if I did not acknowledge that disability—in all its myriad forms—is also stigmatized in the US. Ultimately, it is this stigma, the valorization of the so-called normal, healthy body, that Garland-Thomson and others working in disability studies are hoping to address. Bodies in the twenty-first century are constantly managed, and that management often works on a molecular level that is obsessed with how our bodies function physiologically, and how they could be improved for economic and political ends. We are told how much we should weigh, what we should eat, how we should sleep, whether our genes predict a propensity for any life-altering diseases; these are among just some of the ways we're managed on an individual level in order to generate population-level statistics—and profit. This management is how I'm defining biopolitics for the purpose of this essay. Increasingly, the state is *also* outsourcing the gathering of this information to private corporations and turning the management of our bodies—and diseases—into profit-propelled industries that provide different levels of information and help depending on ability to pay. The withdrawal of the state and the privatization of healthcare is one of the hallmarks of neoliberalism. And when this management of women's reproductive lives and the lives of people with disabilities enters the political sphere is when we see how neoliberalism works hand-in-hand with biopolitics to deem which lives are worth living given their economic and political values.

The Biopolitics of Reproduction and Disability

The key point for me is that a shared biopolitical logic governs both the marginalization of bodies with disabilities and reproductive bodies. Just as the healthy body—the idealized body free of any inhibiting disability—is held up as the norm, the reproductive body that can produce children without economic, social, physical, and emotional constraints is similarly prized. When the disability studies scholars I've been citing critique prenatal testing and the selective abortions that might follow because they deprive us of diversity or harm humanity, they end up replicating the underlying logic that made eugenics such a popular ideology once upon a time: Women need to reproduce for the benefit of the nation-state and the population at large. In other words, our reproductive choices have repercussions that exceed us. In an argument that seems to have endless variations, women's reproductive lives, we are told, hold a greater responsibility because it is through their bodies and reproductive choices that the future of a more utopic (*diverse*) population rests, just as eugenic scientists and politicians argued at one time when justifying racial hierarchies and passing laws for forced sterilization. Even though almost all the critics I cite resist subscribing to the biopolitical norms that shape how disabled bodies are valued, they ultimately reenforce the norms that dictate how women should behave reproductively when they call selective abortions eugenic, morally wrong, or irresponsible.

Such logic is evident, for example, in Erik Parens and Adrienne Asch's *Prenatal Testing and Disability Rights,* which explores the ethics and morality of prenatal testing and the abortion of fetuses considered to have abnormal genetic makeup. An underlying question in all the essays in their anthology is whether abortion is a form of discrimination against people with disabilities. While they included a handful of essays by critics arguing against the position that such selective abortion discriminates against people living with disabilities, Parens and Asch take the position, asserted not only in their opening chapter and but also in a later chapter by Asch, that "prenatal genetic testing followed by selective abortion is morally problematic, and that it is driven by misinformation" (5). Parens and Asch explain in three points why prenatal testing that leads to abortion devalues disability. As they see it, for one, it presents disability as the problem that needs to be solved rather than the social discrimination against people with disabilities. Two, it views disabled children as a disappointment or a departure from the normative parental experience. And three, aborting a fetus with a disability is often a misinformed choice based on the thinking that a child with disabilities won't contribute to the world and familial experience (13). Important to their argument, and to the many critical arguments that follow in the collection, is the point that selective abortion "signals an intolerance of diversity not merely in the society but in the family" (13).

While Asch, Parens, and many of the writers published in their collection make a compelling case for why selective abortion is a discriminatory practice, they do not address whether the elimination of such practices will actually change societal attitudes toward disability. They do not consider how labeling selective abortion after prenatal testing immoral or discriminatory might have the effect of shaming women who will, despite these arguments and for a myriad of reasons, still choose to have selective abortions. And perhaps most important, they do not address how their arguments hold women's reproductive bodies responsible for *improving* the future population and ending discriminatory attitudes. It is an enormous burden to bear.

Marsha Saxton similarly critiques the position held by some reproductive justice feminists, who in constructing arguments for why abortion should be legal present disability as a justification that can convince even those people who might be skeptical of legal and accessible abortion. Saxton's critique of this argument is fair; using disability to argue *for* the legalization of abortion does make assumptions about which lives we value, what kinds of parents we'll be, and what it means to live with disability. However, once we start listing the qualifications explaining why abortion should be legal (in cases of rape, in cases of incest, in cases of disability, etc.), we have already been swayed by antiabortion rhetoric that asks us to justify the necessity of accessible and safe abortion as a basic human right. Saxton's response to that critique similarly adopts this rhetoric when she argues, "A woman's individual decision, when resulting from social pressure, or colluding with a 'trend,' has repercussions for others in the society" (157). In most cases it is impossible to know whether a woman's decision to abort is a result of social pressure, and in fact it may be—but how many of the decisions we make, big and small, aren't? It's precisely these arguments that rely on the pronatalist, neoliberal rhetoric that holds women responsible for the future of the population, the nation, humanity as a whole. Neoliberalism as an ideology excels at placing blame on the individual while obscuring the social conditions that shape us.

In their 1999 book, *Exploding the Gene Myth,* biologist Ruth Hubbard and Elijah Wald present a feminist critique of prenatal testing when they argue against the position that prospective parents are responsible for bearing children who are "physically and mentally sound," and they rightly point out that this rhetoric "places the burden of implementing these so-called rights of fetuses squarely on the shoulders of individual women" (26). For them, prenatal testing unfairly holds women accountable for ensuring that the future nation, population, society (you name it) will *not* encompass disability because disability is often framed as a burden on the state and a blemish in the family. Their argument is an important one, and it is one that has historical and contemporary significance, for women's reproductive bodies have historically been asked to reproduce for the future of the nation or the people or however the population views itself collectively. Yet this argument also holds when the situation is flipped, when women are held accountable for deciding to abort fetuses after prenatal test results. Eva Feder Kittay believes that "the morality of that choice must be weighed in the conscience of the woman who makes that choice. She alone can know just what her act meant and if it was carried out as a consequence of moral sloth and uncaring, or through a responsible choice" (190). While the rhetoric of choice that Kittay relies on has been critiqued by many working in reproductive justice,[8] in essence, Kittay's argument asks for caution when it comes to assessing why women might choose to abort a fetus diagnosed with a disability or disease. While Kittay suggests that only the woman can judge herself, I am arguing that that judgment is misplaced, especially in these neoliberal conditions of austerity where healthcare is rarely guaranteed, economic security is an unreachable goal, and access to education is increasingly at risk. In an ideal world not governed by these conditions of austerity, having a disabled child would not mean expensive healthcare bills that might not be covered, it wouldn't mean that one parent couldn't work so that medical appointments could be kept, it wouldn't mean that childcare or respite care was impossible to find or unaffordable. Until we live in that world, abortion might be the only pragmatic choice available for many women.

The Biopolitical Child

The National Tay-Sachs and Allied Diseases (NTSAD) website, which is primarily designed to help parents with a child recently diagnosed with one of these conditions, has a page called "Prevent." The word, in the context of this site, however, is somewhat misleading because there is no cure or even treatment for the inevitable effects Tay-Sachs and similar disorders will cause. In the case of infants diagnosed with Tay-Sachs, death in early childhood is the sure conclusion. Prevention, then, according to the website, is genetic screening, ideally before pregnancy, but more realistically for most women, during. In the US, routine prenatal screening generally includes a blood test that first looks to see whether the pregnant woman is a carrier for a number of common recessively linked disorders such as a Tay-Sachs. If she is, the next step is to determine whether the fetus would have received another recessive copy linked to the disorder from the gametes contributed by the sperm. While the NTSAD website doesn't say it explicitly, prevention is abortion in the case of a

---

8. For some of the critiques of "choice," the rhetoric that Kittay draws on, see Rickie Solinger's *Beggars and Choosers: How the Politics of Choice Shapes Adoption, Abortion, and Welfare in the United States*; Rosalind Petchesky's *Abortion and Woman's Choice: The State, Sexuality, and Reproductive Freedom;* and Dorothy Roberts's *Killing the Black Body: Race, Reproduction, and the Meaning of Liberty.*

fetus found to have two recessive copies of genes linked to a disorder described on its site. The NTSAD seems to be acknowledging what in our current political moment is often viewed as a radical claim—the fetus is not a child.

In not conflating the fetus with the child, the NTSAD site aligns with an earlier understanding of gestation and birth, one that has not been widely used since the advent of reproductive technologies that allow for the viewing and hearing of the fetus during pregnancy. Lorna Weir describes the shift as follows: "Where previously the birth threshold only definitively concluded at the end of the birth process with the separation of mother and child, the perinatal threshold distinguished mother from the unborn *during* pregnancy and birth" (3). In other words, even as the fetus is physically dependent on the pregnant woman for its life support, a fact that at one point created the widely believed assumption that a fetus could therefore *not* be viewed as an independent being, the more dominant belief today among those advocating against the legalization of abortion is that the fetus deserves personhood. Even among supporters of abortion, as Weir points out, the question is often not whether a fetus is ever a person but *at what point* in pregnancy the fetus passes the threshold of personhood. However, as Lauren Berlant reminds us, "It was not always the case that everyone knew what a fetus looked like" (86). Berlant argues that the pro-life movement has successfully turned the fetus into a person by borrowing from the language of minority rights to present the fetus as "the unprotected person, the citizen without a country or a future, the fetus unjustly imprisoned in its mother's hostile gulag" (97).[9] Implicit in this logic is the belief that if we can save the fetus, then we can save ourselves.

Rebekah Sheldon, continuing this line of thought, argues that the child, and the fetus that often stands in for the child, figures doubly in our biopolitical moment. First, as a figure of our continuity-without-change, it works as a call for protection and safety from future harm. In other words, the figure of the child should remind us to keep what we now have safe, to conserve our resources, our planet, our humanity, and our selves. But Sheldon also argues that in the fetus/child's connection to reproduction, as a product of reproduction, the fetus/child is a reminder of how new forms of biotechnology are refiguring our lives—as we refigure the lives of these technologies. Pregnancy in the twenty-first century is saturated in technological innovation, even in its uncomplicated manifestation, from the pregnancy test to early DNA screening to the sonogram viewing. To be pregnant in the twenty-first-century US is an

---

9. Berlant traces the development of the victimized fetus to the Reagan years, but in fact the fetus was personified and framed as embattled citizen almost as soon as the antiabortion movement began in the US. See also my argument in *Abortion in the American Imagination: Before Life and Choice, 1880–1940*.

experience in technological change. Sheldon thinks that amidst this change, the fetus/child stands in as our response to the biotechnologies that turn us into the genes that supposedly map our destinies, the mutations that turn us into freaks, the numbers and percentages that categorize risks in our imagined futures. The figure of the fetus/child is safe and comforting.

Sheldon's argument provides another framework for understanding why, for example, in the now widely chronicled—and critiqued—story of Ashley X, Ashley's parents desired to turn her into a child forever. Because Ashley was born severely disabled, her parents decided to give her hormones in order to stunt her growth so that she would never look older than a prepubescent child, and her breast buds and ovaries were surgically removed to prevent the onset of bodily changes that come with puberty. Her parents argued that her smaller size would make it easier to care for her in their home, and the halt of puberty would, according to them, reduce the likelihood of her experiencing sexual abuse by future caretakers. You can hear in this story the narratives that Sheldon describes in her work: the desire to prevent future harm, the imagining of the child's body as whole, the child as response to a body that is increasingly medicalized and technologized. In this narrative, however, disability activists have critiqued the turn to infantilizing the disabled body.

Yet there is also another side to this narrative. Alison Kafer calls prenatal testing, which she rightly notes often ends with the abortion of fetuses diagnosed with potential disabilities, "a clear manifestation of compulsory able-bodiedness and able-mindedness" (29) because bodies—both the bodies of the future children *and* the bodies of the pregnant women—are seen as a threat to the future. Building on Lee Edelman's critique of the Child, she notes, "These sites of reproductive futurity demand a Child that both resembles the parents and exceeds them" (29). She also incisively critiques how the focus on disability in our society is a focus on cure, which is always a politics of deferral; implicit in its logic is that the goal is to have a future with no disability, and this politics, she notes, equates disability with failure. Extending this argument, she posits, "Disabled children are not part of this privileged imaginary except as the abject other" (33). However, there is a slipperiness to this argument: In serving as a critique of the selective abortions that follow prenatal testing, it conflates the Child, and the very real children that Kafer imagines, with fetuses. While there is unquestionable truth in Kafer's construction—the Child is often burdened with all parental aspirations—the Child is ultimately not the fetus, and to conflate the two is to implicitly accept the encroachment of rhetoric developed by antiabortion ideologies.

Or consider the quotation that Parens and Asch include from an earlier essay authored by Asch, in which she asserts, "Do not disparage the lives of existing and future disabled people by trying to screen for and prevent the birth of babies with their characteristics" (13). In Asch's construction, the fetus immediately becomes the already born baby, and the pregnant woman's body—her life—doesn't enter the equation in her formulation. There is a danger for women's reproductive lives when fetuses are equated so quickly with babies, even in the name of justice, precisely because, as in this example, Asch erases the woman's lived experiences, her reasons for seeking an abortion, and the material conditions that shape her life.

Mary Ann Baily, who attended the conversations about prenatal testing and disability documented in Parens and Asch's anthology, describes the dichotomy as follows: "Their [disability studies critics in the seminar] picture is of a line of babies waiting to be born, and a quality control officer coming along and throwing 'people like them' out of line so they never make it to earth" (66), whereas her view is of a "disembodied soul" waiting to take the form of a baby. Baily identifies as a pro-choice Catholic, and she readily admits that this view of a disembodied soul stems from her religious ideology. Yet even as a religious woman, she distinguishes between a fetus that is not yet fully human and the status of full personhood assigned to fetuses by the disability rights critics in the Hastings seminar. In other words, implicit in the disability rights critique of abortion in response to prenatal testing is a depiction of the fetus as already child, already embodied human.

Michael Bérubé notes the hypocrisy in antiabortion discourse promoted by many right-wing politicians who are invested in protecting the rights of fetuses, *all* fetuses, until they are actually born. Those same politicians then actively try to destroy or defund early intervention programs, parental leave, and respite programs, not to mention other social welfare laws meant to ease economic constraints. Referring to his son with Down syndrome, he explains, "The danger for children like Jamie does not lie in women's freedom to choose abortion; nor does it lie in prenatal testing. The danger lies in the creation of a society that combines eugenics with enforced fiscal austerity. In such a society, it is quite conceivable that parents who 'choose' to bear disabled children will be seen as selfish and deluded" (52). Yet, on the other hand, will those women who *choose* not to bear disabled children because neoliberalism has dismantled the social safety net by defunding Medicaid, limiting respite services, and cutting social services in schools also be seen as selfish? Bérubé continues to point out how this logic relies on free-market, neoliberal beliefs that distinguish between *productive* and *non-productive* citizens, and that the danger is that the value we place on human life will come to be based on its economic potential. This line of thinking is chilling indeed, and frighteningly, not far from our current reality. However, what is also emerging in our new reality is a system where individuals are seen as responsible for their own healthcare and their own social services, often through private fundraisers or individual wealth. And those who don't have access to such resources? Neoliberal ideology is by design tight-lipped when it comes to answering that question.

There is an important economic critique here based on how the development of capitalism in the West has shifted the role of the child from one worker or contributor in the family to a reflection of a family's wealth, intelligence, and status. But once again, as worrisome as that trend is in the kinds of pressures it imposes on our children, a rejection of prenatal testing is not likely to undo or undermine this shift. It is rooted in an economic and political philosophy with deep stakes in our current culture; it is rooted in the increasing biopoliticization of human life that shapes how we value *both* disability and women's reproductive bodies. As Sheldon tells her readers in a different context: "Causality is richer and stranger than rescue narratives imagine" (83). In other words, *conserving* deafness or Down syndrome or spina bifida is not going to necessarily happen through the elimination of prenatal testing for the presence of genes that cause these conditions. It is not, to use Sheldon's language, the child to come who will save us from this future harm. The truth is, as Kafer recognizes, children's bodies are messy and imperfect too. In many ways, they are even messier and more imperfect in their potentialities than the adult bodies we inhabit. And children are not necessarily our future, as any parent with a seriously ill child could tell you. Parenting is usually at its most disastrous when we project our desires for the future onto our children, even if the imagined future hopes for a world where our disabilities do not impact how we are viewed or what access we have.

My arguments here intend to demonstrate how even the disability studies critique of prenatal testing, one that often positions itself as attuned to the importance of legal and accessible abortion, reinscribes the same reproductive norms for women and assumes personhood for the fetus in much the same way that pronatalists and antiabortionists have over the past century. And while I agree with Rayna Rapp, Alison Piepmeier, and others who argue for the necessity of genetic counseling that is more nuanced, politically attuned, and context-dependent, I also unequivocally believe in access to selective abortion for whatever reason.[10] A world that limits or eliminates prenatal testing or selective abortion in order to protect disability is a world that has surrendered to the biopolitical management of bodies for yet another series of norms, standards, and hierarchies.

---

10. See Rayna Rapp's study on the uses of amniocentesis and the counseling received afterward, where she argues for the importance of genetic counseling that understands the context in which "risk" is communicated. Rapp stresses how important it is for counselors to be able to make room both for cultural variation and for providing a context for any particular diagnosis.

Works Cited

Adams, Rachel et al., editors. *Keywords in Disability Studies.* New York University Press, 2015.

Bailey, Sarah Pulliam, and Michelle Boorstein. "Pope Francis Suggests Contraception Could Be Permissible in Zika Fight." *Washington Post,* 18 Feb. 2016., www.washingtonpost.com/news/acts-of-faith/wp/2016/02/17/mexico-confirms-zika-virus-cases-in-pregnant-women-as-pope-francis-exits-the-country/?utm_term=.3908709c3532.

Baily, Mary Ann. "Why I Had Amniocentesis." *Prenatal Testing and Disability Rights,* edited by Erik Parens and Adrienne Asch, Georgetown University Press, 2000, pp. 64–71.

Balmert, Jessie. "Ohio Passes Bill to Ban Abortion After Down Syndrome Diagnosis." *Cincinnati.com,* 1 Nov. 2017, www.cincinnati.com/story/news/politics/2017/11/01/ohio-house-vote-bill-ban-abortion-after-down-syndrome-diagnosis/818876001/.

Berlant, Lauren. *The Queen of America Goes to Washington City: Essays on Sex and Citizenship.* Duke University Press, 1997.

Bérubé, Michael. *Life as We Know It: A Father, a Family, and an Exceptional Child.* Vintage, 1996.

Cox, Casey. Indiana House Bill 1337. 2016 Session. iga.in.gov/legislative/2016/bills/house/1337#digest-heading.

Fine, Michelle, and Adrienne Asch. "The Question of Disability: No Easy Answers for the Woman's Movement." *Reproductive Rights Newsletter,* vol. 4, no. 3, 1982, pp. 19–20.

Garland-Thomson, Rosemarie. *Extraordinary Bodies: Figuring Physical Disability in American Culture and Literature.* Columbia University Press, 1996.

——. "The Case for Conserving Disability." *Journal of Bioethical Inquiry,* vol. 9 no. 3, 2012, pp. 339–55.

Garsd, Jasmine. "Zika Virus Isn't the First Disease to Spark a Debate about Abortion." *National Public Radio,* 31 Jan. 2016, www.npr.org/sections/goatsandsoda/2016/01/31/464750384/zika-virus-isnt-the-first-disease-to-spark-a-debate-about-abortion.

Hubbard, Ruth, and Elijah Wald. *Exploding the Gene Myth: How Genetic Information Is Produced and Manipulated by Scientists, Physicians, Employers, Insurance Companies, Educators, and Law Enforcers.* Beacon Press, 1999.

Indiana Right to Life. "Pence Commended for Signing Dignity for the Unborn Bill." 24 Mar. 2016, www.irtl.org/2016/03/pence-commended-for-signing-dignity-for-the-unborn-bill/.

Kafer, Alison. *Feminist, Queer, Crip.* Indiana University Press, 2013.

Kelly, Niki. "Judge Strikes Down Indiana Abortion Law." *The Journal Gazette* (Indiana), 30 June 2016, www.journalgazette.net/news/local/indiana/Judge-strikes-down-Indiana-abortion-law-13867401.

Kittay, Eva Feder (with Leo Kittay). "Concerning Expressivity and Ethics of Selective Abortion for Disability: Conversations with My Son." *Prenatal Testing and Disability Rights,* edited by Erik Parens and Adrienne Asch, Georgetown University Press, 2000, pp. 165–95.

Kline, Wendy. *Building a Better Race: Gender, Sexuality, and Eugenics from the Turn of the Century to the Baby Boom.* University of California Press, 2001.

Natoli, Jaime L., et al. "Prenatal Diagnosis of Down Syndrome: A Systematic Review of Termination Rates (1995–2011)." *Prenatal Diagnosis,* vol. 32, no. 2, Feb. 2012, pp. 142–53.

Parens, Erik, and Adrienne Asch. "The Disability Rights Critique of Prenatal Genetic Testing: Reflections and Recommendation." *Prenatal Testing and Disability Rights,* edited by Erik Parens and Adrienne Asch, Georgetown University Press, 2000, pp. 3–43.

Petchesky, Rosalind. *Abortion and Woman's Choice: The State Sexuality, and Reproductive Freedom.* Northeastern University Press, 1990.

Piepmeier, Alison. "Evaluation, Value, and Evidence: Parenting, Narrative, and Our Genetic Future." www.youtube.com/watch?v=fLDOBI7_JKQ.

———. "The Inadequacy of 'Choice': Disability and What's Wrong with Feminist Framings of Reproduction." *Feminist Studies,* vol. 39, no. 1, 2013, pp. 159–86.

Rabin, Roni Caryn. "In Florida, Pregnant Women Cover Up and Stay Inside Amid Zika Fears." *New York Times,* 19 Aug. 2016, www.nytimes.com/2016/08/19/well/in-florida-pregnant-women-cover-up-and-stay-inside-amid-zika-fears.html.

Rapp, Emily. "I Would Have Saved My Son from His Suffering." *Slate,* 27 Feb. 2012, www.slate.com/articles/double_x/doublex/2012/02/rick_santorum_and_prenatal_testing_i_would_have_saved_my_son_from_his_suffering_.html.

———. *Still Point of the Turning World.* Vintage, 2013.

Rapp, Rayna. *Testing the Women, Testing the Fetus: The Social Impact of Amniocentesis in America.* Routledge, 2000.

Reagan, Leslie. *Dangerous Pregnancies: Mothers, Disabilities, and Abortion in Modern America.* University of California Press, 2010.

Roberts, Dorothy. *Killing the Black Body: Race, Reproduction, and the Meaning of Liberty.* Vintage, 1998.

Romero, Simon. "Surge of Zika Virus Has Brazilians Re-examining Strict Abortion Laws." *New York Times,* 3 Feb. 2016, www.nytimes.com/2016/02/04/world/americas/zika-virus-brazil-abortion-laws.html.

Rose, Nikolas. *The Politics of Life Itself: Biopower, Medicine, and Subjectivity.* Princeton University Press, 2006.

Saxton, Marsha. "Why Members of the Disability Community Oppose Prenatal Diagnosis and Selective Abortion." *Prenatal Testing and Disability Rights,* edited by Erik Parens and Adrienne Asch, Georgetown University Press, 2000, pp. 147–64.

Sheldon, Rebekah. *The Child to Come: Life after the Human Catastrophe.* University of Minnesota Press, 2016.

Snyder, Sharon, and Mitchell, David. *Cultural Locations of Disability.* University of Chicago Press, 2006.

Solinger, Rickie. *Beggars and Choosers: How the Politics of Choice Shapes Adoption, Abortion, and Welfare in the United States.* Hill and Wang, 2002.

Sun, Lena H. "WHO: People in Zika-Affected Regions Should Consider Delaying Pregnancy." *Washington Post,* 9 June 2016, www.washingtonpost.com/news/to-your-health/wp/2016/06/09/who-women-in-zika-affected-regions-should-consider-delaying-pregnancy/?utm_term=.646c485c6800.

Weingarten, Karen. *Abortion in the American Imagination: Before Life and Choice, 1880–1940.* Rutgers University Press, 2014.

Weir, Lorna. *Pregnancy, Risk and Biopolitics: On the Threshold of the Living Subject.* Routledge, 2006.

CHAPTER 9

Commodification Anxiety and the Making of American Families in a State-Contracted Adoption and Foster Care Program

MELISSA HARDESTY

CLAUDIA'S CUBICLE was the first in the adoption team aisle at Kids First, a state-contracted child welfare agency in a Midwestern city in the United States. Most agency staff worked in a large room punctuated by a maze of desks and partitions. The aesthetic screamed call center rather than social service agency, but as I learned over fifteen months of ethnographic observations aimed at understanding how caseworkers assess prospective adoptive parents applying for domestic infant or foster care adoption, the setup was good for building community among workers. Claudia kept a Froot Loops–themed bowl at her desk. During hectic periods, like this cloudy February afternoon in 2012, when work prevented her from walking across the street to Popeye's or McDonald's, she used the bowl to cook ramen noodles. After holding countless batches of soup, the white plastic background behind Toucan Sam had taken on the color and sheen of a chicken bouillon cube. As Claudia trudged through paperwork, her managers, Ivy and Val, dropped a new case file on her desk. Meanwhile, Beth, an intern, was enlisted to transport the child in question, an infant, to an emergency foster care placement. Soon, the entire adoption aisle was abuzz with baby excitement. Infants were not unheard of in foster care adoption, a state-mediated form of family-making where abused or neglected children whose rights have been terminated are placed in permanent homes, but this was a healthy infant—a rare, sought-after demographic for would-be adoptive parents. "The birth mom was selling the baby outside a liquor store," Claudia told her lingering coworkers.

Child welfare workers were rarely shocked by the circumstances that prompted entanglements between parents and the child welfare system, but this case was unusual. The addicted parent can be sent to drug or alcohol rehab, the abusive or neglectful parent to parent training classes. The baby-selling parent was an altogether different character. Workers were speculating about her motivations when Val walked through the aisle with a grocery bag full of onesies. "Is it true she was trying to sell her?" Beth asked. "Yep," Val quipped, "outside a liquor store to the highest bidder. She's in jail now."

Workers' emotions ranged from befuddlement to anger. There were no bidders, or the police arrived before a baby sale could take place. The details of the liquor store incident remained murky because the usual confounders of child abuse and neglect cases—parent mental illness and missing or unreliable witnesses—made it difficult to pin down what actually happened. Neverthe-less, in the context of child adoption, where tens of thousands of dollars may be exchanged in the process of transferring parental rights from one person to another, this incident raises the question of how the act of offering a child for sale can lead a birth mother to be criminalized, while exchanges of money in adoption and foster care are regular operating procedure.

In the US and abroad, the flow of children into and out of adoption and foster care is undergirded by socioeconomic inequality. Economic hardship is among the most common reasons women place children for adoption in the US (Oaks ch. 3), and poverty is entwined with the forms of child abuse and neglect that prompt the state to take custody of children and sometimes ter-minate parental rights, making them available for foster care adoption (Rob-erts). At the same time, private and agency-based domestic infant adoption and international adoption are costly, and therefore off limits, to poor appli-cants. Foster care adoption is frequently subsidized (sometimes entirely) by the state as a means to incentivize adoption of children whose histories of trauma and older age render them less desirable to would-be adoptive parents. Subsidies, in turn, attenuate economic barriers for potential adoptive parents. In a Western culture that, according to Igor Kopytoff, likes to maintain a "cat-egorical and moral distinction between people and things," market valuations of family relationships create commodification anxiety—the fear that intimate and sentimental relationships will be tainted or corrupted by the presence of money (271).

The moral valence of money in regulating social relationships has been the subject of sociological inquiry for the past few decades. In *Pricing the*

Priceless Child: The Changing Social Value of Children, Viviana Zelizer detailed the historical process at the turn of the twentieth century whereby American children transitioned from laborers who were expected to contribute wages to their families to "economically useless but emotionally priceless" members of the family (57). Paradoxically, the economically useless child came with a much higher price tag than her wage-earning counterpart (201). Whereas parents had to pay others to take custody of unwanted infants and toddlers in the mid- to late 1800s (195), adoptive parents hoping to gain custody of an infant today can expect to pay tens of thousands of dollars to an attorney or adoption agency. Commercial attributes of adoption violate the moral distinction between people and things identified by Kopytoff, and what Zelizer refers to in "The Purchase of Intimacy" as a Hostile Worlds perspective on the intersection of money and intimate ties (818). The Hostile Worlds perspective contends that social relationships and economic exchange are so different that any intersection of the two can only lead to "moral contamination and degradation" (818).

Despite overwhelming evidence demonstrating links between sentiment and money in all families, the cultural fiction that these two moral registers can and should be separate persists. At the same time, the monetary exchanges that regularly occur in biological, nuclear families, in addition to indirect government-family transfers written into the tax code and private health insurance subsidies in America, are far less obvious than the financial exchanges that transpire when families are created and regulated through public and government-contracted social service agencies. Monetary exchanges in adoption and foster care are far more visible and appear as a breach of deep-seated cultural values. I argue that child welfare workers manage the dicey intersection between money and families by performing *ethical labor*—that is, they carefully manage the way they talk about and define money and teach would-be adoptive parents to think about money in similar ways. These linguistic management strategies normalize adoptive families by downplaying the market and making recourse to an understanding of healthy families as private, self-sufficient, biological, and child-centered. Within *normal* families, money supposedly has nothing to do with whether or not people become parents and how they parent. In reality, the availability of children in domestic infant and foster care adoption is linked to birth parents' inabilities to be self-sufficient. Child welfare workers' attempts to normalize families by downplaying market forces in adoption inevitably lead them to patch over forms of social inequality already entrenched in the adoption market.

The concept of an adoption market found its way into academic literature in 1978 when Elisabeth Landes and Richard Posner published "The Economics of the Baby Shortage." The article was a response to the shortage of adoptable (white, healthy) infants, a problem the authors attributed to decreased stigma around unwed childbearing and increased availability of birth control and abortion. They proposed giving pregnant women financial incentives to forgo abortion in cases of unwanted pregnancy and instead carry fetuses to term so that they could be adopted by waiting families. Academic and popular audiences, who tended to view market logics as incompatible with family-making, were offended by what they dubbed "the baby-selling article." The controversy was so heated and long-standing that Posner was still responding to the baby-selling accusation nine years after the article's publication (59). In the decades since, increased demands for any healthy infant—not just white infants—has racialized the anxiety around commodifying children. Michele Bratcher Goodwin noted that market comparisons in adoption are offensive, in part, because of their alleged similarity to the auction block of slavery (2). Similarly, the Adoption and Safe Families Act of 1997 (ASFA) and the Multi-Ethnic Placement Act of 1994 (MEPA)—pieces of federal legislation aimed at regulating adoption and foster care—and the Personal Responsibility and Work Opportunity Reconciliation Act of 1996 (PRWORA, or welfare reform), which limited federal economic support for poor families, have been criticized for hastening the removal of poor, disproportionately African American children from the custody of their mothers and making it easier for white and middle-class families to attain custody (Briggs ch. 3). Poverty and child welfare involvement disproportionately affect African American families, and support for welfare reform was garnered, in part, by appealing to the stereotype of the welfare queen, commonly portrayed as an African American woman who gives birth to multiple children so that she can live on welfare checks. ASFA asks states to terminate parental rights on children who have been in state foster care for fifteen out of the last twenty-two months (if parents have not made reasonable progress toward achieving treatment goals) and incentivizes adoption. MEPA prohibits agencies from making decisions about foster care and adoptive placements on the basis of race, thus making it easier for white families to adopt children of color. ASFA was passed just one year after PRWORA and three years after MEPA, leading opponents of welfare and adoption reform to conclude that these policies were motivated by racism, or that they would have racist effects.

PRWORA defined parental poverty as an individual problem of dependency that could be solved through procuring waged work in the market economy. Widely considered a punitive, neoliberal reform because it offered free market solutions to social problems, PRWORA made the economics of parenting more precarious, while ASFA expedited adoption of children already in state care. In sum, legislative reforms of the mid-1990s simultaneously decreased state financial support for poor families—a move that was likely to increase the number of children placed in foster care due to neglect—while pushing the state to terminate parental rights on foster children more quickly, and to place these legally free children in adoptive homes. Such policies hasten the flow of children from poor to relatively wealthier families.

Scholars have also linked international adoption to neoliberal reforms, particularly cuts to state welfare spending. Wealth inequality in the former USSR led some parents to relinquish custody of their children, while the availability of such children, according to Sadowski-Smith, spawned an uptick in predatory and unethical adoption practices (3–5). According to Laura Briggs, the neoliberal structural adjustments demanded by the International Monetary Fund and World Bank in exchange for loan money to bail out fledgling national economies in Latin America had a similarly pernicious impact on adoption practices. Structural adjustments—a catchall term describing policies such as privatization of state services, cuts to welfare subsidy spending, and liberalization of trade—created political and economic conditions rife for adoption profiteering, and allegedly, child stealing (chs. 4–6). The neoliberal policy context makes it increasingly difficult for poor and working-class parents to manage the demands of child-rearing and work, all the while neoliberal understandings of family foreground freedom and choice, as if one's choices about when and whether to parent can be divested from a global economy that has hastened economic inequality.

Public and Private Adoption at Kids First

My interest in learning about adoption sensitized me to some of the everyday sights that often seemed unremarkable in the city where this study was conducted—bulletins for Family Tree, a local adoption agency, posted in the window of a Planned Parenthood Clinic, and subway ads and billboards inviting women to contact various adoption agencies. "Pregnant? Scared? We can help," an ad proclaimed in bold script written across the bulbous abdomen of a despondent-looking woman. In contrast, the city adoption team at Kids First did little to recruit birth mothers interested in making an adoption plan. Adoption team manager Val told me that it was rare for pregnant women to approach the city program for adoption services. "I'm not sure why that is," she said, though I had already begun to suspect that it was because the program did not market itself to them. Given a large supply of foster care children whose rights were likely to be terminated, they did not need to. Kids First was situated in a blighted community, in a city punctuated by pockets of concentrated poverty and its attendant social problems, so they focused on providing social services through the public child welfare system. In the post-ASFA environment, foster care adoption services fulfilled the federal government's demand to shorten the time children spent in foster care and to increase adoption. While Kids First had been doing domestic infant adoptions for over a century, the city's foster care–centered adoption program was started as a direct response to ASFA's demands.

Questions of social inequality are foregrounded in foster care adoption work, in part because child welfare workers' recommendations about who ought to have custody of children—birth parents or foster parents—are inextricably tied to the social problems that accompany concentrated poverty. At the same time, the co-occurrence of domestic and international fee-for-service adoption and state-subsidized foster care adoption in Kids First's adoption program, an unusual programmatic arrangement, made this a fruitful site for understanding how adoption markets affect family-making in a neoliberal era.

Doing the Math: Adoption and Foster Care in the US

According to *Adoptive Families* magazine, the average cost of adopting a child in 2015–2016 was more than $35,000, or nearly 60 percent of the median family income in US dollars, making adoption a substantial financial burden on many prospective parents and completely inaccessible to others ("Adoption Cost"). The Adoption Tax Credit substantially reduces the burden of adoption expenses, as adoptive parents can claim up to $13,810 (in 2018) in allowable expenses for the year in which an adoption was completed (IRS). However, the credit does not diminish the up-front costs of pursuing adoption. Consider the creative strategies used by some middle- and working-class people to cobble together the tens of thousands of dollars often required to adopt. Readers of *Adoptive Families* reportedly pulled from their 401(k) accounts, took advances on anticipated inheritances, and threw adoption carnivals through their churches. One woman charged adoption expenses on a no-interest credit card and later referred to her child as "my Visa baby." Many use the fundraising platform GoFundMe to crowdsource adoption expenses ("Affording Adoption").

Notably, workers at Kids First did not consciously consider domestic adoption fees or foster care adoption subsidies an important part of the everyday work of assessing prospective parents and managing foster care and pre-adoptive relationships; yet I observed numerous exchanges in which workers spoke bluntly and incisively about how money impacts applicants' access to different modes of adoptive family-making.

On an unseasonably hot day in March, the adoption team was suffering in cramped cubicles without air conditioning when Janet called across the aisle to ask Elise how her initial paperwork meeting with a new client went. "She was a *mess*," Elise responded, with the tender, empathic tone of voice usually reserved for babies and pets. "She was so emotional. She brought her mom with her, and they held hands the entire time. That's how nervous she was. She makes thirty thousand dollars a year, and she wants to adopt an infant with no legal risk." The term *legal risk* was commonly used by Kids First's adoption workers to characterize concurrent planning foster care adoption, which places a foster child with *pre-adoptive parents* before the rights of the birth parent(s) are terminated, but this termination is not a given. The process of actually adopting a child through this system is lengthy, emotional, and uncertain. Elise did not think her new client could handle it. Domestic infant adoption was the best option for her, but she couldn't afford it.

Lizzy, who had recently left her job at a traditional adoption agency, interjected, "I always hated it when single moms would call [her prior agency], even those that had incomes of a hundred and fifty thousand dollars a year." Other workers rolled their desk chairs toward the center aisle to listen. "Most international countries won't let single [US] women adopt, and it's difficult with domestic infant[s], too," she explained. "A lot of single women don't get picked out of the album by birth moms. They're more likely to pick a traditional family." "It's very difficult for single women," Elise nodded in agreement, but quickly changed the focus back to money, "especially if they have low income. There aren't really any options out there. You're *buying* a baby. That's just how it is." Murmurs of agreement trickled through the aisle before chairs were slowly wheeled back in front of computer screens and piles of paperwork. While workers ordinarily tried to downplay the money required to access domestic infant and international adoption, this example highlights the stark reality that applicants have to buy the *opportunity* to adopt a baby, if not the baby itself.

Adoptions from foster care are fully subsidized by the government, and prospective parents do not incur the enormous fees common to domestic and international infant adoption. Theoretically, this means that the pool of suitable adoptive parents is more socioeconomically diverse. Given the links between race and income, this also meant that Kids First's applicants for foster care adoption were also more racially and ethnically diverse than the typical adoptive parent. "Some of our parents are a little rough around the edges," Sue once told me. "I have gone into some areas. I mean, remember when we went to the one home study, I think it was in—I don't know if it was in [a lower-income, predominantly African American neighborhood] or—." "Was it Violet?" I asked, referring to a middle-aged, working-class African American woman. "Yeah, yeah," she continued. "The area was not that great. It's not the white picket fence you picture an adoptive parent having. So, some of the— but I don't think that means they wouldn't be good parents, and I don't think it means the child would be unsafe."

Several months later, when Sue was about to leave Kids First for a job in domestic infant adoption, she prepared to contend with a different kind of parent. "Even at my interview, she [the new manager] made it sound like there's some pretty entitled people, and I'm picturing, you know, white, middle class, we want our baby now—I don't feel like that's what our clientele here is completely."

Implicit in Sue's description of the clientele at Kids First versus "regular" adoption agencies is a dynamic where wealthy, white parents demand imme- diate access to available babies, as working-class prospective adoptive parents bump up against Norman Rockwell images of the ideal American family, as they try to prove that they can be good parents and keep children safe in dangerous neighborhoods. Workers at Kids First, hoping to temper the anxi- ety that low-income applicants experienced when submitting their financial information, often assured clients, "We're not looking for the richest parents. We just want to make sure that taking in another child is not going to make you or break you." Yet the make-or-break metric suggests that workers are also on the lookout for applicants who want to improve their financial lot by taking in a child who comes with a subsidy from the state. Taken together, these examples show how evaluations of parents cohere around two opposite but equally pernicious stereotypes—the *purchasing parent* who thinks that money entitles them to a child and the *profiteering parent*[1] who could be *made* or financially benefit from a child placement. These composite bad parents delimit the boundaries of normal parenting and show how the moral calculus of the kinship/cash nexus determines who gets access to children and who does not.

Elise's case of the well-meaning but under-resourced single woman stood out as a rare instance at Kids First in which the inability of an applicant to *pay* for domestic adoption services, and her presumed inability to withstand emotionally the *legal risk* of foster care adoption, limited her access to a child. Her case casts light on the market dynamics lurking beneath the surface of

---

1. I discuss the implications of the profiteering foster parent in a recently published arti- cle, "It's Not a Job! Foster Care Board Payments and the Logic of the Profiteering Parent."

a social service system intent on minimizing their impact. State-subsidized adoption lessens economic discrimination against prospective parents, but this leveling effect is incidental to the actual purpose of foster care subsidies; they exist because foster kids are considered riskier sentimental investments (i.e., less valuable).

The woman described by Elise and the workers' discussion of her underscore the ambivalence with which many adoption workers fulfill their role as agents of surveillance. Declining a prospective parent based upon factors such as a failed background check, "unrealistic expectations" of the adoption process, or even "getting a bad feeling" about somebody seemed to be less ethically troublesome to workers at Kids First than having to turn somebody away because of money. Elise had the power to refuse her client for government-funded foster care adoption, but she was powerless to overlook that client's inability to pay the service fees for domestic adoption. "You're buying a baby" in this context bluntly marks economic discrimination as something endemic to the adoption system.

Creating and Disciplining the Purchasing Parent

The payment required from prospective parents in domestic or international adoption elicits commodification anxiety—fear of baby selling—at the cultural level, and according to workers, can elicit feelings of entitlement at the individual level. Under market logic, payments and fees demand a product or service in return. At first glance, regular adoption looks a lot like a simple purchase; a sum of money is paid to the agency in exchange for an adoptive child. However, agencies, workers, and birth parents have discretion when it comes to determining who is and is not a suitable parent, and this means that a client could spend a lot of money and still not get a placement. Agencies need people who are willing and able to pay money to adopt a child, but they also face a cultural imperative to downplay market forces and a practical impetus to regulate the expectations of clients. Thus, workers employ strategies to discipline the *purchasing parents* the adoption market has itself created.

Regular adoption fee schedules are an important tool in the disciplinary apparatus. They are the most obvious indicators of market dynamics in adoption, and they help educate the public and potential clients about the distinctions between ethical child adoption and baby markets. A typical adoption fee schedule has separate fees for application, home study, programming and training, and child placement. The itemization of fees serves the practical purpose of anticipating and making payments over time, which allows the agency or the client to opt out of the process midway. Categories also accomplish the moral work of separating money from babies.

In particular, attaching fees to *services* and *expenses* is a common strategy employed by workers to discursively situate agencies outside baby markets and to constitute clients as consumers of *services for the child* who have no entitlement to an actual child placement. Yet most of the services provided by adoption agencies—helping pregnant women manage their healthcare and choose adoptive parents, assessing prospective adoptive parents and helping them create family profiles—are geared toward birth parents and adoptive parents, respectively. At information and orientation sessions held for prospective parents, Kids First's workers cautioned attendees, "Our job is not to find the perfect child for you. We're trying to find the best home for the child."

The administrator at another local agency, Family Tree, espoused a similar warning: "Children are not an *entitlement*. Our job is to safeguard children against harm, not to find you children or please birth parents." The implicit argument that unmediated transfers of parental rights are a danger to children was not questioned by participants in this session or addressed by the administrator. It is remarkable that birth parents are automatically assumed to be fit and that a birth parent could forgo agency-mediated adoption altogether and transfer parental rights via an attorney. Indeed, these dynamics suggest that adoption agencies, particularly those that specialize in domestic infant and international adoption, act more like a professional matchmaking service for families than as a *child* welfare service.

The idea that an agency can collect adoption fees from an applicant, then use their discretion to deny adoption based upon loosely regulated criteria, is rendered more rhetorically sound when it is done under the auspices of promoting a child's best interests. Agencies have other compelling reasons for setting boundaries on the expectations of *purchasing parents* and highlighting the cost of the vetting process. Adoption staff know all too well that birth mothers and fathers can decide against surrendering a child, thus disrupting the exchange and causing prospective adoptive parents to incur costs without receiving a child in return. In fact, the money and labor required to transfer parental rights from biological parents to adoptive parents reveal the hegemony of biological parenthood, which is figured as a legal and natural right. In contrast to the Family Tree administrator's assertion, children *are* an entitlement—for biological parents. This has both positive and negative implications for birth and adoptive parents.

As Barbara Katz Rothman pointed out, property ownership models have been useful for securing reproductive freedom for women in liberal society and for protecting against state intrusion in the family, but they do not render the female body or maternal labors valuable under capitalism and patriarchy; hence the high cost of adoptable children and low income-generating potential of surrogacy for birth mothers (21–25). Additionally, one can have legal rights over one's body and children but lack the economic and cultural resources to fully exercise these rights. The limitations of the property rights model can be seen in UNICEF's attempt to decrease or limit international adoption by arguing that children have a right to grow up with their birth parents. This so-called right is unenforceable because some birth parents are unwilling or unable to parent. UNICEF's argument may be an attempt to protect poor parents suffering in the wake of neoliberal structural adjustments and/or wars from having their children rescued by people from more economically and politically powerful countries, but it does not name or address the neoliberal policies driving the phenomenon.

Neoliberal child welfare policies in the US have similarly undercut the effectiveness of property ownership models in protecting some families, particularly African American families, from state intrusion. Dorothy Roberts takes issue with the package of child welfare laws passed under the Clinton administration—ASFA, MEPA, and PRWORA—for precisely this reason. PRWORA values labor force participation over parental labor and makes it more difficult for poor women to successfully parent their children. When women cannot parent adequately, the state may step in to remove their children. ASFA makes it more difficult for poor parents to regain custody of children who have been removed from the home by speeding up child welfare timelines. MEPA, in turn, ignores the racial disproportionality of the child welfare system and makes it easier for white families to adopt black children. Hence Roberts argues that these policies represent a pernicious mix of free market ideology and de facto racism rooted in the devaluation of black children and their parents (76). Ownership rights to one's children have no teeth when structural inequality and countervailing policies enable government intrusion in the family under the banner of child protection.

While attending prospective adoptive parent information sessions, I found that many of the educational documents that agencies used to introduce applicants to the adoption world tacitly defined the criteria for assessing parents. These criteria strongly implied that parenting is separable from economics. One notable example included a self-assessment checklist from an adoption magazine, according to which a charitable impulse—wanting to adopt because adoptive children are often disadvantaged—was specifically flagged as an inappropriate motivation for family-making through adoption; only a deeply felt desire to parent was considered appropriate. This intrinsically motivated parental impulse closely aligns with the neoliberal ethic of self-actualization through carefully weighed individual choices. It also sidesteps any consideration of the market dynamics that delimit choices—especially in the wake of global capitalism—about who gets to parent and how. Through written and verbal discourse, adoption agencies thus instill in prospective parents a narrowly defined orientation to the adoption transaction and frame as a matter of fact and objectivity a morally loaded process.

Self-Sufficient, Private, and Normal Families

If prospective adoptive parents are subject to surveillance and discipline though adoption's discourse about money, this very language is also used to defend adoption as a normal means of family-making. Oftentimes, in order to normalize adoptive parents and distance them from the image of making a purchase, agencies rhetorically draw analogies between payments made in the adoption process and medical fees incurred by biological parents. For example, in an article from *Adoptive Families* magazine, Carney asserts, "I'm often struck that the same folks who inquire how much our adoption cost would never dream of asking proud parents who've just given birth in a hospital how much they (or their insurance) paid in medical bills" ("The Truth"). The person who asks the price of an adoptive child commits a social/moral error, the article implies, because she associates payment with a child. Like the adoption workers I observed, Carney links payment to services and further normalizes the market and adoptive parents by drawing an analogy between adoption expenses and the fees paid for medical services by biological families. The implicit message is that adoptive families are *normal,* just like biological families.

Again, these normalizing moves are not recognized as such. Instead, Carney makes reference to "adoption myths," which can be countered by facts. "To a degree, such blundering remarks reflect a simple lack of information," she writes. "For those with no direct adoption experience, a little education can go a long way. But just beneath the surface of these myths lurk some unpleasant value judgments." The person who asks the price of a child makes "unpleasant *value* judgments," while those who (re)educate them are simply shoring up the *facts.* Better exposure to adoption, she implies, allows one to properly categorize the money being exchanged. For her, the right category is a matter of accuracy, but Carney's mission to disseminate adoption facts is punctuated by language that reveals the moral underpinnings of this task. The stakes of correcting misconceptions, she asserts, lie in protecting the adopted child from harmful remarks, showing her (the child) that "adoption is a *normal* way to build a family."

In contrast to Carney's assertion, the answer to the question of whether adoption entails buying a child is a matter of interpretation. There is little doubt that market dynamics infuse adoption practices, that a sizeable proportion of adoptions involve the transfer of children from poor women to wealthier people, and that one must pay large sums of money to access domestic infant adoption. At the same time, adoption offers transformative possibilities for family because it disrupts the naturalization of parental labor and the economic devaluation that often accompanies denaturalization. When it comes to expensive and labor-intensive acts such as pregnancy and parenting, naturalization discourses have been mobilized to defend America's stingy social safety net via PRWORA and other pieces of national and state-level legislation that restrict access to affordable birth control and abortion. As these policies show, access to normal, private family life comes with a very real and often unaffordable price tag.

Advocates like Carney wash over the fact that *normal* families are differently subsidized by the government, employee health insurance plans, and hospitals. Carney contends that after the Adoption Tax Credit, the cost of adopting a child is comparable to giving birth in a hospital. However, her analysis fails to account for the fact that the majority of prenatal clinic and delivery charges are covered by insurance and the fact that the Adoption Tax Credit is a *reimbursement*. Birth parents may incur medical bills, but this is not going to stop them from receiving hospital services or gaining immediate custody of a child.

The point here is not that biological parents should face the same economic barriers as adoptive parents. Rather, it is to demonstrate that normalcy excludes even while it legitimates. Normalizing strategies may be increasingly successful for incorporating some adoptive parents into the fold of American family, but they also wash over the structural economic conditions that lead many birth mothers to make adoption plans (or have parental rights involuntarily revoked) and the financial barriers faced by working-class and poor would-be adoptive parents. Indeed, attempts to enclave children from the commodity sphere do not rid the adoption world of market dynamics, they merely leave unmarked the normal ways markets privilege those with the most resources.

Moreover, even when the adoption world and its participants acknowledge the socioeconomic and racial inequalities in their wake, they advocate for adoption by relying upon less explicitly economic norms that nevertheless perpetuate inequality. For example, adoption workers commonly stress that their *services* are primarily focused on the child, not would-be adoptive parents or birth parents. And children, we're told, "are not an entitlement." All of these assertions are consistent with a child-centric American culture that excludes children from the labor market and constructs them as costly financial liabilities. Responsibility for this burden is placed on private, self-sufficient parents. Children may deserve grants and entitlements, but adults do not. In the midst of the self-sufficient family's failure, children are shunted from one parent to another, thousands of dollars are exchanged, and economic responsibilities and failures remain the private property of adults.

Adoptive Families: Radical and Regressive

This analysis shows that inequality is perpetuated not just through policies that are beyond the purview of child welfare workers, but also through the complicated intersection of cultural norms about money and family that get rehashed in their day-to-day language. By shoring up the market and downplaying its significance, adoption workers leave uninterrogated the social inequality that undergirds adoption, which in turn allows the market to further propagate inequality. As Kopytoff observed, the very idea that the family could be a sphere of pure sentiment, relatively free from economic constraints, is a luxury afforded to relatively wealthy people (273).

Nivedita Menon argued that adoption can be a radical endeavor because it denaturalizes family-making by showing that the biological nuclear family is not inevitable. In adoption, the link between genetic transmission, gestation, and parenting is disrupted. A woman can give birth without becoming a mother and vice versa. A man can *mother* and/or *father*. Absent social and economic barriers, adoption could lead to more inclusive, alternative family structures—those not explicitly structured around the gender binary and heterosexuality. Yet few of the workers in this study viewed adoption as radical because its radical possibilities are bound to a decidedly regressive economic reality; a sizeable proportion of birth parents in domestic infant and foster care adoption are poor women with few social and economic resources. Yet, adoption workers and parents are embedded in a cultural and normative professional context that renders these realities unspeakable. To protect the sanctity of parenthood and children, and the cultural fiction that money and family belong to separate realms, workers engage in a laborious exercise of properly categorizing payment and containing the market.

Despite their best efforts, the practice of containing the market without explicitly confronting its propensity to exacerbate inequality leads child wel-

fare workers to become unwitting participants in the cycle of marginalization. Undervalued children remain underpriced, as we see in the example of
foster care adoption, and prospective parents who must pay to gain access
to children are stigmatized if they expect anything in return for their costly
investment in adoption. Yet workers are committed to normalizing adoptive
families and removing the social stigma to which they are sometimes subject.
Unfortunately, their moves to legitimize adoption hinge on normalizing private, self-sufficient biological families without contesting the social and economic exclusions the hegemony of this family form entails. This unintended
outcome stems in part from adoption workers and participants' perceptions
that they are simply engaged in the work of educating an ignorant public—
they are not engaged in moral or normative work at all.

Discrimination against impoverished birth parents is also indirectly
enacted by adoption agencies working to promote *the best interests of the child*.
Family Tree's administrator told prospective parents that adoption is exciting
but also very sad. Most birth mothers, he informed them, are adult women
who already have children but cannot afford the expenses associated with an
additional child. Adoptive parents should be prepared for the tough questions,
he said, recalling the story of a child who learned that his birth mother was
living in poverty and asked his adoptive parents why they couldn't give her
money.

There is no satisfying answer to the child's question because it underscores
the fact that in adoption and in society at large, social inequality is treated
as a given, sometimes rationalized as just desserts for poor choices or one's
inability to compete in the job market. Adults may have a vested interest in
caring for a child, both emotionally and financially, and many will pay enormous sums of money for access to the most coveted available children. However, prior to adoption, these prospective parents will never be entitled to
children to whom they are not biological parents, and women who make an
adoption plan will never be entitled to the money others have paid for the
chance to parent their children. Welfare spending cuts and welfare-to-work
programs push parents into the labor force without giving them access to
adequate childcare, thus increasing the risk that poor parents will lose their
children due to allegations of neglect. When poor parents lose custody of
children, removal is commonly chalked up to individual failure rather than
systematic injustice. In fact, baby markets should not be interrogated only or
primarily because they entail the commodification of children. Also important
is the way adoption markets perpetuate and ignore the suffering and marginalization of birth parents. Within a legal and cultural system that prohibits
baby sales under the auspices of protecting women from sexual and reproduc-

tive exploitation all the while operating a stingy and inadequate welfare state, adoption workers can inadvertently become handmaidens of the status quo.

While commodification anxiety has a long history in the US, the Hostile Worlds perspective (Zelizer, "Purchase" 818) that asks us to bracket pregnancy, adoption, and child-rearing from the market can perpetuate inequality in a neoliberal social and economic system in which freedom itself is cast in market terms. As Nancy Fraser observed, exploitation in the Marxist sense can be appealing to those who have been prevented from selling their labor in the capitalist marketplace due to racist or sexist domination (9). Fraser's point about commodification and my arguments in this essay are not meant to minimize the dangers of that commodification; rather, they imply that in a capitalist system, we have to attend to rather than downplay market forces if we want to redress inequality.

To be fair, the social policies that hasten socioeconomic inequality can feel far removed from day-to-day adoption work, such that the links between neoliberal social and economic reforms and the availability of adoptive children remain tacit and under-conceptualized by child welfare workers. As an ideology, neoliberalism attains its success by lodging itself into our cultural lenses, concealing the contingency of its logics by appearing to be inevitable. However, neoliberalism, much like the families that adoption workers reconstruct through their day-to-day work, is not natural or inevitable. Policy makers and advocates can do something to attenuate its impact on parents and children. The process of parsing through commodification anxiety may be uncomfortable for workers and adoption advocates, but it allows us to better understand how families are regulated in the wake of global capitalism, and how we might intervene in the service of social and reproductive justice.

Works Cited

Adoptive Families. "Adoption Cost and Timing in 2015–2016." *Adoptive Families,* www.adoptive-families.com/resources/adoption-news/adoption-cost-and-timing-2015-2016/.

———. "Affording Adoption." *Adoptive Families,* www.adoptivefamilies.com/how-to-adopt/financing-adoption-creative-fundraisers/.

———. "The Truth about Domestic Adoption." *Adoptive Families,* www.adoptivefamilies.com/articles.php?aid=522.

Briggs, Laura. *Somebody's Children: The Politics of Transnational and Transracial Adoption.* Duke University Press, 2012.

Fraser, Nancy. "Can Society Be Commodities All the Way Down? Polanyian Reflections on Capitalist Crisis." Working paper FMSH-WP-2012–18, Fondation Maison des sciences de l'homme, Paris, France, 2012, pp. 1–13.

Goodwin, Michelle Bratcher. "Baby Markets." *Baby Markets: Money and the New Politics of Creating Families,* edited by Michelle Bratcher Goodwin, Cambridge University Press, 2000, pp. 2–22.

Hardesty, Melissa. "'It's Not a Job!' Foster Care Board Payments and the Logic of the Profiteering Parent." *Social Service Review,* vol. 92, no. 1, pp. 93–133.

IRS. Topic Number 607. Adoption Credit and Adoption Assistance Programs. www.irs.gov/taxtopics/tc607

Kopytoff, Igor. "Commoditizing Kinship in America." *Consuming Motherhood,* edited by Janelle S. Taylor et al., Rutgers University Press, 2004, pp. 271–78.

Landes, Elisabeth M., and Richard A. Posner. "The Economics of the Baby Shortage." *The Journal of Legal Studies,* vol. 7, no. 2, 1978, pp. 323–48.

Menon, Nivedita. "Science in the Laboratory of Politics: Commercial Surrogacy and the Question of the Natural," Symposium, The Center for the Study of Gender and Sexuality, 4 Apr. 2012, The University of Chicago, Classics Building, Chicago, IL.

Oaks, Laury. *Giving Up Baby: Safe Haven Laws, Motherhood, and Reproductive Justice.* New York University Press, 2015.

Posner, Richard A. "The Regulation of the Market in Adoptions." *67 Boston University Law Review,* 1987, pp. 59–72.

Roberts, Dorothy E. "Poverty, Race, and New Directions in Child Welfare Policy." *Washington University Journal of Law and Policy,* vol. 1, no. 63, 1999, pp. 63–77.

Rothman, Barbara Katz. "Motherhood under Capitalism. *Consuming Motherhood,* edited by Janelle S. Taylor et al., Rutgers University Press, 2004, pp. 19–30.

Sadowski-Smith, Claudia. "Neoliberalism, Global 'Whiteness,' and the Desire for Adoptive Invisibility in US Parental Memoirs of Eastern European Adoption." *Journal of Transnational American Studies,* no. 3, vol. 2, 2011.

Zelizer, Viviana. *Pricing the Priceless Child: The Changing Social Value of Children.* Princeton University Press, 1985.

———. "The Purchase of Intimacy." *Law and Social Inquiry,* vol. 25, no. 3, 2000, pp. 817–48.

CHAPTER 10

"It's Your Choice, But . . ."

Paradoxes of Neoliberal Reproduction for
Indigenous Women in Oaxaca, Mexico

REBECCA HOWES-MISCHEL

> "One of the problems we face here is that women are too passive in
> the face of doctors, they need to understand themselves as consum-
> ers. Something this group [*Parto Libre*] can do is work to improve
> women's capacity to demand choices."
>
> —Sonia,[1] nurse-midwife

MIDWAY THROUGH a year of anthropological fieldwork focused on the politics of reproduction in Oaxaca, Mexico, in 2008, I found myself sitting on the
floor with a group of midwifery activists, doulas, and feminist doctors. By this
point in the circle, personal introductions had shifted into a discussion about
how each participant identified the cultural and institutional obstacles Oaxacan women—particularly rural and indigenous ones—face in their ability to
plan and birth children in safe and culturally competent settings. The group's
main critique focused on the normative birth model's emphasis on medical
authority and technological intervention rather than on pregnant women's
bodily experiences, cultural traditions, and personal preferences. Their challenge to this institutional birth paradigm reflects Mexican feminists' embrace
of an increasingly global movement for *parto humano* (humanized birth),
which is sometimes translated as "respectful care." Activists using the framework of parto humano emphasize that birth is a normal and embodied process
that the laboring person should direct, and they stress that such women (and
family)-centered approaches are in line with evidence-based medical guide-

---

1. All direct quotations were either audio recorded and later transcribed or noted verba-
tim in field notes and then translated into English by me. Field note excerpts are elaborated
versions of real time jottings I made. All communities and individuals have been given pseud-
onyms, per the ethics review conducted by New York University's Institutional Review Board.

lines to improve obstetrical outcomes. Articulated alongside movements to resurrect indigenous midwifery traditions, parto humano is a campaign that often centers challenges to medical institutional authority as both feminist health practice and collective cultural heritage preservation.

For Sonia, empowering rural women to make choices as medical *consumers* instead of as patients was key to improving their birth experiences. Her argument was framed around the differential rate of caesarean sections between local private and public hospitals (according to her presentation, 80 to 90 percent and 40 to 45 percent, respectively), which she argued partially reflects women not claiming the *right* to make choices. As she concluded: "It's an issue of fear and misinformation for women about their biological capacity to give birth, so we should work to empower them through this capacity." At the time I understood this narrative as a call toward encouraging indigenous women to embody the *possessive individualism* of neoliberal subjectivity. It also seemed to reflect a trend in discourses about modern human rights and reproduction that address people as individuals and that stress the value of traditional practices as reflections of consumer choice (Craven; Rothman).

But a month later, in June, I began to rethink how Sonia's promotion of consumer choice-making as feminist aspiration expressed a particular understanding of the aftereffects of neoliberalism in southern Mexico and about contexts in which an *incitement* to choose does not always accompany the *ability* to choose.

On a hot afternoon in a small rural community further south in the central valley, Lucia, a nurse, ushered a mother clutching her young son's hand to where Erica, the social worker, was standing on the edge of a crowd on a cement patio in front of the temporary health clinic. Addressing Erica, Lucia explained that "she [the mother, Rosa] has doubts about the campaign. Explain to her why he needs the shot [the measles, mumps, and rubella vaccine]." Without waiting to hear Rosa's doubts, Erica replied matter-of-factly: "Ultimately it's your choice, but you are his mother and you are responsible for his health, so you should be educated and make the *right* choice." Here Erica positioned Rosa as both someone whose choices mattered (i.e., as an autonomous choice-maker) and as someone who needed moral and scientific suasion to make the right choice (i.e., as an unreliable choice-maker). Contextualizing these two interactions within broader shifts in Mexican public health institutions, I suggest that we can understand the invocation of *choice* alongside disciplining discourses of *risk, responsibility,* and (implicitly) *maternal love* in negotiations over reproductive and mothering practices as an illustration of the contradictory ways Oaxacan indigenous women experience a kind of state-driven cultural neoliberalism.

Contexts of Neoliberalism and Reproduction

The southern state of Oaxaca is rural, with a large indigenous population representing sixteen different ethnolinguistic groups. In the national imaginary, these communities are typified simultaneously as central to Mexico's nationalist cultural heritage and as lagging in modern development. It is the source of large-scale migration to the north (both to northern Mexico and to the US) in the aftermath of NAFTA-imposed neoliberal market reforms.[2] The women at the center of this analysis experience neoliberalism as they build transnational families and as their reproductive choices are symbolically overdetermined in public health institutions. Their experiences support Solinger's argument that the sociopolitical designation of "good" and "bad" choice-makers (7) is a key to the way neoliberal discursive and governing regimes target reproductive practices (i.e., to fail to make the right choice is to reveal oneself an "inadequate mother"; 191). Yet, contrary to analyses of neoliberalism that attend to privatization and the evacuation of a public sphere, it is within public institutions (and the expansion of social welfare) that these women are asked to be good choice-makers.

This essay attends to contexts in which women are encouraged to make good choices, are shamed for not making good choices, and perhaps, refuse to choose at all.[3] I conclude by asking questions about how to understand the gap between institutional pressure to make choices and women's responses deferring them. This analysis of the specific contours through which neoliberalism takes shape in Oaxacan public health practices relies on thirteen months of ethnographic fieldwork I conducted between 2006 and 2013 that was focused on the routine politics of reproduction in rural Oaxaca. The data gathered over the course of this research include long stretches of participant observation in and around public health spaces—specifically a regional hospital (Hospital Rural) and two community clinics—as well as extended participant observation in a surrounding indigenous community; semi-structured interviews with medical professionals, policy makers, feminist activists, and community members; and content analysis of public media about pregnancy

---

2. Economic reforms in Mexico in the 1980s and 1990s, culminating in 1994's North American Free Trade Agreement (NAFTA), challenged the sustainability of Oaxacan agriculture by placing small-scale farmers in direct competition with multinational corporations. With American food (particularly corn) cheaper than local produce, Oaxacans from agriculturally focused regions increasingly migrated north for economic opportunity.

3. *Good choices* or *the right choice* are contingent and precarious categories that shift to reflect normative expectations expressed in institutional socialization. Throughout this chapter, I place them in quotes only when repeating direct speech. However, this is not to suggest static, settled, or self-evident constructs.

and reproduction. Employing a perspective that acknowledges interview content as a discursive production of self-in-context, I analyzed these narrative
interactions as collaborative and co-constructed encounters.[4] I draw on this
archive to consider how narratives about making responsible choices reveal
the uneven ways that forms of neoliberalism take shape in Oaxacan women's
reproductive experiences.

Good choice-making is a central link between neoliberalism as a form
of economic privatization and neoliberalism as a form of gendered subjectivity. Neoliberal models of health encourage individuals to internalize
sets of norms in the name of responsible citizenship. They learn to calculate risk (as prescribed by institutional experts), to take responsibility for
self-optimization projects, and to become subjects who can appropriately
make use of state resources in the service of a larger body politic (Rose). This
neoliberal subjectivity is gendered, as mothers are tasked with acting as consumers (Craven), who make responsible and future-oriented decisions to optimize both their own and their children's outcomes (Reich)—particularly while
pregnant (Lupton). Women are tasked with reliably consuming information
(even when unavailable or inaccessible) and making "'free choice[s]' in terms
of safe/unsafe, order/disorder, life/death . . . [that frame] women's mothering
identities as good/bad" (Bryant et al. 1199). In this schema, the self-maximiz-
ing individual experiences agency through personal *empowerment* rather than
as part of public collectives. Thus, as Cruikshank argues, one of the key modes
through which neoliberalism works is by hailing individual subjects into the
subject position of rational consumers who may be more and less *empowered*
to act on this array of choices. Accordingly, feminist analyses of reproductive politics in an age of neoliberalism(s) stress the stratifying effects of the
presentation of a purported world of innumerable—yet constrained and constraining—choices to women who are encouraged to act as self-actualizing,
self-sacrificing, and self-caring individuals (Lowe).

As such, Sonia's narrative appears to very much illustrate a particular kind
of activism that positions *consumer* relationship to a market of choices as a
central way to shift the classically hierarchical relationship between doctor
and patient (Rothman). It is also part of a long tradition in Mexico in which
indigenous women are encouraged to adopt modern or mestiza[5] maternal
sensibilities to demonstrate their civic and moral fitness in their health, chil-

---

4. See Charmaz for extended discussion of the relationship between narrative construction and grounded theory interviews.

5. The alignment between ideas about modernity and *mestizaje* (a national ideology of
racial mixing) is a post-Revolution argument valorizing the national body as given form in the
figure of the mestizo—ethnically mixing indigenous and Spanish "blood" (Stern).

drearing, and nutritional choices (Stern; Smith-Oka). Yet, in the encounter recounted above, Rosa was neither the empowered choice-making figure of Sonia's remedy nor a docile subject to Erica's dictates. Instead, I suggest that analyses of reproduction amidst the aftereffects of neoliberalism benefit from greater attention to the contradictory ways that Mexican indigenous women are invited to choose in public health settings though practitioners' repetitions of "it's your choice, but . . ." Attending to the gap between the incitement to choose and women's active choice-making—or their deferral of choice—illustrates the contradictory logics of neoliberalism in Mexican public health settings.

Oaxacan Public Health in a Time of Neoliberalism

Public health institutions and mothering practices have been key elements of state-building throughout rural communities since the Mexican Revolution—exemplified by the inclusion of a national right to health in the 1917 constitution. As Birn argues, "Public health offered a concrete, feasible area through which the state could enlarge its authority by meeting revolutionary expectations for improved social conditions, build a sense of citizenship—particularly among rural populations—and tether science and scientific professionals to renewed national goals" (*Marriage of Convenience* 15). Between the 1930s and 1980s, the Federal Health Ministry slowly extended its reach through the newly built clinics and hospitals that brought services to rural areas and brought rural areas into federally centralized health campaigns. In the mid-twentieth century, Mexico turned its policy attention to questions of (over)population and child health concerns and stressed the importance of integrating rural indigenous communities into the national body politic through an expanded public health services infrastructure that supported community education programs (Birn, *Marriage of Convenience*). In 1983, facing a debt crisis and under pressure from international politics and economic forces, the Mexican government initiated neoliberal restructuring of the public healthcare system. Despite maintaining public commitment to quality universal coverage, these reforms exacerbated discrepancies in human development indices (health, poverty, literacy) between the wealthier (and whiter) North and impoverished (and indigenous) South (Laurell).

Constructed in 1980, Hospital Rural's outpatient wing, which served as my primary research site, embodied the ambivalent intersection between Mexico's national commitment to health (and reliance on population health as a key marker of modernity) and its neoliberal dismantling of the publicly financed social services infrastructure. Ironically, for rural Oaxacan women the period inaugurating large-scale and national privatization of public services is the same period in which they finally gained access to them. Illustrating what Schwegler describes as Mexico's negotiated and "hybrid forms of neoliberal governmentality" (684), medical personnel simultaneously emphasized the importance of their community service to underserved populations and stressed the importance of such communities learning to embody a neoliberal ethos of *autocuidado* (self-care). This dual-pronged emphasis reflected changes in the funding and organization of health provision that encouraged the development of newly accountable subjects in the name of moral citizenship (Birn, "Federalist Flirtations"). Thus, the rippling effects of neoliberalism within public health institutions most acutely manifest in ideological rather than political and economic forms. Maintaining the federal health system's centralizing force and framing good health as a collective project, rural public health institutions through national health campaigns integrate indigenous women into a modern body politic as responsible choice-makers who need to develop an ethos in alignment with public standards. Even as the rural communities surrounding Hospital Rural have experienced greater inclusion into the formalized public health system, full enfranchisement is discursively hedged as invocations of *risk,* and *choices* that move the locus of accountability from the public sector to embodied and individual actions.

While risk discourse animates a general neoliberal ethos of health, in southern Mexico it intersects with long-standing Mexican public health and policy concerns about rural women's reproductive health. The alignment between the bodily health of gendered bodies, their cultural practices, and the symbolic health of the nation continues to reverberate through the importance health institutions place on the risk indices that serve as contemporary instruments of modernity claims—notably, the vital statistics of population and maternal and infant mortality (Andaya; Howes-Mischel). Thus, while indigenous women's reproductive practices have long been the terrain in which Mexican state claims to modernness are rendered uneven and unsettled, in the aftereffects of neoliberalism the close alignment of private decisions and collective morality is ever tightened.

"The Ones Who Come All Eventually Make the Right Choice . . ."

The confrontation between Rosa and Erica came at the end of a long, hot day. Early that June morning, the *equipo de salud* (the mobile clinical team of a medical resident, several nurses, a nutritionist, and a social worker) set out from the public hospital for their biweekly visits to the small community less than twenty kilometers away. The equipo operates as an auxiliary force in Mexico's centralized public health system to offer communities regular access to basic healthcare targeted at mothers, children, and the elderly and to coordinate nationally directed community health initiatives. Upon our arrival, Erica had stressed to the group of *promotoras* (middle-aged women tasked with implementing health campaigns) the importance of the entire community's participation in that week's national vaccine drive. Midday, Erica called the promotoras together and gave them community census lists with the names of the women whose children were not yet vaccinated highlighted, sending them off to retrieve them. She told them, "It is important to do this with enthusiasm because you are my people here. Your participation is for your community and the project of health is bigger than individuals because it is for all of us. So, it's important that you communicate these things [compliance with vaccines] as science, not as beliefs." Speaking in the voice of national interests, Erica aligned good health choices with advancing the national body politic. This is ideological, but also institutional, reflecting the way public welfare programs align individuals' clinical compliance to social benefits.

Progresa (Progress), the contemporary social welfare system launched in 1997, from the first directly linked public services to neoliberal models of health and personal responsibility to state expectations of, and on, its population. In 2002 it was renamed *Oportunidades* (Opportunities) and shifted to a conditional cash transfer program that made direct payments to mothers as "responsible caregivers" as long as they satisfied program requirements, including children's regular school attendance and medical visits for both children and pregnant women.[6] Considered the region's most successfully restructured social welfare program, it relies on aligning deeply maternalist expectations with neoliberal frames: "basing its programme on normatively ascribed maternal responsibilities, in effect making transfers conditional on 'good motherhood'" (Molyneux 438). It is now rebranded *Prospera* (Prosperity). As a form of governance, it encourages women to learn and internalize these expectations as a *civic* duty that is consistent with long-standing narratives of maternal caregiving that are foundational to gendered citizenship claims (Molyneux).

Thus, all day a steady stream of women and children passed through the central plaza to receive the shot or to present proof of their prior compli-

---

6. Frenk et al. offer a comprehensive history of the policy developments that led to these policy reforms, while Molyneux's and Smith-Oka's analyses highlight the way motherhood in particular is mobilized within them.

ance—rendering their evidence of good choices forms of public civic virtue. Rosa instead arrived with questions raised by a neighbor about the vaccine's risk and thus wasn't sure that she wanted to participate in *this* campaign at *this* moment—although she did leave open the possibility for future participation once she had thought more about it. Erica's response was swift and emphatic:

> Who told you that? Really you should do it. It's a national campaign, and if you don't, there's a risk he will get sick. But, ultimately, it's your choice. You are his mother, and you are responsible for his health. Of course, it's your choice, but if you do not, he could get very sick, and it would be because he wasn't vaccinated.

Without attempting to explain herself further, Rosa walked away for a short while. Finally, nodding at Erica, she and her son joined the line in front of the vaccinating nurse. As we piled into the back of the hospital's truck at the day's end, I asked Erica whether any woman had refused to participate in the campaign, and she replied: "No, the ones who come all eventually make the right choice. It's only the ones we can't find, the ones who don't come, those we don't know about." Linking individual choices to national health, Erica positions the women in the community as subjects capable of making rational choices, but unreliably so. Further, she suggests that making good choices is simultaneously a demonstration of individual desire to participate in the modern body politic and not actually a choice. Rather than a scenario with good or bad choices, the only way to not make a good choice was to refuse to make a choice.

"It's Important to Make Good Choices"

Small color-coded *cartillas* (booklets) titled "Your passport to health" were a ubiquitous presence in the clinical and para-clinical spaces in and around Hospital Rural, where I observed the quotidian politics of prenatal care. As do national passports, these cartillas classified individuals by age and gender and facilitated their access to the public facilities. The cartillas not only served as a personal record of health and an access point, they operated as a kind of surveillance device that enabled hospital personnel to review at a glance women's compliance with Oportunidades requirements. While as rural citizens, all pregnant women were eligible for free basic prenatal care, low-income households also received conditional cash transfers through the program. About half of the people served by the outpatient wing of Hospital Rural received these benefits, and all were treated as if they did.

Oportunidades perhaps best illustrates rural indigenous women's experiences of the contradictory aftereffects of neoliberalism in Oaxaca: On the one hand, it radically expanded the material reach of the public welfare state; on the other hand, its benefits required individuals' acquiescence with institutionally mandated practices. Oportunidades' gendered focus offers indigenous women a clear carrot (cash benefits) and stick (the removal of such benefits), yet Smith-Oka's analysis of how "the underlying structure of Oportunidades is aimed at rationalizing poor people's behavior and self-care" (48) points to a subtle second carrot. In addition to its conditional cash benefits, the public welfare system encourages women to find empowerment in their increased capacity for responsible mothering that results from their participation in its programs. This reliance on the buzzwords of neoliberal development exposes the gendered and illusionary nature of agency as promoted within the program. Further, the evolution of the initiative's name from *progress* to *opportunity* and now to *prosperity* reflects a proposition that ties individual and national long-term economic welfare to both material and ideological advancements in their caregiving.

Margarita, a nutritionist, began one mandated community workshop in the outpatient wing's multipurpose room by reminding the assembled women that "it's important to make good choices." The group of eight women included a first-time participant barely showing at nine weeks' gestation, two first-time teenage mothers, and a thirty-two-year-old mother of three, who drew on her experience to counsel another participant, whose thirty-five-week pregnant belly inspired a long side conversation about natural remedies to alleviate the physical discomfort of the final stretch. For Margarita, the importance of making good choices was reflected in small daily decisions about what to eat, and she encouraged women to choose nutrient-dense unprocessed food from local markets rather than commercial food. But more importantly, they were reflected in what she termed "a broad sensibility." More significant than what kind of food they purchased was understanding their daily choices as demonstrations of maternal love, starting with breastfeeding: "We're going to talk about many details you can choose, but first the most important thing is to offer your breast. Like this, you hold it like a 'C' [she demonstrates cupping her own breast] and offer it with love. That's the most important choice you can make." Throughout her presentation, Margarita returned to the theme of classifying the kinds of choices women would be asked to make as new parents, teaching them in each case which choice was the caring one. Good choices like breastfeeding or local vegetables thus enroll the domestic spaces of family nutrition into clinical discourses of responsible care, rendering the former newly modern and scientifically informed (Yates-Doerr).

In another workshop held in a neighboring small town, the clinic's director even more explicitly reminded women that the nutritional choices they make are direct manifestations of their maternal responsibility. At the end·of a presentation about the cultural importance of reincorporating amaranth (a cheap and nutrient-dense heritage grain that a local NGO promotes to address child malnutrition) into the community's diet, she switched from explaining its benefits over processed food to castigating women for making irresponsible choices:

> The reason there are so many problems in this community is that people are lazy and forgot how to make the right choices. They lost that sensibility. It's important to pay attention at these workshops because, if not, it's too easy not to make the right choices, and we already see the problems with that.

She went on to tie unspecified "bad choices" to the rise of childhood illness and cancer, suggesting that these things (and not the town's location next to the municipal dump) were causal agents of an ill community.

Again and again, in the didactic spaces of Oportunidades medical professionals held out the carrot of good choices to reshape what Smith-Oka refers to as indigenous women's "reproductive habitus" (16). With this term, she highlights the ways social, political, economic, and medical institutions socialize women's preconscious dispositions toward "reproductive and sexual practices, contraceptive choices, childcare practices, and mothering practices" (79). Addressing predominantly indigenous communities, instructors encourage women to embody a broad sensibility of good mothering that is defined by compliance with institutional practices. To receive public benefits is to be encouraged to develop a new sensibility—one whose good choices demonstrate responsible maternal love. Selectively invoking lost cultural heritage, they suggest that modernization has both introduced new bad choices and offers a means of making good ones.

As Oportunidades expanded rural women's inclusion into the public welfare system, it expanded the degree to which their private practices could be framed as matters of national and moral concern. This broad sensibility is classically neoliberal as women's private choices—rather than public and structuring contexts of food-insecure poverty, ethnic marginalization, and transnational displacement—are rendered the salient domain of child outcomes. Yet, I think it is crucial to note that in each of these instances, women

only learned about good choices,[7] and that in the face of an incitement to publicly choose, most often women participants were silent. Thus, understanding
how neoliberalism works in rural Oaxacan prenatal health is to attend to what
Rapp terms the "existential gaps" (693) between institutional narratives about
the need to make good choices and the embodied contexts of deferring (or
refusing) choice.

"What Kind of Birth Control Will You Choose?"

In 1977, three years after family planning was made the constitutional right
of all couples, Mexico established a National Family Planning Program that
was integrated into existing maternal and child health services (Rodriguez-
Barocio et al.). Since then, Mexican health policy has heavily promoted birth
control—particularly long-acting forms—as a means of modernizing the
nation and the family (Laveaga). This is illustrated by colorful murals promoting birth control that are now a ubiquitous part of villages' public spaces,
sponsored by the national education institution and created by local health
committees. One common mural directly links the nuclear family to emotional well-being with the slogan "A small family is a happy family" above two
cartoon figures embracing with a small child encircled between them. And,
posters with similar language linking familial *care* to family *planning* have
proliferated throughout clinical spaces. Discursively highlighting the individual practice of planning as a demonstration of maternal worth and love,
public health media encourage women to internalize a sensibility of responsible motherhood in the service of a modern body politic. This was reinforced
in medical encounters as doctors used health information tools to socialize
patients' reproductive sensibility.

During the nine months I spent at Hospital Rural, I observed and recorded
almost fifty women's prenatal exams with two cohorts[8] of the four family med-

---

7. It is worth noting that although in my Oaxacan fieldwork clinical dictates were framed
in discourses of *responsible* and *loving* motherhood, Smith-Oka observed a dominant narrative
of "bad mothers" in her fieldwork in the neighboring state of Veracruz. One explanation for
this variance is the influence of locally specific cultural histories and politics of indigeneity in
southern Mexico on interactions between clinics and communities (personal communication).

8. All of the residents who staffed the outpatient wing were completing their mandatory
national service period. This requirement ensured that Mexico made good on its national commitment to public health. Doctors are assigned their locale, which meant that their duration in
the community was limited. This program also meant that the cultural gap between the clinical institution and their patients was exacerbated as only two of the residents I shadowed were
Oaxacan, and none of them were indigenous.

icine residents and obstetrical specialists who staffed the outpatient wing. The exams involved periods of highly standardized interactions while doctors completed an individualized risk profile and periods of idiosyncratic questions and observations during the physical exam. In the former, doctors asked women for information about their age, marital status, number of pregnancies, and number of children. At the end, the doctor used this to calculate a risk score, which structured the woman's prenatal care. While assigning a risk score to each pregnancy is a purportedly neutral assessment to guide women's clinical care, it ultimately gave doctors a language to contextualize possible future harm in women's daily practices rather than in the forms of social and economic marginalization that make Oaxacan reproduction risky (Howes-Mischel). Thus, the standardizing instruments of the national public health system encourage a maternal neoliberal subjectivity that centers the individual as the prime locus of positive and negative outcomes.

The risk form also served as a launch point for further, seemingly informal, conversations between doctors and patients as they shifted from the interview toward the physical exam. Questions about *this* pregnancy easily became questions about the next (potential) one, as Dr. Augustin explained to me after an exam:

> It's important that they think about their choices now for two reasons. The first is when else will we see them so often, will they need to listen to this way of thinking. The second is that sometimes people have romantic ideas, but this is a time when it is very practical and very physical. So, for both reasons, it's an opportunity to think about the future and encourage good choices.

He couched these questions in terms of offering information and encouragement—of empowering women to act on their own futures. Yet, in practice and in interactions in which women's rhetorical affect was primarily one of passive reception, questions about using birth control were more often commands to use birth control. In its most neutral form, this routine exchange looked like this one between Dr. Pamela and a woman named Edeline:

> DR. P: "And what method of planning will you use after this one?"
> E: "An IUD?"
> DR. P: "Correct."

This exchange of "What kind of method will you choose . . . Correct" was echoed in twenty-four of the forty-seven cases I recorded. Sometimes doctors incorporated additional narratives that connected proper family planning to a vision of a good life, as reflected in the following utterance by Dr. Augustin:

> OK, so this is your second baby? So, two is good, right? Good for everyone. What kind of birth control do you and your husband choose for afterwards? [He pauses for response; she is silent.] Talk about it with him. It's good to do.

Repeating the optimal nature of only two children "for everyone," he enrolls Felicia and her absent husband in the process of making good choices on behalf of the future of their family. Yet, given the way family planning campaigns evoked responsibility to a larger collective, his invocation of "everyone" suggests that this choice also is one to benefit the national body politic.

Rarely did women directly oppose doctors' imperatives to make the good choice. Instead, they deferred or displaced it to an unspecified future. Such a strategy of postponement is evident in the patient Juana's statement, "My husband and I, we've talked, but we haven't decided [here she trailed off]." Notably, Juana leaves open the possibility of resolving these discussions in favor of the right choice, but she reclassifies it as a marital—not a medical—concern. Only in one instance did a man—a rare presence at these exams—participate in the exchange at the end of the exam. As Estela (the man's pregnant teenage daughter) began to gather her belongings, the doctor engaged him as follows:

> DR. PAMELA: "And after the baby? Tell [Estela's partner] that it is a simple thing."
> ESTELA'S FATHER: "We want another baby."
> DR. PAMELA [TURNING BACK TO ESTELA]: "You may want more, but talk to him about how to make good choices that serve your future."
> [Estela nods, and she and her father leave.]

Often invoking absent partners' implicitly uncertain participation in the making of "good choices that serve your future," doctors enrolled women as subjects who had the capacity—if not yet the determination—to act as choice-making consumers. That is, while doctors' narratives about the importance of choice were largely performative in practice, they seemed genuinely invested in women's ultimate capacity to make choices, as long as they made good ones.

Doctors in prenatal spaces rarely followed up on this issue of post-birth contraceptive plans.[9] Instead, they emphasized the importance of a future-

---

9. This is partially a limitation of the data as I did not follow women into the maternity ward on the other side of the hospital; however, Castro's research suggests that patients in public hospitals are most likely to receive long-acting contraceptive methods at birth.

oriented planning sensibility that encompassed both women's dietary and contraceptive choices. Dr. Delfina's speech to nineteen-year-old Paola reflects doctors' rhetorical framing of the importance of choosing as part of women's responsibility to craft an empowered future:

> Now, what kind of birth control do you and your boyfriend use? None?! And this is your first pregnancy? Well, you've had a lot of luck, that's good. It's good when women have babies because they want to be pregnant, because they want to be a mother. But the desire is good for when you're ready; it's good to use birth control and then we can plan and it's not something that just happens. And if you plan, we can make sure that everything's OK.

Illustrated by her repeated insistence on the goodness of planning, Dr. Delfina encourages Paola to internalize a future-oriented sensibility in which choice-making is a key indicator of success. Notably, even when partners were occasionally invoked or involved, the responsibility to make contraceptive choices was firmly attached to women's lives, reinforcing Gutmann's argument that Mexican family planning plans men out of the center of domestic choices. In part, this echoes the gendered dynamics of Oportunidades' cash benefit flows that designate women as empowered beneficiaries *and* as potentially "backwards" individuals who require institutional socialization through expectations of "good motherhood" (Smith-Oka). Thus, it is important to consider not only the constraining circumstances in which women were encouraged to make *good choices* but also the stakes of choosing not to make choices at all.

"The Doctor Hasn't Told Me Yet"

Throughout my research in Hospital Rural, I attempted to conduct interviews with the women whose exams I had just observed, listening for the ways they internalized, contested, or elaborated on the forms of embodied socialization encouraged by medical professionals. Women were generally minimally responsive, offering only short affirmations of an institutional narrative that could be summed up as: "The doctors are good, the treatment is good, there's nothing I would change." Conscious of the contested status of the high rates of caesarian sections in public hospitals, I added a query about the form of birth they desired, receiving a uniform answer that "the doctor hasn't told me yet." Originally I dismissed these interviews as *bad data* and decided that within the hospital, I was too closely positioned as an institutional figure to receive answers that sounded like (my idea of) authentic reflection.

However, I continued to hear this demurral of choice in my more extended conversations with community members with whom I developed relationships, causing me to return to the implications of "my doctor hasn't told me yet." Rather than a statement of docile passivity, I ultimately conclude that it lays bare the fictitiousness of incitements to choose within public health spaces—the illusionary nature of *choice* that Solinger shows haunts stratifying discourses within neoliberalism generally.

As medical professionals presented women with decisions about fertility control or children's vaccines, they simultaneously positioned them as autonomous choice-makers *and* as potentially unruly and unmodern ones who might make nonscientific and therefore bad choices. As medical professionals drew on expectations about proper maternal affect by stressing the importance of making *good, loving,* and *responsible* choices in their disciplining invocations of risk, the social worker Erica was proven right. The only women who did not make "good" choices were ones who refused to choose. Thus, while neoliberal expectations introduced the discursive possibility of an array of choices in the course of their medical encounters, seldom could these women not make good choices.

Much of the scholarship on reproduction in the aftereffects of neoliberalism emphasizes the relationship between conditions of economic austerity and the push to privatize risk and responsibility in the individual actor. To consider the forms of neoliberalism at work in Oaxacan public health spaces is to consider how these same privatizing logics are deployed in the provision (and expansion) of public services. For a population whose reproductive practices and outcomes have long garnered suspicion within Mexican health policy, it is striking how well current concerns about making good choices about vaccines, prenatal diet, and birth control extend long-standing ones rather than constitute novel phenomena. As Oaxaca has experienced a hybrid form of neoliberalism in the expansion of public welfare services alongside economic privatization, indigenous women are simultaneously positioned as (potentially) autonomous modern subjects and as unreliable ones. This hybridity points to the unevenness through which neoliberalism takes shape, as well as to the continuing salience of looking at reproduction and intimate decisions as a central domain in which multiple forms of power operate. Thus, the incitement to choose contains both a kind of aspiration (i.e., "Be the kind of person who can make good choices") and caution (i.e., "If you don't, bad things can happen"). Not making a good choice is to risk censure, whereas not making a choice defers it. Indigenous women's statement that "my doctor hasn't told me yet" thus constitutes recognition of the dynamics of this form of neoliberal governance.

Amidst this cacophony of narratives about choosing well, a final return to where this essay began in the circle of Mexican feminists: What, then, of Sonia's original proposition that Oaxacan women are not yet, but need to be, empowered to demand choices as consumers? Perhaps she points to a paradoxical strategy for shifting the politics of reproduction in an arena already structured by an ethos of neoliberal consumerism. As Sharma's research in India shows, dissonant fissures created by paradoxical forms of neoliberalism in practice may at times create spaces for women to resignify empowerment discourses as a form of "moral citizenship talk" (xxxv). Alongside their birth activism that is couched not in direct opposition to public facilities but in restoring cultural heritage practices to communities, perhaps these Oaxacan feminists are crafting new frameworks for reproductive agency in which the right to demand choices may look like the right to make *not good* choices.

Works Cited

Andaya, Elise. *Conceiving Cuba: Reproduction, Women, and the State in the Post-Soviet Era.* Rutgers University Press, 2014.

Birn, Anne-Emanuelle. "Federalist Flirtations: the Politics and Execution of Health Services Decentralization for the Uninsured Population in Mexico, 1985–1995." *Journal of Public Health Policy,* vol. 20, no. 1, 1999, pp. 81–108.

———. *Marriage of Convenience: Rockefeller International Health and Revolutionary Mexico.* University of Rochester Press, 2006.

Bryant, Joanne, et al. "Caesarean Birth: Consumption, Safety, Order, and Good Mothering." *Social Science & Medicine,* vol. 65, no. 6, 2007, pp. 1192–1201.

Castro, Arachu. "Contracepting at Childbirth: The Integration of Reproductive Health and Population Policies in Mexico." *Unhealthy Health Policy: A Critical Anthropological Examination,* edited by Merrill Singer and Arachu Castro, Rowman Altamira, 2004, pp. 133–44.

Charmaz, Kathy. "Qualitative Interviewing and Grounded Theory Analysis." *Handbook of Interview Research: Context and Method,* edited by Jaber Gubrium and James A. Holstein, Sage, 2002, pp. 675–94.

Craven, Christa. "A 'Consumer's Right' to Choose a Midwife: Shifting Meanings for Reproductive Rights under Neoliberalism." *American Anthropologist,* vol. 109, no. 4, pp. 701–12.

Cruikshank, Barbara. *The Will to Empower: Democratic Citizens and Other Subjects.* Cornell University Press, 1999.

Frenk, Julio, et al. "Evidence-Based Health Policy: Three Generations of Reform in Mexico." *The Lancet,* vol. 362, no. 9396, 2003, pp. 1667–71.

Gutmann, Matthew. "Planning Men out of Family Planning: A Case Study from Mexico." *Reproduction, Globalization, and the State,* edited by Carole H. Browner and Carolyn F. Sargent, Duke University Press, 2011, pp. 53–67.

Howes-Mischel, Rebecca. "Local Contours of Reproductive Risk and Responsibility in Rural Oaxaca." *Risk, Reproduction and Narratives of Experience,* edited by Aminata Maraesa and Lauren Fordyce, Vanderbilt University Press, 2012, pp. 123–40.

Laurell, Asa Cristina. "Health Reform in Mexico: The Promotion of Inequality." *International Journal of Health Services,* vol. 31, no. 2, 2001, pp. 291–321.

Laveaga, Gabriela Soto. "'Let's Become Fewer': Soap Operas, Contraception, and Nationalizing the Mexican family in an Overpopulated World." *Sexuality Research & Social Policy,* vol. 4, no. 3, 2007, pp. 19–33.

Lowe, Pam. *Reproductive Health and Maternal Sacrifice: Women, Choice and Responsibility.* Springer, 2016.

Lupton, Deborah. "'Precious Cargo': Foetal Subjects, Risk and Reproductive Citizenship." *Critical Public Health,* vol. 22, no. 3, 2012, pp. 329–40.

Molyneux, Maxine. "Mothers at the Service of the New Poverty Agenda: Progresa/ Oportunidades, Mexico's Conditional Transfer Programme." *Social Policy and Administration,* vol. 40, no. 4, 2006, pp. 425–49.

Rapp, Rayna. "Reproductive Entanglements: Body, State, and Culture in the Dys/regulation of Child-Bearing." *Social Research,* vol. 78, no. 3, 2011, pp. 693–718.

Reich, Jennifer. "Neoliberal Mothering and Vaccine Refusal Imagined Gated Communities and the Privilege of Choice." *Gender & Society,* vol. 28, no. 5, 2014, pp. 679–704.

Rodriguez-Barocio, Raul, et al. "Fertility and Family Planning in Mexico." *International Family Planning Perspectives,* vol. 6, no. 1, 1980, pp. 2–9.

Rose, Nikolas. *The Politics of Life Itself: Biomedicine, Power, and Subjectivity in the Twenty-First Century.* Princeton University Press, 2009.

Rothman, Barbara Katz. "Motherhood under Capitalism." *Consuming Motherhood,* edited by Janelle Taylor et al., Rutgers University Press, 2004, pp. 19–30.

Schwegler, Tara. "Take It from the Top (Down)? Rethinking Neoliberalism and Political Hierarchy in Mexico." *American Ethnologist,* vol. 35, no. 4, 2008, pp. 682–700.

Sharma, Aradhana. *Logics of Empowerment: Development, Gender, and Governance in Neoliberal India.* University of Minnesota Press, 2008.

Smith-Oka, Vania. *Shaping the Motherhood of Indigenous Mexico.* Vanderbilt Press, 2013.

Solinger, Rickie. *Beggars and Choosers: How the Politics of Choice Shapes Abortion, Adoption, and Welfare in the United States.* Hill and Wang, 2001.

Stern, Alexandra M. "Responsible Mothers and Normal Children: Eugenics, Nationalism, and Welfare in Post-Revolutionary Mexico, 1920–1940." *Journal of Historical Sociology,* vol. 12, no. 4, 1999, pp. 369–97.

Yates-Doerr, Emily. *The Weight of Obesity: Hunger and Global Health in Postwar Guatemala.* University of California Press, 2015.

CHAPTER 11

The Globalization of Assisted Reproduction

Vulnerability and Regulation

RACHEL ANNE FENTON

WE LIVE in an age where dreams of reproduction can be bought and sold. Human gametes, fertility treatments of every type, and surrogates are available in the billion-dollar, unregulated global marketplace. For reproductive *consumers,* the global marketplace becomes an attractive option when restrictive regulation and policies prohibit the fulfillment of their reproductive dreams at home. For those involved in supplying the global market with eggs, sperm, and wombs to rent, ethical issues about commodification and exploitation arise, particularly when that supply originates in developing countries in the global South—increasingly the destination of choice for fertility travelers from the global North. The realities, *good-news* stories, and particularly the tragedies that globalized reproduction potentially entails are never far from media consumption. The stories of baby Manji, born in India and whose gestational and commissioning mothers relinquished any claim to her (Roy 54), and baby Gammy, who was allegedly left behind in Thailand according to newspaper reports (an account later rejected by an Australian court) when the Australian commissioning couple collected only his twin sister, are only two recent tales of surrogacy *gone wrong* (Callaghan and Newson; Photopoulos). Likewise, international media interest was sparked by the Italian case of elderly parents

The author is indebted to Martha Albertson Fineman.

achieving a postmenopausal pregnancy abroad with consequent removal of the child by the Italian authorities (Margaria and Sheldon). These news stories are a preview of the vulnerabilities that can ensue, for all parties involved, from the transnational reproduction trade.

Reproduction is an area characterized by the increasing medicalization of women's bodies and state control over their decision-making. In seeking to establish control over reproductive choices, it is unsurprising that scholars and activists focused on the acquisition of bodily autonomy and formal equality. In positioning women as fully functioning liberal subjects for whom reproductive liberty has become synonymous with autonomous choice-making and freedom to contract (Fineman, "Vulnerability" 17), law has led to some valuable gains in terms of formal equality in the way in which assisted reproductive technologies (ARTs) have been regulated by the state in many developed countries. However, what this chapter is concerned with is the extent to which "an adherence to formal equality has seemingly eclipsed our moral and political aspirations for *social justice*" (Fineman, "Equality"; my emphasis), and what aspirational social justice and well-being might look like in the context of ARTs. Fineman's concept of vulnerability is an "alternative vision for justice" based on the understanding that vulnerability is a constant, shared, and "universal, inevitable, enduring aspect of the human condition," arising from our embodiment ("Vulnerability" 20) and our differential embeddedness "in social relationships and within societal institutions" ("Equality" 613). Fineman suggests that replacing the mythical, autonomous, fully functioning liberal subject with the vulnerable subject in politico-legal discourse necessitates a mandate for a responsive state, "one with a clear duty to effectively ensure realistic equality of access and opportunity to society's resource-generating institutions for everyone" ("Equality" 613). In this essay, I position ART provision, including surrogacy, firmly within the context of vulnerability, inequality, globalization, and the discourse of social injustice and exploitation. From the stance of Fineman's vulnerability thesis, I will explore how the gains made by the liberal order's focus on formal equality and autonomy in reproductive decision-making regulation may be set against the state's unresponsiveness to the embodied vulnerability of ART users, exposing actual inequalities and limitations on opportunity. I explore how law and policy perpetuate and facilitate globalization and continue to *other* some types of mothering. I use Fineman's vulnerability analysis to question states' accountability for their unethical domestic regulation and the consequent vulnerabilities—predominantly of women—that this facilitates and perpetuates along global geographic trajectories as a result.

The Vulnerability Thesis and Assisted Reproduction

Our need for connection and care is part of our humanity, which will include for some, but not all, a desire to reproduce, situated within particular social, cultural, and religious contexts. Such contexts may affect women more than men. It is precisely within these contexts that an inability to reproduce without assistance, whether for clinical or social reasons,[1] will be lived. It is crucial to understand that Fineman detaches vulnerability from its association with "victimhood, deprivation, dependency or pathology" ("Vulnerable Subject" 266), and therefore to be vulnerable is *not to be stigmatized*. Rather, all of us are universally vulnerable simply because we are human, simply because we are embodied. Infertility arises from our embodiment and is characterized by its very universality and ubiquity: It may genuinely affect anyone regardless of gender, sexuality, race, religion, disability, or able-bodiedness, wherever they are globally situated. While infertility is universal, it, like vulnerability itself, is "experienced uniquely" (Fineman, "Vulnerable Subject" 269) because we are differentially and uniquely embodied, and differently situated. Our vulnerability can be mitigated by our access to assets that provide us with resilience or resources to respond to vulnerability, including the state and societal institutions. For some, the lure of ARTs, including surrogacy, may represent a solution to infertility, but in turn may both exacerbate their own vulnerability and create vulnerabilities in others: ART and surrogacy users become subject to constraints imposed by law and institutions such as healthcare providers—which gain legitimacy and authority through the state and law—and through the medicalization of infertility, which may contribute to inequalities and disparities in treatment through social exclusion (Bell). The role of the state from a vulnerability stance must be to increase our resilience, be responsive to ART and surrogacy users' vulnerability in order not to unduly privilege some and disadvantage others, and ensure genuine equality of opportunity is realized by all.

Infertility and the (Un)responsive UK State

The Legal Regulation of ARTs

The state defines and regulates the constitution of the family. Access to ARTs is often constrained by regulation in conformity with the privileged normatively preferred family ideal, most often the sexually affiliated two-parent hetero-

---

1. Note that this is my meaning when I use the word *infertility* in the context of this chapter.

sexual patriarchal model, to the exclusion of others. The Human Fertilisation and Embryology Act of 1990, as updated in 2008, regulates assisted reproduction in the UK. The UK has made significant progress in the inclusivity of diverse family forms since its initial regulation in 1990. The privileging of the heterosexual family was clear under s.13(5) HFE Act of 1990, which required clinics to consider "*the need of that child for a father*" (my emphasis), and provided justification for the exclusion of single and lesbian women from infertility treatment in line with the general concern of the liberal order with the *dangerousness* of *manless* mothers apparent within much of family law (see Fineman, *Autonomy* chs. 4 and 5). This criterion was jettisoned in 2008, in recognition of both the positive findings of the literature on lesbian and solo parenting and of the unacceptable discrimination on grounds of sexual orientation (Fenton et al. 249). There has been a significant increase in the number of same-sex female couples receiving treatment in the UK in recent times (Human Fertilisation and Embryology Authority).

In addition to newfound inclusivity in terms of access, the new 2008 parentage regime brings the legal position of lesbian couples into line with that of heterosexual married and unmarried couples, although, as it is set out as a mirror image of the sexually affiliated heterosexual model, it might be thought symbolically suggestive of the notion that the alternative model is secondary or even *other* (Fenton et al. 249). More radically, however, the reform also permits a nonsexual partner to be named as the father or as the second legal parent of a child. Sexual affiliation is thus not the only determinant of family, something Fineman has argued for at least two decades (Fineman, *Neutered* and *Autonomy*). Although the new regime still maintains the normative primacy of the biogenetic two-parent model so fundamental to the liberal order, the UK approach is to be applauded for its significant and positive recognition of alternative family forms. By contrast, in the US, fertility clinics are free to refuse to treat single and lesbian women, and "studies indicate that many infertility clinics will deny access to single men, gay couples and poor couples" (Storrow, "Medical" 376–77), thus reifying heteronormative bias (Storrow, "Marital" 100).

The 2008 reform has enacted valuable and responsive gains in reproductive choice by granting access to previously excluded groups, which to a certain extent mitigates vulnerability by transitioning previously conceptualized subversive or *dangerous* mothering into the mainstream. However, a vulnerability perspective reveals that what the law actually does is permit those previously excluded to be reclassified as the liberal autonomous subject, and inclusion therefore *looks like* formal equality. Such single, male-partner-less women begin to *look like* the liberal subjects and the lesbian family begins to *look like* its heterosexual equivalent. The alternative nonsexual two-parent family takes on the *appearance* of an accepted family form (Fenton 134). But, as Fineman states, "we have merely expanded the group to whom this version of equality is to be applied" (*Autonomy* 24). The symbolic recognition of formerly excluded groups *is* important but may be deceptive: Law does not operate in a vacuum, and a vulnerability analysis, in its pursuit of social justice, requires us to explore the wider healthcare context and barriers to access of ARTs as a social good.

Resource Availability and Equality of Access: State Responsiveness

Law legitimates those societal institutions that distribute significant social goods and that, says Fineman, provide us with "assets" that give us "resilience" when faced with vulnerability (Fineman *Vulnerability* 22–23). In the realm of ART provision, the most important societal institutions are healthcare providers. The vulnerability thesis therefore suggests that the state and healthcare providers—as societal institutions—have a duty to be responsive and "a responsibility to structure conditions in which individuals can aspire to meaningfully realize their individual capabilities as fully as possible" ("Vulnerable Subject" 274)—in this case, parenthood.

Health inequalities exist across different socioeconomic groups, genders, and ethnicities in the UK (House of Commons Health Committee 5). Poverty and social exclusion—which may be related to sociocultural or racial groups and access to basic medical care—are determinants of women's reproductive health (Earle and Letherby 234; Cahn 35), and similar patterns of inequality are evident globally. Further, Bell argues that one of the consequences of the medicalization of infertility is the focus on the treatment of infertility as opposed to its preventable causes, which are more common among women of low socioeconomic status (635). This correlation between general healthcare access and fertility substantiates the argument that infertility patterns are of appropriate concern to a responsive state and indicates that reproductive health can be protected through equal healthcare provision provided by systems such as the National Health Service (NHS), which provides healthcare free of charge to all in the UK.[2] The NHS is a social asset, important

---

2. The NHS provides healthcare free of charge in the UK based on clinical need and not ability to pay. This includes primary and secondary care, including emergency treatment. Some means-tested contributions are required, such as a small standardized prescription charge for medication irrespective of the actual cost of the medication. It is possible to purchase private healthcare and insurance to cover private healthcare.

in its provision of shelter and resilience against citizens' vulnerabilities, but equal *availability* of healthcare is not sufficient under a vulnerability analysis: It must take into account the ability of differently situated groups in society to *access* and *utilize* such healthcare. Genuine equality of opportunity and access, then, obviates the privilege of the least vulnerable in society. Such concerns and patterns are distinctively structural, and not merely individual—and the state is connected as the moderator of social resources in the production of the general health-provision conditions under which fertility, or infertility, is facilitated (Fenton 132).

While law may now formally include in its gaze those previously excluded on the grounds of identity, genuine equality is unlikely to result from forced conformity to the autonomous liberal subject model. Unless resources are actually available, and utilization possible, access to ARTs is merely symbolic: The questions, then, become, what does genuine equality in ART provision look like in a post-identity and post-autonomy context, and how do "asset-conferring" (Fineman, "Vulnerability" 23) societal institutions—namely, the NHS—distribute ARTs as a social good?

In the UK, some ART treatment should be theoretically available under the NHS. The National Institute for Clinical Excellence (NICE) determines the effectiveness and appropriateness of treatments for use by the NHS using best clinical and economic evidence, and the constitution of the NHS sets out the use of NICE-recommended treatment where clinically indicated as a right for patients (UK Department of Health and Social Care). NICE recommends that public healthcare should provide three full cycles of in vitro fertilization (IVF) for women under forty years and one full cycle for women aged forty to forty-two (NICE, "Fertility Problems"). Treatment for same-sex couples is included. However, research has consistently indicated that regional commissioning bodies do not provide the recommended cycles of IVF, and the trend is in a continuing decline in healthcare provision. By 2016, the Fertility Fairness audit had found that of the Clinical Commissioning Groups (regional commissioning bodies—CCGs), just 16 percent offered three cycles and 22 percent offered two cycles, with a majority of 60 percent offering only one cycle (Fertility Fairness). Five CCGs have now cut NHS IVF completely (2.4 percent) (Fertility Fairness), and 13 areas have cut or are consulting on reducing IVF provision since the start of 2017 (Marsh). This essentially means that access to ARTs is governed by one's geographic location—a *postcode lottery*. Access is thus fundamentally unequal and is further exacerbated by a range of arbitrary and unsubstantiated nonclinical and non-evidence-based social *deservingness* criteria by CCGs (such as excluding cases where one partner already had a child) and the imposition of age limits, many as low as thirty-five years. The *postcode lottery* is being worsened by the CCGs. In response to these cuts, NICE has issued a new quality standard calling for the end to the *postcode lottery* and emphasizing the importance of treating infertility (NICE, "NICE Calls"). Pressure has also been put on CCGs by a successful legal challenge against a CCG's refusal to fund oocyte cryopreservation as recommended by NICE for a woman undergoing chemotherapy: Here the CCG's policy was found to be unlawful, and it is possible that this decision will spark further legal challenges where the NICE guidance is not followed (*R [on the application of Elizabeth Rose] v. Thanet Clinical Commissioning Group*). While the effect of these current developments remains to be seen, in the meantime fertility treatment remains an ever-decreasing priority for commissioners, resulting in significant inequality of access to public resources distributed by a societal institution, which unjustifiably exacerbates vulnerability.

Although the regeneration of society is valuable and productive in itself, the discourses surrounding healthcare provision are of cost and effectiveness. Thus, this reduction in public funding of IVF by CCGs is always justified under the guise of reducing public spending. Ideologically we might question whether economic productivity arguments have any place in a vulnerability analysis, but nonetheless, pragmatically, we might contest them and reveal them to be illusory. Indeed, research into the fiscal implications relating to achieving ART-conceived children demonstrates an eightfold return on investment for government, and thus "appropriate funding of ART services appears to represent sound fiscal policy" (Connolly et al. 603). It is suggested that the call for a more responsive state should also involve a requirement to recognize the long-term economic advantages—particularly in the era of the increasing trend in below-replacement fertility experienced across the world—rather than entrusting the distribution of significant social goods to regional microeconomic, short-term budgeting by CCGs. Even more important should be the focus on the babies inevitably not born as a result of cuts and thus on the people who are precluded from becoming parents, and the economic context in which cuts are made. As Connolly et al. point out, "'financial access' plays a critical role in overall access to fertility treatment" (607)—not just in terms of actual cost but in affordability. In times of austerity, affordability and thus utilization declines, and of course, austerity affects different socioeconomic and cultural groups differently, with women being particularly disadvantaged (Karamessini and Rubery). The correlation between affordability and utilization is well illustrated by the US, which has one of the lowest utilization rates of developed countries and also the highest direct cost of ART treatment (by a large margin) but almost no public financing (Connolly et al. 604, 607). The lack of public funding thus creates inequality based on ability to pay, which affects different socioeconomic and cultural groups unequally. It is no surprise that financial access is used to police the norms of motherhood. Indeed, there are other structural inequalities that operate social exclusion from infertility treatment. US research demonstrates that ART treatment is utilized more by educated, white, older women and that "racial, ethnic and educational disparities in access to fertility care are not generally reduced by state insurance mandates to cover fertility treatment" (Connolly et al. 607). Bell argues that medicine not only reinforces norms of family but also controls the application of those norms. She suggests that "not only does it do so explicitly through the private medicalized market in which only a few individuals can afford treatment, medicalization also implicitly reinforces stratified reproduction through its inherent characteristics" (634).

In addition to its nonimplementation, the NICE guideline itself raises an issue about the age limit restrictions. Although this has now been extended from thirty-nine years to forty-two years, it nonetheless limits treatment for forty to forty-two years. The law imposes no age limit, while CCGs impose their own arbitrary, often lower, age limits. The rationality of NICE's imposition of age limits has been discussed elsewhere (Fenton 136–37), but it can still be questioned whether they are at odds with social reality: There has been a consistent increase in women giving birth over the age of forty years (Office for National Statistics). The recognition of the vulnerable subject at the forefront of decision-making about the allocation of scarce resources (rationing) might suggest that older women should be prioritized, as they need treatment more than younger women. The recourse to exclusion of older mothering as a money-saving exercise, in the guise of rationing, is strongly reminiscent of the discourses that portray older mothers as subversive and morally unsuitable (Fenton et al. 246)—and perhaps bad, and even dangerous. Furthermore, early motherhood is restrained by socioeconomic actualities—exacerbated in the era of austerity—that lead women to the impasse of early pregnancy and lost career positioning or potential infertility. Through this lens, the promise of ARTs in the eventuality of infertility, coupled with the subsequent exclusion from NHS treatment, simply exacerbates vulnerability. Such vulnerability is perpetuated by large businesses such as Apple and Facebook, who now offer egg freezing to female employees for retention purposes (Tran). Such practices simply increase the normalization of late childbearing, lure career women into infertility with the promise of (successful) ARTs, and simultaneously entrench patriarchal norms regarding caregiving and family. NHS rules create an excluded yet privileged class of infertile women—those with the economic resilience to afford private treatment (in the UK, private clinics will treat women up until the age of around fifty years, for example). The infertile woman who is not economically self-sufficient is effectively punished for her inability to buy herself out of the state's control.

Despite the gains made by law in terms of reproductive freedom and autonomy, the centering of the vulnerable subject reveals reproductive *choice* to be, in substantive terms, illusory. The vulnerable subject is certainly not the liberal actor that the traditional identity-based formal equality analysis portrays her to be. The operation of NHS rationing reflects underlying inequality, unevenness, and discrimination in the distribution of resources that deny actual autonomy and equality. Thus, while law has certainly lessened the barriers to access to ARTs, we remain bound by the familiar liberal scenario as described by Fineman: "We gain the right to be treated the same as the historic figure of our foundational myths—the white, free, propertied, educated, heterosexual (at least married), and autonomous male. We do not gain, however, the right to have some of his property and privilege redistributed so as to achieve more material and economic parity" (*Autonomy* 23). Formal autonomy, after all, is merely symbolic without actual access to treatment. Discrimination on formal identity grounds may now be unlawful, but discrimination due to geographic location is not, and thus what is missing is the recognition of our sameness, our humanness. Although currently a poor representation of social responsibility, the NHS as an institution *could* provide assets and resilience against vulnerability in this arena. However, as Fineman suggests, institutions themselves are vulnerable; they are not "foolproof shelters," but are "potentially unstable and susceptible to challenges from both internal and external forces" ("Vulnerable Subject" 273). The NHS is vulnerable to the privilege and disadvantage created by the state and exacerbated by political choices around austerity. The responsibility of the state therefore needs to be reconceptualized to establish a more equal access to resourcing and utilization, unpolluted by privilege and inequality. We need to create a paradigm in which "the state is not a default (therefore stigmatized) port of last resort, but an active partner with the individual in realizing her or his capabilities and capacities to the fullest extent" (Fineman, *Autonomy* 271). In this context, that includes becoming a parent.

Surrogacy and the Abdication of State Responsibility

Whilst the law on ARTs may now be relevant to the twenty-first century, the same cannot be said of the law relating to surrogacy in the UK. The UK reveals itself unresponsive to surrogacy both domestically and transnationally.

The UK prohibits commercial surrogacy (as do many European countries) and allows altruistic surrogacy but fails to provide a statutory regime for its regulation and for the legal enforceability of surrogacy agreements (Surrogacy Arrangements Act 1985). The law has been unable—or unwilling—to grapple with the ethics of surrogacy and therefore has chosen to simply ignore it, creating and exacerbating vulnerability in its wake and leaving the courts, who are consequently themselves rendered vulnerable, to attend to the aftermath once the child is born. The ban has meant that surrogacy arrangements not only are unenforceable but cannot be arranged professionally on a commercial basis, leaving commissioning parents without proper legal guidance and unaware of the legal complexities they are about to enter into, exacerbated by international conflict of laws.

While there is older case law on resolution of custody when the surrogacy agreement fails and the surrogate—often also the biological mother in those older cases—does not want to give up the child, the courts today have been predominantly (although not exclusively) occupied with different issues surrounding parentage transfers arising from transnational surrogacy where (intended) parentage is not necessarily contested. Where the child's living arrangements have been contested, courts must apply the welfare of the child principle, which is paramount in English law. The problem is that the parentage rules under the 2008 Act simply do not consider surrogacy, and in UK law, the legal mother of the child is always the surrogate as she is the birth mother, regardless of genetics or intended parentage. Some recognition of alternative surrogacy-created families has been achieved since 2008: Parental orders, which transfer legal parenthood to the commissioning or intended parents in a surrogacy arrangement, can be issued to same-sex couples as well as heterosexual ones, provided there is a genetic tie to one of the intended parents (s.54 HFE 2008). Single people, however, remain excluded by the law. The government has announced its intention to reform the law following the 2016 decision by the High Court in the case of *Re Z* that the provision is incompatible with the European Convention on Human Rights (House of Commons). Discrimination on grounds of identity is to be remedied—here the exclusion of singles—and again in this realm of law, we see the emphasis upon formal equality. The UK finds itself in a rather curious, and arguably untenable, position in which, on the one hand, it prohibits commercial surrogacy yet, on the other, it makes some provision for the eventuality—and proven reality—of surrogacy occurring. Awards of parental orders have doubled since 2012, and there has been considerable judicial criticism of the current legal regime, with judges being forced to manipulate orders to give effect to the welfare principle and the parentage intentions of those involved.

The law on parental orders also requires that the surrogate must not have been paid, other than reasonable expenses. However, the courts have faced a steady stream of cases in which monies that exceed reasonable expenses have been paid. Under the welfare of the child principle, the courts have sanctioned such payments so that the parental order can be made. As the judiciary has pointed out, it is practically impossible that parental orders will now be withheld (*Re L*). Despite the ban on commercial surrogacy, arrangements are in essence being sanctioned through the *back door* as they are in effect authorized by the courts and the ban is, as Jackson points out, "completely ineffective" (892). The limitations of the regulatory regime have been further exacerbated by the High Court ruling that the time limit for making applications for parental orders set down by law as within six months of birth cannot prevent the court making an order in late applications (*Re X*). The statutory regime is fundamentally flawed in its assumption that surrogacy can be regulated by after-the-fact transfers of parentage, and the law reveals itself troublingly unethical, blinkered, and unresponsive to the realities of surrogacy, which, in today's world, mostly involves cross-border arrangements. The uncertainty caused by this approach renders children, commissioning parents, and surrogates vulnerable, and courts in many countries worldwide, at all levels, including the European Court of Human Rights, are increasingly being called upon to regulate the results of cross-border surrogacy.

Cross-Border Reproduction and Cross-Border Surrogacy[3]

Neoliberal globalization situates states within a global market and their citizens as global consumers, for whom the internet provides access to a flourishing global market for clinics, gametes, embryos, and surrogates. The globalization and the commercialization of assisted reproduction and surrogacy expedites cross-border reproduction and surrogacy (CBRS)—the movement of persons between jurisdictions in the quest for a child—under different conditions from those available domestically (Gürtin and Inhorn). The trajectories of CBRS are fueled by four main reasons for fertility travel: actual (non-chosen) exclusion by regulation in terms of access and treatment availability, chosen exclusion, long waiting lists, and economic costs. Differ-

---

3. I include cross-border surrogacy in this discussion as it mainly concerns gestational surrogacy that requires IVF treatment and is, for this discussion, another way to achieve conception and birth of a child for those unable to conceive or carry a pregnancy. While I am not suggesting that all the issues are the same or raise the same level of concern, for ease of discussion I am discussing them together under the heading of cross-border reproduction and surrogacy (CBRS).

ent destinations become attractive to different types of fertility traveler, and as a consequence, individual state policies and regulation have repercussions beyond their domestic jurisdictional borders through juridical globalization. The universality of the vulnerability thesis requires that we consider vulnerabilities created by legislative behaviors that have global impact, in this case through CBRS. Our starting point may be to consider the construction of CBRS as a positive means of alleviating vulnerability, followed by an exploration of how CBRS may exacerbate vulnerabilities.

CBRS as an Asset

We might think that CBRS could be constructed as an asset supplying resilience in the face of vulnerability attributable to local restrictions on ARTs and surrogacy. Importantly, states themselves may purposely construct and rely upon CBRS as "a moral safety valve" (Storrow, "Quests" 305). Those who are excluded from local treatment by being rendered *other* (such as by sexuality) are able to purchase the means of reproduction on the international market. Likewise, those excluded because a treatment type is simply not available, such as sex selection or commercial surrogacy, can locate such treatment elsewhere. Thus, sidestepping of local regulation is an important function of CBRS and may in fact be an ally of reproductive rights. The thriving global market, under this analysis, allows access by excluded groups, facilitating alternative family forms, and thus offering resilience against vulnerability. The global market facilitates access to cheaper treatment abroad—cutting economic costs and increasing the availability of reproduction for those who are privileged to have some means to purchase treatment. It makes up for shortages in local markets and allows for the purchase of autonomy by allowing choice for those who, while not actually excluded from treatment, simply disagree with the local conditions for treatment.

In its mitigation of adversity for marginalized groups, CBRS might be constructed as an important market-based asset promoting reproductive freedom, autonomy, and choice. But this market-model is flawed: It reflects a liberal construction of the parties as liberal autonomous actors, consumers, and providers operating in a context of supply and demand, able to freely contract without coercion, from a position of equality. It presumes genuine equality and opportunity of the parties involved. A vulnerability analysis mandates inquiry beyond this construction, this commodity trading, and the exploration of systematic disadvantage in access and equality, "amplified in the context of the globalised neoliberal order" (Grear 54).

CBRS as Exacerbating Vulnerability

A vulnerability analysis of CBRS must question the law's role and adequacy. First, it must examine how the law functions in acting as a market driver, a facilitator of CBRS by exclusory regulation and policy, and consequently as the creator of a dual regime in which the rich can contract out of local laws and subvert the ethical preferences of the home state, but the poor cannot. Secondly, the law's role in regulating CBRS itself both in terms of its practices and standards (such as the number of embryo transfers) and in terms of its outcomes (such as legal parentage, legal recognition, and welfare of the child) must be questioned.

The way in which CBRS operates gives rise to many potential vulnerabilities. First, the fertility tourist exits the home state in their quest for reproduction. This travel is likely to subvert home state regulation and policy and is only open to those who can pay. The tourist may find cheaper treatment abroad, but that treatment may come with welfare hazards for the traveler herself, such as the transfer of multiple embryos. Here we witness the correlation between cheaper treatment and value for money; as Connolly et al. note: The "level of affordability is an important driver of utilization, treatment choices, embryo transfer practices and ultimately multiple birth rates" (603). The risks in terms of the lack of safety standards become clear. Multiple pregnancies resulting from treatment abroad are both high risk and high cost, which has consequences both for pregnant mother and fetuses. Second, the home state may be rendered vulnerable in that the costs will be borne by its healthcare system as the pregnancy proceeds. University College London Hospital, for example, has seen an increase in high-order multiple pregnancies from treatment abroad (Shenfield).

Third, gamete donation may be required to achieve pregnancy. This factor in itself may be a motivator for travel when anonymous donation is unlawful in home states and in short supply, as is the case in the UK. While UK regulation recognizes the principle of biological truth—that is, for a child to know its genetic origins—an exception is made when a citizen chooses to travel abroad for treatment. In the absence of any sanctions for using anonymous gametes abroad, the law is complicit in the privileging of the rich's ability to circumvent national rules, contributing to the vulnerability of the resulting child. Egg donors are vulnerable in terms of the health risks of donation itself and potential ovary overstimulation to maximize profit. Nahman discusses "reverse traffic repro-migration," a practice in which clinics retrieve eggs and import them to their own country to save women travel, in which she suggests "tissues/embryos/eggs and recipients are prioritized over the well-being of the oocyte seller herself," perhaps more than in other forms of CBRS (633). The market for egg donation can thus be criticized for turning "some women into available resources and others into consuming bodies" (Nahman 633), a differential exacerbated by inequalities between differently situated women in the global market. Whilst some trajectories for CBRS are relatively localized—such as within Europe, where there are established trajectories between similarly situated economies (Shenfield)[4]—there is a constant direction of reproductive traffic from poor to rich, from global South to global North. The intersection between developed and developing countries in the global market, and the potential exploitation of the economically vulnerable and disempowered women, raise particular concerns for a vulnerability analysis. Even a brief perusal of websites offering egg donation across the world reveals the immense price differential—of tens of thousands of dollars—for eggs between the global South and global North. The vulnerability analysis must address the invisibility of women donors and the commodification of their reproductive material both generally and particularly at the juncture of South and North, ensuring that these global donors develop visibility. These donors must be accounted for by states as part of ethical legislative behavior in their own regulation of ART.

Where pregnancy is achieved abroad, and the pregnant mother is the intended social mother, the law is relatively unproblematic in regulating the issue of birth mother parentage. It is not averse to stepping in, however, in an attempt to enforce its national moral perspectives retrospectively in relation to surrogacy outcomes.[5] For those unable to realize a pregnancy, surrogacy may be the only answer, and it is heavily restricted in many developed countries either by law or by cost. Generally, where it is permissible, such as in the US, it remains an opportunity only for the very rich, with costs estimated to be over £100,000 (Horsey). International surrogacy becomes normalized, endorsed, and perhaps even glamourized through utilization by celebrities such as Elton John, who used a surrogate in California. The attraction of developing countries such as India or the Ukraine for cheap surrogacy is therefore predictable and potentially illustrative of how "the poorest peoples and nations of the earth are forced disproportionately to bear the deepening social costs of capitalism" (Grear 59). Surrogacy arrangements are often brokered by agencies or clinics for high fees (of which the surrogate is likely to receive only a small

---

4. For example, the trajectory is from Italy to Spain for egg donation, and from France to Belgium for sperm donation (Shenfield 1366).

5. For example, in the French cases of *Mennesson v. France* and *Labassee v. France*, France refused birth certificates to children born in the US. The European Court of Human Rights found that France had breached the children's human rights (Jackson 905; Brooks).

part) and surrogacy is predominantly gestational. Because the commissioning parents are likely to be significantly more financially resilient and advantaged than the surrogate, regardless of their respective socioeconomic statuses at home, the specter of abuse and inequality of bargaining power is always looming. Much disquiet has been expressed about the exploitation of women, who are structurally and socioeconomically disadvantaged in developing countries and who, for example, indicate that hunger motivates their participation in egg donation, surrogacy, and similar types of "work" (Pande 161). It is notable that as the ethical issues play out in reality, developing country surrogacy "hotspots" have begun to wind down or terminate their access to foreigners, but this simply shifts trajectories, with the same issues, as new markets open their doors (Horsey).

Can free choice ever genuinely be said to operate in such contexts? Some facts are inexorable, such as high levels of poverty and that surrogacy and egg donation in the host countries are often highly stigmatized. Ironically, part of the appeal for clients is exactly that surveillance and loss of autonomy under which poor foreign surrogates can be held during pregnancy, as demonstrated in the documentary *Google Baby* (Franz): Indian surrogates are shown living communally, lined up close to one another, provoking an image of *battery-baby-farming*, family and existing children left behind. Such surveillance is abhorrent to the basic notions of autonomy and dignity enjoyed in the developed world. Further concerns are raised about illiteracy, lack of bargaining power, and lack of (the Westernized concept of) informed consent. In the case of *AB v. CT*, for example, the legal agreement was *signed* by the surrogate's thumbprint, raising questions about whether the surrogate could ever have understood or been made to understand what was a complex contract. While on the one hand some authors document illiteracy (Pande), others report some surrogates as both literate and questioning (Deomampo); however, even literate women have no bargaining power and are fearful of jeopardizing their surrogacy contracts by asking questions of doctors and lawyers. Further, while the women are paid and this payment may allow them to purchase education or commodities otherwise out of reach, such as a home, the surrogacy market does not better the conditions of women, their reproductive health, and their communities (Mohapatra).

In addition to the vulnerability of the bio-available women, surrogacy creates issues for the children who become entangled in its web of consequences. The situating of Indian surrogates out of sight and away from their families during their socially unacceptable and subversive, othered pregnancies means that any existing children of the surrogate are likely to be deprived of mothering while their mother *mothers* for another. The law's operation can leave the children born through surrogacy vulnerable. The law may render children stateless and legally parentless because of conflict of laws, where neither of the relevant jurisdictions recognizes the commissioning couple or the surrogate as the legal parents (such as in *Re X and Y*). In one recent case, twins were unable to leave India for over a year (*Re Z* in 2015) due to immigration issues. Some states have refused to recognize surrogate-born children: Germany, in the case of twins born to German parents in *Balaz v. Anand* 2009 (Crockin); and the European Court of Human Rights, to protect the Article 8 rights of surrogate born children refused citizenship by France (see European Court of Human Rights; Brooks). Children may remain uncollected with agreements unenforceable at law, as in the case of baby Gammy (mentioned at the beginning of this essay), while some children may be taken from their parents, who are retrospectively deemed unsuitable by the state (Margaria and Sheldon). Legal reforms in India have sought to ban foreign and commercial surrogacy, although the exact legal status of such reform attempts is not clear (*Indian Express*, "New Surrogacy Bill"). Such unilateral revocation of surrogacy is problematic when arrangements are already in course: For example, one British couple was told to leave their surrogate-born baby in an orphanage (Patel), and two US couples had to begin legal action to reclaim embryos stored in India (Taylor). Such responses of the host state, perhaps somewhat ironically, expose the vulnerability of the fertility tourist.

States reveal themselves unresponsive to the vulnerabilities of their own citizens and their children born through surrogacy. Western inequality in provision and the unresponsive, unethical developed nation-state, combined with corporeal vulnerability, create and perpetuate various trajectories of exploitation and commodification of all those involved in CBRS in the name of the free neoliberal global market, to the detriment of human populations predominantly in the global South.

Conclusion

The law's role in ART and surrogacy provision, as a domestic regulator, as a driver to transnational markets, and as a *fixer* of cross-border outcomes, needs careful examination. While the UK's local provision is seemingly progressive and inclusive, a focus on vulnerability's reconstruction of the politico-legal subject as vulnerable reveals the UK state is unresponsive and unethical in its approach. Genuine equality is mythical and illusory, and privilege and disadvantage abound, from which the embodied vulnerability of the global, socioeconomically disadvantaged is readily forseeable.

A more substantive vision of equality, as demanded by Fineman, can only be achieved by moving beyond autonomy—and beyond mere formal equality—to include an examination of the realities and vulnerabilities created by ART and surrogacy regulation and policy on a global scale. Vulnerability therefore requires us not only to demand the elimination of inequality, privilege, and disadvantage created by our own state's local provision, but also to call upon states to be responsive to globalized structural inequalities and to demand accountability for the vulnerabilities created externally by their own domestic legislation. Vulnerability facilitates the search for a more just and equal global social order, and while vulnerability might not give us ready solutions to the ethics of ARTs, it can be used to argue for fertility justice in the forms of global standards, ethics, and regulation in recognition of our universal embodied vulnerability.

Works Cited

AB v. CT [2015] EWFC 12.

Bell, Ann V. "Beyond (Financial) Accessibility: Inequalities within the Medicalisation of Infertility." *Sociology of Health & Illness*, vol. 32, no. 4, 2010, pp. 631–46.

Brooks, James. "France to Recognise Children Born via Surrogates Abroad." *BioNews*, vol. 761, 2014, https://www.bionews.org.uk/page_94659.

Cahn, Naomi. *Test Tube Families: Why the Fertility Market Needs Legal Regulation.* NYU Press, 2009.

Callaghan, Sascha, and Newson, Ainsley. "Surrogacy, Motherhood and Baby Gammy." *BioNews*, vol. 766, 2014, https://www.bionews.org.uk/page_94709.

Connolly, Mark P., et al. "The Costs and Consequences of Assisted Reproductive Technology: An Economic Perspective." *Human Reproduction Update*, vol. 16, no. 6, 2010, pp. 603–13.

Crockin, Susan L. "Growing Families in a Shrinking World: Legal and Ethical Challenges in Cross-Border Surrogacy." *Reproductive Biomedicine Online*, vol. 27, no. 6, 2013, pp. 733–41.

Deomampo, Daisy. "Transnational Surrogacy in India: Interrogating Power and Women's Agency." *Frontiers: A Journal of Women Studies*, vol. 34, no. 3, 2013, pp. 167–88.

Earle, Sarah, and Gayle Letherby. "Conceiving Time? Women Who Do or Do Not Conceive." *Sociology of Health & Illness*, vol. 29, no. 2, 2007, pp. 233–50.

European Court of Human Rights. *Research Report: Bioethics and the Case-Law of the Court.* Council of Europe/European Court of Human Rights, 2016, echr.coe.int/Documents/Research_report_bioethics_ENG.pdf.

Fenton, Rachel. "Assisted Reproductive Technology Provision and the Vulnerability Thesis: From the UK to the Global Market." *Vulnerability: Reflections on a New Ethical Foundation for Law and Politics*, edited by Martha Fineman and Anna Grear, Ashgate, 2013, pp. 125–46.

Fenton, Rachel, et al. "Shall I Be Mother?" *Gender, Sexualities and Law*, edited by Jackie Jones et al., Routledge, 2011, pp. 241–54

Fertility Fairness. "Cheshire CCGs Slash NHS IVF." 11 May 2017, www.fertilityfairness.co.uk/cheshire-ccgs-slash-nhs-ivf/.

Fineman, Martha. *The Autonomy Myth: A Theory of Dependency.* The New Press, 2004.

———. *The Neutered Mother, the Sexual Family, and Other Twentieth Century Tragedies.* Psychology Press, 1995.

———. "The Vulnerable Subject and the Responsive State." *Emory Law Journal,* vol. 60, 2010, p. 251–75

———. "Equality and Difference." *Alabama Law Review,* vol. 66 (3): 609–26

———. "Equality, Autonomy, and the Vulnerable Subject in Law and Politics." *Vulnerability: Reflections on a New Ethical Foundation for Law and Politics,* edited by Martha Fineman and Anna Grear, Ashgate, 2013, pp. 13–27.

Frank, Z. B. *Google Baby.* HBO Documentary Films, 2009.

Grear, Anna. "Vulnerability, Advanced Global Capitalism and Co-symptomatic Injustice: Locating the Vulnerable Subject." *Vulnerability: Reflections on a New Ethical Foundation for Law and Politics,* edited by Martha Fineman and Anna Grear, Ashgate, 2013, pp. 41–60.

Gürtin, Zeynep B., and Marcia C. Inhorn. "Introduction: Travelling for Conception and the Global Assisted Reproduction Market." *Reproductive Biomedicine Online,* vol. 23, no. 5, 2011, 535–37.

Horsey, Kirsty. "Fraying at the Edges: UK Surrogacy Law in 2015." *Medical Law Review,* vol. 42, no. 4, 2016, pp. 608–21.

House of Commons Health Committee. *Health Inequalities: Third Report of Session 2008–09.* Vol. 1, 26 Feb. 2009, publications.parliament.uk/pa/cm200809/cmselect/cmhealth/286/286.pdf.

House of Commons Library. *Children: Surrogacy—Single People and Parental Orders (UK).* 10 Dec. 2018, researchbriefings.files.parliament.uk/documents/CBP-8076/CBP-8076.pdf.

Human Fertilisation and Embryology Authority. *Fertility Treatment 2014: Trends and Figures.* March 2016, ifqtesting.blob.core.windows.net/umbraco-website/1783/fertility-treatment-2014-trends-and-figures.pdf.

The Indian Express. "New Surrogacy Bill Bars Married Couples with Kids, NRIs, Gays, Live-ins, Foreigners." *Indian Express,* 25 Aug. 2016, indianexpress.com/article/india/india-news-india/surrogacy-bill-sushma-swaraj-married-couples-can-now-opt-homosexuals/.

Jackson, Emily. *Medical Law.* 4th ed., Oxford University Press, 2016.

Karamessini, Maria, and Jill Rubery, editors. *Women and Austerity: The Economic Crisis and the Future for Gender Equality,* vol. 11, Routledge, 2013.

Margaria, Alice, and Sheldon, Sally. "Parenting Post IVF: Is Age Not So Relevant After All?" *Reproductive Biomedicine Online,* vol. 29, no. 1, 2014, pp. 10–13.

Marsh, Sarah. "IVF Cut Back in 13 Areas of England to Save Money, New Data Shows." *The Guardian,* 6 Aug. 2017, www.theguardian.com/society/2017/aug/06/ivf-cut-back-in-13-areas-of-england-in-bid-to-save-money-new-data-shows.

Mohapatra, Seema. "Achieving Reproductive Justice in the International Surrogacy Market" *Annals of Health Law,* vol. 21, 2012, pp. 191–200.

Nahman, Michal. "Reverse Traffic: Intersecting Inequalities in Human Egg Donation." *Reproductive Biomedicine Online,* vol. 23, no. 5, 2011, pp. 626–33.

National Institute for Health and Care Excellence. "Fertility Problems: Assessment and Treatment." Feb. 2013, www.nice.org.uk/guidance/CG156.

———. "NICE Calls for an End to Postcode Lottery of IVF Treatment." 23 Oct. 2014, www.nice.org.uk/news/article/nice-calls-for-an-end-to-postcode-lottery-of-ivf-treatment.

Office for National Statistics. "Births in England and Wales: 2016." 29 July 2017, www.ons.gov.uk/peoplepopulationandcommunity/birthsdeathsandmarriages/livebirths/bulletins/birthsummarytablesenglandandwales/2016.

Pande, Amrita. "Not an 'Angel,' Not a 'Whore': Surrogates as 'Dirty' Workers in India." *Indian Journal of Gender Studies,* vol. 16, no. 2, 2009, pp. 141–73.

Patel, Rikita. "Indian Minister Intervenes to Help British Couple Take Home Surrogate Baby." *BioNews,* vol. 869, 2016, https://www.bionews.org.uk/page_95691.

Photopoulos, Julianna. "Judge: 'Baby Gammy' Was Not Abandoned and Sister Can Stay with Parents." *BioNews,* vol. 847, 2016, https://www.bionews.org.uk/page_95472.

R (on the application of Elizabeth Rose) v. Thanet Clinical Commissioning Group [2014] EWHC 1182.

Re L (A Minor) [2010] EWHC 3146 (Fam).

Re X (A Child) (Surrogacy: Time limit) [2014] EWHC 3135 (Fam).

Re X and Y (Foreign Surrogacy) [2008] EWHC 3030 (Fam).

Re Z [2015] EWFC 90.

Re Z (A Child) (No. 2) [2016] EWHC 1191 (Fam).

Roy, Modhumita. "Foreign Babies/Indian Make: Outsourcing Reproduction in the Age of Globalization." *Locating Cultural Change: Theory, Method, Process,* edited by Partha Pratim Basu and Ipshita Chanda, SAGE India, 2011, pp. 54–72.

Shenfield, Françoise, et al. "Cross Border Reproductive Care in Six European Countries." *Human Reproduction,* vol. 25, no. 6, 2010, pp. 1361–68.

Storrow, Richard F. "Marital Status and Sexual Orientation Discrimination in Infertility Care." *Law Journal for Social Justice,* vol. 3, 2012, pp. 99–120

———. "Medical Conscience and the Policing of Parenthood." *William and Mary Journal of Race, Gender, and Social Justice,* vol. 16, 2009, pp. 369–93

———. "Quests for Conception: Fertility Tourists, Globalization and Feminist Legal Theory." *Hastings Law Journal,* vol. 57, 2005, pp. 295–330.

Taylor, Lucas. "Embryos from Overseas Couples 'Stuck' in India." *BioNews,* vol. 874, 2016, https://www.bionews.org.uk/page_95741.

Tran, Mark. "Apple and Facebook Offer to Freeze Eggs for Female Employees." *The Guardian,* 15 Oct. 2014, www.theguardian.com/technology/2014/oct/15/apple-facebook-offer-freeze-eggs-female-employees.

UK Department of Health and Social Care. *The NHS Constitution for England.* Updated 14 Oct. 2015, www.gov.uk/government/publications/the-nhs-constitution-for-england/the-nhs-constitution-for-england.

CHAPTER 12

Dangerous Desires and Abjected Lives

Baby-Hunger, Coerced Surrogacy, and Family-Making in Michael Robotham's *The Night Ferry*

MODHUMITA ROY

IN LATE AUGUST of 2015, the world was yet again shocked by the discovery of a truck in Austria with dozens of decomposing bodies in it. With multiple continuing wars across the globe—in Syria, Iraq, Afghanistan, and the Sudan, to mention a few—and a deepening global economic crisis, desperate populations began to make efforts to escape the instabilities and reach safe havens. Many became easy targets of ruthless human traffickers, as was clearly the case in Austria. The refrigerated truck, with Hungarian number plates, had apparently been parked off the highway for a number of days before authorities made the gruesome discovery. The German chancellor, Angela Merkel, and her Austrian counterpart at the time, Werner Faymann, who were both at a summit in Vienna, expressed their horror. "The refugees who died today wanted to save their own lives by fleeing, but instead lost their lives at the hands of traffickers," Faymann was quoted as saying ("Dozens of Refugees").

This and similar accounts of migrants fleeing war zones and dying in their attempt to reach safety rang an eerie bell as I sat down to write this essay on coerced surrogacy in Michael Robotham's 2007 thriller, *The Night Ferry*. Indeed, the novel appears remarkably prescient in its foregrounding of a world destabilized by war, where refugee populations are forced to make grim choices just to survive. A mass-market, middlebrow read, the novel, though positively reviewed in several newspapers, has yet to receive any scholarly attention. In many ways, the novel replicates the familiar "death-detective-explanation" of detective fiction (Horsley 12). What sets Robotham's thriller apart, as reviews have noted, are the serious ethical questions it raises. The novel takes us, says the *Sydney Morning Herald* quoted on the back cover of the paperback edition, "deep into a set of humanitarian concerns." Unlike most garden-variety thrillers that steer clear of politics, *The Night Ferry* doggedly connects the dots of social, economic, and geopolitical instabilities, and shows them to be the grounds upon which criminal activities flourish.

As in detective novels with a political viewpoint, the crime under investigation in *The Night Ferry* is revealed to be part of a "network of problematic social and institutional mechanisms of which the crime itself is only one manifestation" (Tomc 46). The novel focuses on the never-ending Afghan war and the refugee *crisis* in Europe and links these geopolitical catastrophes to the creation of a new, vulnerable class of exploitable people. Many, as the novel shows, are forced to fulfill metropolitan demands and desires, especially for *intimate labor*—be it caretaking, sex, or reproduction via surrogacy. Robotham bravely wades into the troubled waters of reproductive politics, connecting coerced reproductive labor to the desperation of some for genetically related offspring.

The thriller is one of only a handful of novels published in recent years that explore the murky underbelly of surrogacy arrangements. For the most part, commercial surrogacy, especially in popular cultural representations, gets treated rather positively. It would be hard to find a situation comedy, serialized drama, or even a reality show in the last decade that did not have at least one subplot that favorably examined parenthood via surrogacy.[1] As artificial reproductive technologies (ARTs) have advanced and as vulnerabilities of populations, especially in the global South, have increased—not only as a result of geopolitical instabilities, as in Robotham's novel, but also due to draconian Structural Adjustment Programs (SAPs) and neoliberal policies that have, among other things, increased labor market volatilities and inequality—womb renting has become an alternative survival strategy for some women. As the wealthy embrace commerce in what Anne Phillips calls "intimate bodily services" (*Our Bodies* 66), stigma attached to renting poor women's wombs seems to have diminished. Instead, such practices have come to be accepted as a means of family-making, especially for those experiencing what is often referred to as *intractable* or *involuntary* infertility. This acceptance coincides rather conveniently with increased vulnerabilities of populations.

---

1. These include *Modern Family, Glee, The Good Wife, Ugly Betty,* and *Dancing with the Stars,* among many others.

The series of intertwined criminalities that the novel presents challenges the reader to consider the thriller not simply as a crime-solving exercise, but as a political commentary about the ethics of commercial surrogacy, though it should be noted that the instances of surrogacy in the novel are criminally coerced and not a commercial transaction as such. More broadly, the novel can be read as engaging the latent question of what fuels the demand for such labor; that is, it focuses on the core issue of baby-hunger or the all-consuming desire to have *genetically related* offspring. *The Night Ferry* instantiates what such desires can let loose in a radically unequal world of "reproscapes" or global landscapes and circuits across which technologies, labor, biocapital, and ideologies of race and family now travel (Inhorn 90). To be sure, Robotham raises the stakes by interjecting into arguments about the morality and ethics of commercialized reproduction (whose pros and cons continue to be debated in scholarly journals), the extreme—perhaps improbable—circumstance of war refugees terrorized into becoming reluctant surrogates. I argue, however, that Robotham's focus forces readers to consider how far the blast radius of the globalized war on terror reaches; furthermore, the novel compels us, at the very least, to consider where and how and with what consequences abjected and precarious lives and *dangerous* desire for "custom-made, ready-to-order" babies intersect (Robotham 57).

In a 2013 essay, Tavia Nyong'o expressed his worry around the "sudden acceleration" of the term *precarity* in academic writing (157). The overuse of the term, he rightly warned, "threatens to generalize precarity as ubiquitous and therefore an undifferentiated human condition" (157). At first glance, the novel too appears to be making such an indiscriminate claim, implying that bodies, especially female bodies, are all precarious because they are especially susceptible to violence: from murder victim Cate Elliot's damaged body; to her mother's paralyzed one; to the detective Alisha Barba's, whose spine is held together with steel; not to mention the Afghani refugees in Amsterdam, who are forced to become surrogates. On the one hand, such precarity—the exposure to assaults that diminish the body's capacities (for speech or childbirth or *normal* movement)—suggests a modicum of equality. On the other hand, as the novel illustrates in excruciating detail, only *some* are much more defenseless than others, and this differential in vulnerabilities has everything to do with the complex unfolding of geopolitical realities and unevenly dispersed economic opportunities and life chances. What the novel demonstrates throughout is that while *vulnerability* may well be a universal human condition, *precarity* is not; it is—and ought to be—reserved as a description of inequitably distributed risk and harm, terror and abjection. The novel's intricate plot knits together the effects of war, displacement, and economic hopelessness that produce precarious subjects, and the relentless pursuit of profit, which exploit their vulnerability and turn them into disposable populations. In other words, the novel does appear to remain "scrupulously attentive" to "the constitutive and uneven distribution of . . . vulnerability," as Nyong'o urges, by taking into account "the full violence of global capitalism" (157).

Mad . . .

The Night Ferry opens with Detective Constable Alisha Barba, of the London Metropolitan police, receiving a cryptic note from her estranged friend Cate. It reads, "Dear Ali, I'm in trouble. I must see you. Please come to the reunion. Love, Cate" (3). Alisha attends the reunion and meets a heavily pregnant Cate, who only has time to whisper to Ali that she desperately needs help: "They want to take my baby . . . You have to stop them . . ." (15). Before Ali can ask any questions, Cate and her husband Felix are struck by a taxi. Felix is killed instantly, and though Cate is still alive, her body is so damaged it seems unlikely that she will survive. In their attempt to save her life and that of the unborn baby, the paramedics tear away her clothes and make a shocking discovery: Cate had been faking her pregnancy. The paramedics find "a large piece of upholstery foam, trimmed to fit over her stomach," and once the "prosthetic belly" is pulled away, Cate is "'pregnant' no more" (21). Ali sets out to piece together the *why* of Cate's faked pregnancy and her desperate appeal for help. Above all, she wants to find the reason for what Ali suspects to be the deliberate and premeditated murder of Cate and her husband. Why had Cate faked her pregnancy? If she wasn't pregnant, how could her *baby* be in danger? Why was she murdered? By whom? To find answers, Ali and her former boss and mentor, the retired Detective Inspector Vincent Ruiz, travel to Amsterdam and to the dark, violent world of human traffickers, baby-sellers, refugees, corrupt doctors, and childless couples, desperate to have babies.

Narrated by Ali, the novel shocks us at the outset with Cate's death and the discovery of her secret and takes the reader on a long, murky journey of discovery. The plot moves back and forth in time, and we get to know Cate and Ali and their intimate friendship in slowly unfolding flashbacks, which helps to emphasize their closeness and similarity, as it also reminds us of their differences. This oscillation between their similarity, and ultimately their difference, becomes the key to understanding the death of one and the survival of the other. We learn that though Cate Eliott and Alisha Barba "were born at the same hospital and raised in Bethnal Green in London's East End" (10), they belonged to quite different worlds. They first met when they were thirteen years old when Cate transferred to Ali's school and they "became inseparable" (30). Despite their closeness, and despite Ali's avowal that they were "like Siamese twins," or like "milk and cookies" (30), the girls are separated by race and class: Cate is white and middle class; Ali is working class and of Indian descent. What also distinguished them from each other are their physical appearances. Ali consistently emphasizes Cate's feminine desirability in contrast to her self-assessed "rather ungirlie" (204) appearance. She casts herself as Cate's physical opposite, a "skinny Indian girl with braces and glasses," with a lean, muscular, athletic body (29); Cate, on the other hand, was "the coolest, most desirable girl in the whole school" (25), "born with the ability to make men admire her" (14). Though Ali does not have "Cate's luminous beauty or infinite sadness," (60) what she has, and what stands her in good stead, perhaps even guarantees her survival, is that she has, as she puts it, "wisdom, determination and steel" (60). Of greater moment than appearance, class, or ethnicity is what Ali *does not* share with Cate: baby-hunger—the burning, all-consuming, desperate yearning to have a child, and not just any child, but one's "own genetic offspring" (199).

The novel flirts with the idea of a romantic-sexual attraction between Ali and Cate and therefore with the possibility of *alternative* bonds and kinships. Indeed, Ali's first experience of an erotic kiss is with Cate: "Sitting in the darkness, our shoulders touched, and her fingers found mine. She squeezed my hand. I squeezed hers. And that was the start of it" (30). While the "start of it" could have blossomed into a romantic relationship between them, which might have allowed Cate to reexamine her aspirations for the future, the novel turns away from such an option. Instead, Ali states categorically, "I loved her. Not in a sexual way" (34). What abruptly ends their friendship is Cate's discovery of her father's sexual seduction of Ali; it shatters the placidity of their shared childhood and irreparably ruptures their closeness. But neither the shocking discovery, nor her parents' loveless marriage, shakes Cate's faith in and desire for a conventional family; that is, Cate holds on to the fantasy of an idyllic, normative life with a husband and especially children who, she imagines, would love her unconditionally. Although the novel is disinclined to shed its heteronormative ideology, it does, in the end, call into question Cate's idealization of familial life, and replaces the nuclear family with a more capacious version of kinship, about which I will have more to say later in the essay.

Despite their differences, the novel is invested also in setting up Cate and Ali as parallels. Since much of the narrative present is interlaced with the past, the flashbacks serve as constant reminders to readers of their intimacy and their similarities. This mirroring, as Sandra Tomc has maintained, between a murder victim and the female detective often has a specific ideological function, especially in feminist detective novels (46). It "adjusts our reading of the woman detective in a crucial way" (46). Tomc finds the substitutions, or what she calls "moments of metaphoric confusion" (46), help to establish the text's political options. Tomc's exemplary instance is Jane Tennison (played memorably by Helen Mirren) in Granada television's hugely successful crime series *Prime Suspect* (1999–2006). Pointing to the many moments in the series where DCI Jane Tension is mistaken for a prostitute or a victim of crime, Tomc argues that these moments "insist on a seemingly arbitrary analogy between the woman detective and the young women whose murders she is investigating. . . . For a split second . . . she and the dead girl are dangerously interchangeable" (46). While metaphoric confusion underscores the vulnerability of women—the detective could as easily have been the victim—such confusions, in fact, draw our attention to what makes the difference. Cate and Ali—Siamese twins, telepathic best friends, same age and the same rhythm ("we were synchronized" [145])—almost share the same fate.

Even with their potential interchangeability, however, what is of significance is that one woman is the victim of a crime that the other will solve. This is a carefully deliberate feature of the novel: to explore, as it were, the reason why one survives while the other does not. And the death of one, as much as the survival of the other, I argue, holds the key to the texts' horizon of understanding of the dangers of certain obsessions—to make genetically related children at any cost, for example.

We meet Ali in this novel, a sequel to the earlier *Shattered* (2008), in which she breaks her back; she tells us matter-of-factly, "Somebody dropped me onto a wall, crushing my spine" (6). Ali had lain in a hospital bed, recovering from life-threatening injuries that had taken six operations and nine months of physiotherapy (6) to be able to resume a normal life. Her spine had to be reconstructed with steel plates, and as a result (we learn later in the novel), she will not be able to have children. Cate's broken body in the hospital is eerily reminiscent of Ali's: "Cate lies . . . hostage to a tangle of tubing, plasma bags and stainless steel. Needles are driven into her veins and her head is swathed in bandages. Monitors and machines buzz and blink" (33). Ali is reminded of her own ordeal in the hospital, when she, too, had lain helpless, hooked to monitors and machines. Reporting on Cate's condition, Ali tell us, "Now they say her pelvis is so badly shattered that even if she survives she'll never be able to carry a baby" (38). This, too, is a moment of deliberate "metaphoric confusion": "Something shudders in me. A déjà vu from another hospital and a different time, when *my* bones were being mended," says Ali (38).

While Ali's shattered body has been patched together, Cate's body "is broken in too many places to fix" (21) and she dies. Robotham makes their conditions deliberately and uncannily similar and uses the "metaphoric confusion" to stress the *differences* between the two women to suggest why one dies while the other survives. Ali herself signals the limits of the interchangeability of identities. Cate, the girl with "a casual, almost unwanted beauty," had always seemed set in her life goal: "I am going to have lots of babies because they will love me and never leave me" (31). Even as a teenager, Cate had steadfastly expressed this normative vision of her future: "She would map out our paths, which included careers, boyfriends, weddings, husbands and children" (34). Ali, child of immigrant Sikh parents, though encouraged to be feminine and to desire marriage and a family of her own someday, harbored instead fantasies of wining the marathon in the Olympics: "At sixteen I wanted to win Olympic gold" (68). We know, of course, that Ali's Olympic dream proves as elusive as Cate's desire for babies. But after the devastating injury, Ali had come to terms with her disappointment and accepted that she would never run again at a competitive level. She had slowly and painfully built back her stamina and continued to run, not as a compulsion or obsession, but as a healing and restorative exercise.

Cate, on the other hand, marries Felix and attempts to start a family, as she had always declared she would. But she is unable to have children. Cate, we are told, became "a walking bloody textbook on infertility," having tried everything, "IVF, drugs, injections, herbal remedies" (49). But nothing worked. Here, again, the novel reminds us of the quite different life goals and temperaments of Cate and Ali. Alisha knows that her "patched pelvis and a reinforced spine" cannot "withstand the trials of pregnancy and labor" and acknowledges, "Wanting children is a dangerous ambition for me" (39). It is dangerous for Cate, too, of course, but unlike Ali, who accepts the consequences of her injury, Cate's repeated attempts and failure to become pregnant made her "obsessed. Desperate" (50). Biology had betrayed Cate, for whom pregnancy "was theoretically possible but realistically unlikely" (89). Such a prognosis did not deter Cate; she was determined to have a baby, no matter the cost.

After Cate's death, Ali, with considerable risk to her own safety, pieces together Cate's story of repeated failed attempts at getting pregnant and her subsequent mental breakdown. Cate had "spent a fortnight in a psych ward" (57), and in her fragile mental state is arrested for stealing baby clothes from Mothercare. A compassionate magistrate, taking pity, gave Cate a suspended sentence and ordered her to seek counseling. When she finally turned to adoption to create a family, the shoplifting conviction disqualified her as a fit parent. At her lowest moment of distress and desperation, Cate had "met someone who convinced her that for £80,000 another woman would have a baby for her. *Not just any baby. Her own genetic offspring*" (183; my emphasis).

And, it was the prospect of *genetic* offspring that had made Cate set aside all qualms and embark on a perilous journey that ended in her murder. Since commercial surrogacy is illegal in Britain, Cate had traveled to Amsterdam, where gestational surrogacy is permitted, to carry out her plan. With whom and under what circumstances had she been able to broker such an arrangement? How would she have brought the babies back into Britain? She had almost got away with it—but how?

It turns out, Cate had been encouraged and aided by Julian Shawcroft, the head of an evangelical organization, whose own obsession is to save *unborn babies,* for which he doesn't mind breaking the law, and by her unscrupulous fertility doctor, who also believes that the end justifies the means. Cate faked her pregnancy while she put in place a convoluted plan not only to circumvent British law, which does not permit paid surrogacy, but also to engage in human trafficking: With the help of other criminal elements, Cate had planned on smuggling the pregnant surrogate into the UK to give birth "in the same country as prospective parents" (266). The home birth, without the involvement of hospitals, would go untraced and the newborn could be registered later by Cate as hers. If it worked as planned, the nefarious, illegal activity would be undetectable, for once the genetic parents take "possession of the baby . . . [b]lood samples, DNA and paternity test could all confirm their *ownership*" (226; my emphasis). It is in the concoction of this mad and criminal plot to realize her lifelong obsession that Cate's otherwise unremarkable middle-class life intersected with pronatalist zealots, who claimed to care about life, and with criminals, who cared little. All the actors had their own reasons for participating and each had rationalized their part in the inhumane nexus of coercion, torture, and even death. With the help of Shawcroft, Cate found a surrogate *willing* to carry her last two viable embryos, created with her eggs and her husband's sperm.[2]

When things went terribly wrong, and she realized that her partners in crime might sell the babies to the highest bidder, Cate reached out to Ali. "As I tell the story," Ali confides in the readers, "it strikes me how implausible it all sounds. An Englishwoman transports fertilized embryos to Amsterdam inside a small cooler box. The eggs are placed in the womb of an unwilling surrogate" for Cate to become a mother (184). Yet, in reality, the trade and traffic in baby-making, which includes a brisk market in *body bits,* make Cate's (and the novel's) scenario almost plausible. Even if Robotham presents an extreme, even lurid, case of international human trafficking, blackmail, and murder, the

---

2. Cate was not aware that Samira, the young Afghani refugee, who would serve as a surrogate, was pregnant with twins. Hence, her plea to Ali to save her "baby."

legal market in bio-materials and in commercial surrogacy is only marginally less sensational. To the vignette with which this anthology begins, of the Lius and their gestational carrier, Jessica Allen, can be added such shocking cases as Baby Manji in India,[3] or Baby Gammy in Thailand,[4] and too many instances that make headlines on a worryingly regular basis. In addition to disputes over payment, unwanted and abandoned babies, and legal challenges about embryos are the growing numbers of appalling reports such as the one about "nine babies found in mysterious circumstances in a Bangkok apartment," without any documents or identifiable parents.[5] Or *baby farms* discovered in various parts of the world: Nigeria, India, Thailand.[6]

Medical technological innovations have fragmented reproduction—dividing the necessary raw materials and labor into discrete components: genetic, gestational, legal, and social—rendering the labor and meaning of gestation culturally and legally ambiguous and locationally separated. The sale of reproductive materials (eggs and sperm) and the renting of wombs is a booming global trade. It is now possible to buy human eggs in Turkey, buy sperm in the US, and hire a woman in India to carry the embryo to term to have one's *own* child. This dispersed form of reproduction inevitably challenges, if not reframes, older, more settled, legal definitions of parenthood, especially motherhood. Babies can be created now with one person's egg, with a fertilized embryo implanted in another woman's womb, to fulfill the desire of parents unrelated to either. Aided in no small measure by the liberalization and deregulation of medical technologies in places like India, ART has found a willing partner in neoliberalism, which encourages the commoditizing of everything. It should not be overlooked, however, that the surrogates who carry the fetus to term and for which labor they are given a (paltry) sum of money come overwhelmingly from the low-paid, informal, casualized work sectors, where employment is hazardous, when available, and the pay is dismal. In the global South, in particular, womb renters sign contracts they cannot read or understand and have no say in any medical decisions that are made about their bodies and reproductive capacities.[7] In the US alone, the number of infants born to gestational surrogates is rising. Nonetheless,

---

3. See Roy.

4. See, for example, https://www.bionews.org.uk/page_95472.

5. *Sunday Morning Herald,* August 8, 2014, https://www.smh.com.au/world/thailand-launches-human-trafficking-probe-after-nine-surrogacy-babies-found-in-apartment-20140808-1026bo.html.

6. See, for example, http://www.vagabomb.com/Baby-Farms-Discovered-in-Gwalior-Where-Newborns-Can-Be-Bought-for-1-Lakh-Each/ or https://www.theguardian.com/law/2011/jun/02/nigeria-baby-farm-raided-human-trafficking, among many others.

7. See, among others, Roy; Rudrappa and Collins; Phillips, *Our Bodies.*

as Deborah Spar and Ana Harrington note in their detailed study of assisted reproductive markets in the US, ART "remains largely the province of the rich, or at least the well-to-do" (50).

It is important also to remind ourselves that the availability of this particular employment *choice* is not only driven by biotechnological innovations; it is also the result of neoliberal policies that, as many have pointed out, are reversing the trajectory of economic development that had once been aimed at the greater common good. This reversal, in addition to wars and forced dislocations, has created immiseration and desperation on a grand scale. It is surely within these contexts that we ought to understand what Melinda Cooper calls "the rise of transactional reproductive work," which, as she argues, "demands that we rethink some of the key assumptions of feminist bioethics, displacing the salient questions from the realm of care, dignity, respect, and the liberal ethical contract (of informed consent) to that of labor relations and unequal exchange" (138).

While debates about reproductive justice often focus on economic conditions, and rightly so, much less attention has been paid to the consequences of war, civil war, and repression, related though these may be. The appropriation of poor, vulnerable women's bodies—especially their reproductive capacities—to fulfill the individual, privatized desire to have one's *own* children (Judith Daar's phrase for it is "individual procreative aspiration" [105]) is what the confluence of war, instability, and neoliberal economic policies produces. The unending war in Afghanistan is one instance of the destabilization that leads to the horrors this novel catalogues. It is not difficult to see why cheap, outsourced ART would become an *attractive* option for those closed out of expensive surrogacy markets, such as in the US, or for those who, for a variety of reasons, are legally prohibited from going the womb-renting route. But Robotham's novel, as I have been arguing, raises a different, if related, set of ethical and legal questions. By presenting an extreme instance—coerced surrogacy—the novel asks us to reconsider the question of *choice*. Too often what is foregrounded is the desperation of the childless, to which the novel adds the desperation of abjected populations to ask us to consider whose desperation is the greater. The novel poses stark questions: Can one person's desperation be sufficient reason to circumvent the law (as Cate did)? And should such cases of baby-making be punished under law? Whom would the law hold accountable?

BAD . . .

In order to track down Cate's surrogate, Ali travels to Amsterdam, where she finds the pregnant Samira, a teenaged Afghan refugee, a devout Muslim, and a virgin. Having lost all her family, except her brother Hasan, in an endless cycle of war and occupation, she was desperate to secure their safety, especially Hasan's. Trafficked to Amsterdam and owing the traffickers a large sum of money, Samira could repay her debt in one of two ways: prostitution or surrogacy. Unwilling to violate the religious prohibition against prostitution, Samira submitted instead to "medical rape" (260) in the hope that it would safeguard her brother's entry into the UK. Instead, Hasan, along with others, had been found dead by suffocation in a freight truck registered to a Dutch company, parked in the port of Harwich (134). Ali, in fact, might never have been able to unearth Cate's "implausible" scheme if not for the discovery of the truck full of dead bodies, none carrying any identification—except for Hasan. The police find, carefully sewn into his shirt, Ali's name and address. Once again, in a moment of metaphoric confusion, Ali, instead of Cate, is suspected of human trafficking. Like Cate, she travels to Amsterdam, to retrace her friend's footsteps and to uncover her crime. Once in Amsterdam, Ali (and the reader) begins to understand how volatile the intercalation of individual procreative aspirations with the desperation of the abjected is. As much as those killed by bombs and drones, Samira, her friend Zala, and countless other women are equally the War on Terror's unremarked collateral damage. "Orphans. Illegal immigrants. What a perfect combination of the unwanted and the desperate," remarks the inspector in Amsterdam (249). They are what Georgio Agamben calls *homines sacri*: unmourned, disposable populations, whose status as refugees—*nonpersons*—renders them valueless, a burden on the state. It is equally their status as nonpersons that creates a different measure of value for a different constituency. Throughout the novel, we see stateless people fleeing terror become the reserve army of labor, from whom value is ruthlessly extracted by a thriving underworld of criminals.

Samira's abjection, for example, is a direct result of the superpower rivalries in Afghanistan. The successive assaults on the region result in the utter decimation of any recognizable civic life. Samira was born during the Soviet occupation of the country. Her life and the fate of her family are inextricably tied to instabilities brought about by geopolitical conflicts and successive wars of occupation—the Soviets, the Taliban, the US forces. Each new conflict prompted another involuntary dislocation and robbed Afghanis of family and future. The upheaval has left Samira no choice but to submit to unspeakable exploitation: "People traffickers smuggle them out of Afghanistan as far as Amsterdam. They are told they owed a debt for their escape. Either they become prostitutes or carried a baby for a childless couple" (260). In a bid to survive, if barely, young women—girls—are transformed into baby-making machines: "Virgins were implanted with embryos in a ritualized form of medical rape. They are the perfect incubators. Factories. Couriers" (260). The choice for Samira, her friend Zala, and countless others is stark: sex slavery or medical rape. Other migrants, as the novel recounts in some detail, from Surinam and elsewhere, have also faced these alternatives and are all part of the real, if overlooked, collateral damage of combined but unevenly dispersed geopolitical power and peril.

The twists and turns of the plot eventually lead to some answers: Ali is able to pinpoint the principals in "this evil trade" (367)—the choice of words connecting *this* trade to that other, older evil trade, slavery. The contemporary *traders* are Nigerian, German-Swiss, Moroccan, Irish, English—a global, multiracial cast of characters, as befits a globalized, albeit illegal, trade. Ali shudders at the horrific possibility that "there could be others. Babies born at a price, ushered into the world with threats and blackmail" (184). In fact, Ali successfully identifies fourteen infants born through coerced surrogacy, and it leads to the disquieting question: "Who *owns* the babies?" (187; my emphasis). Though "appalled by this evil trade" (367), and despite sufficient evidence, Adam Greenburg, QC, refuses to prosecute the criminals. "A case such as this," he tells a shocked Ali, "raises moral and ethical issues. Fourteen infants, born as a result of illegal surrogacy, have been identified. These children are now living with their biological parents in stable loving families" (367). While he concedes that prosecution is legally permissible, he is also quick to warn that such a move will tear families apart: "Parents will be charged as co-conspirators and their children will be taken into care, perhaps permanently. In prosecuting one individual, we risk destroying the lives of many more" (367). The Dutch and German authorities face a similar dilemma, and the implication is that they, too, reach a similar conclusion. The overarching, one might say, irresistible ideology of *family*—nuclear and especially bio-essentialized—trumps the prosecution of criminality and lawless profiteering. The children, after all, *belong* now to their *families,* and breaking up the nuclear family appears to authorities as an unthinkable option. The nuclear family, of course, is not a biological necessity; it is, Laura Mamo contends, "enforced by regulations and reinforced by legal discourse, medical practices, and cultural norms" (5). Yet, it is the nuclear family that has come to represent "social order, idealized kinship, and legitimate relations" (5). The novel, despite its unflinching examination of a grammar of violence—the linked violence of war, human trafficking, debt (extracted by traffickers), and the unspeakable suffering of the abjected populations—recoils from taking the radical step of declaring the hunger for genetically related families also as one kind of founding violence. After all, it is worth remembering that it was Cate's obsessive attempts "to give Felix his *own* child—a perfect genetic match" (186) that had unleashed the series of events leading to her murder.

Even if, within the space of the novel, there can be no solution to the "evil trade," to its credit *The Night Ferry* does provide an alternative vision of *family*. The ending of the novel presents a capacious network, brought together by chance, choice, affection, and even genetics. The creation of this family is an act of social renovation that revises, even subverts, the hegemonic nuclear family, and this subversion, therefore, explicitly repudiates Cate's obsession. We are left with a multiracial household that includes Ali and her partner, "new boy" Dave; her brother and Samira, who are in love; Ali's mother, who can't stay away from the household; and even Inspector Ruiz, the part-gypsy, surrogate father figure and mentor to Ali. At the center of it all are the twins—who have many mothers: Samira, who is not genetically related to them but is their legal mother,[8] having given birth to them; Cate, who, had she lived, would have been their *genetic* mother; and Ali, their surrogate mother, who is not only appointed their guardian in Cate's will ("I direct her to love and care for them" [357]), but finds herself "besotted. Spellbound by the twins" (406).

Having rejected the obsession for genetically related children—in a final ironic twist, we discover that Felix was not the biological father—and positing a viable alternative for weaving a family together, the novel nonetheless at best, is conflicted and ambivalent about motherhood. By making Ali, who had steadfastly rejected the yearning to be a mother, confess, "I realize now that I wanted one too. I *want* to be a mother" (239), the novel reinforces the ideology of motherhood as something women desire naturally or instinctively. Thus, despite its repudiation of Cate's version of family-making, the novel settles for the familiar and comforting arc of redemptive sentimentality, representing the expectation that *family* is the shield from worldly harm, the haven in a heartless world.

Set aside and sublimated by this sentimental conclusion are Ali's—and by extension our own—shock and horror throughout the harrowing novel. We are meant somehow to overlook that Samira's life, her body, is a living map of political and economic vulnerabilities. When Ali finally finds a very pregnant Samira hiding in a rundown, seedy apartment in Amsterdam, she asks, "I need to know why you are doing this. What did they offer you?" To which Samira simply responds, "Freedom." "From what?" Ali persists. "She looks at me as though I'll never understand. 'Slavery'" (172). That searing answer must now, at the end of the novel, be set aside.

---

8. Both in the Netherlands and in the UK, the woman who gives birth is considered the legal mother, even if she is genetically unrelated to the baby.

And Dangerous

For Rayna Rapp, reproductive technologies are a part of the larger picture of "the age of highly selective and exquisitely stratified globalization" (695). While some yearn for biologically related offspring—however fabricated and illusory that relation may be, as we see vividly in the novel—and are willing to pursue such a possibility no matter the cost, others, abjected populations among them, are "increasingly mobilized as 'natural resources' whose own future reproduction or health does not enter into sales, surveillance, or any vestige of monitoring or access to care" (Rapp 709). The "radical reconception of the biology of conception" (Kahn and Chavkin 39) has given rise to a globalized marketplace of baby-making that is unevenly regulated, when regulated at all. The global trade in commercial surrogacy or *womb renting* has increasingly taken on the features of industrialized production, and yet more and more it is presented as a *choice* that some women are *free* to make. Anne Phillips argues, for example, that the normalization of market logics should not be understood as instantiation of the exercise of *choice*. She argues, "Where kidney markets have been normalised, for example, there is evidence that debt collectors put pressure on borrowers to sell a kidney in order to repay a debt. The opportunity for some to sell then reduces the opportunity for others to refuse to do so" ("Inequality" 153). This inability to *refuse* is often obscured in the dominant narratives of bodily sales, including commercial surrogacy, which too often casts unequal and unfair market relation as a double gain, a win-win, rather than, as is the case in many parts of the world, a desperate survival strategy.

One reason why commercial surrogacy is able to recast market relations into discourses of altruism and gift is that it comes suffused in the warm glow of selflessness, of helping someone achieve a happy ending.[9] "I was doing a good thing," says Samira to Ali, ignoring, of course, the horrific circumstances under which she had acquiesced and even the violence of the impregnating process to which she undoubtedly had been subjected; she was, after all, "*forced* to get pregnant" (209) and was only kept physically alive as long as she was the incubator. Samira's sole value to the gang of human traffickers is her reproductive body. Indeed, the source of terror for the refugees hiding out in Amsterdam is the disposability of their lives. Yet, even Samira recasts her terror through the discourse of "doing a good thing."

"Market-driven bodily sales" (Rapp 695) are a global, cutthroat business that exploits the language of emotions: hope, longing, desire, fulfillment. Prefaced often by such narratives of loss and sorrow of involuntary infertility as

---

9. See Rudrappa and Collins.

Cate's, this market ultimately relies on what Sara Ahmed calls "the promise of happiness." In the introduction to her 2010 book *The Promise of Happiness*, Ahmed contends that "happiness is consistently described as the object of human desires, as being what we aim for, as being what gives purpose, meaning and order to human life" (1). Expressing what she calls a "skeptical disbelief in happiness as a technique for living well" (2), Ahmed wants to focus instead on "how happiness is associated with some life choices and not others, how happiness is imagined as being what follows a certain kind of being" (2). It should be noted, of course, that *un*happiness, as well as happiness, is *produced* through social scripts that endorse some choices over others, and the production entails rituals and performances that are socially recognizable: marriage and parenthood chief among them. In fact, happiness and unhappiness are both "regulatory effect[s] of a social belief" (7)—the widely held belief, which Cate shared, that childlessness is an unbearable burden, rendering life worthless. While childlessness evokes sympathy or pity, in the present moment with the availability of medical technologies to assist reproduction, not having children can equally be construed as selfishness or worse. Indeed, Sheila Jasanoff usefully reminds us, "*Not* using the available technologies—by choosing to remain childless, for example—thus becomes the marked, or unnatural behavior" (161).

We attach or associate happiness with certain objects that circulate as social goods—children, for example. And this desire—for children, which we imagine will lead to happiness, and which is legitimated and encouraged by society in a variety of different ways—often rationalizes exploitation of others. In trying to defend Cate's actions, Ali had speculated that perhaps "she didn't realize that Samira would be forced to co-operate" (221). In the end, however, having uncovered the nefarious plot, Ali concluded that Cate "broke the law. She rented a womb" (221) and that she "was an inept thief . . . a foolish dreamer. I don't want to think about her anymore" (396). But Cate's venture is neither unique nor abnormal. Societies are so invested in pronatalism, what Lee Edelman in a related if somewhat different context calls "the compulsory narrative of reproductive futurism" (12), that human *decisions* to have children are recast as biological reproductive *instincts,* beyond our control. The inability to have children is constructed—and experienced—as a *failure* that gives rise to what Charis Thompson evocatively labels a "monopoly of desperation" (207). Robotham's novel, however, refuses to award such monopoly to the childless alone. Instead, it carefully computes different claims to "desperation" that intersect—Samira's for survival, Cate's for motherhood, Shawcroft's to prevent abortions—and suggests that in effect it is the *entanglement* of different kinds and degrees of desperation that leads to the harrowing trail of violence, abjection, and death.

Works Cited

Agamben, Georgio. *Homo Sacer: Sovereign Power and Bare Life.* Stanford University Press, 1998.

Ahmed, Sara. *The Promise of Happiness.* Duke University Press, 2010.

Cooper, Melinda. *Life as Surplus: Biotechnology and Capitalism in the Neoliberal Era.* University of Washington Press, 2008.

Daar, Judith. *The New Eugenics: Selective Breeding in an Era of Reproductive Technologies.* Yale University Press, 2017.

"Dozens of Refugees Found Dead in a Truck." *Aljazeera,* 27 Aug. 2015, www.aljazeera.com/news/2015/08/dozens-refugees-dead-truck-austria-150827094349613.html.

Edelman, Lee. *No Future: Queer Theory and the Death Drive.* Duke University Press, 2004.

Horsley, Lee. *Twentieth-Century Crime Fiction.* Oxford University Press, 2005.

Inhorn, Marcia. "Globalization and Gametes: Reproductive 'Tourism,' Islamic Bioethics, and Middle Eastern Modernity." *Anthropology and Medicine,* vol. 18, no. 1, 2011, pp. 87–103.

Jasanoff, Shelia. "Taking Life: Private Rights in Public Nature." *Lively Capital: Biotechnologies, Ethics, and Governance in Global Markets,* edited by Kaushik Sunder Rajan, Duke University Press, 2012, pp. 155–83.

Kahn, Linda G., and Wendy Chavkin. "Assisted Reproductive Technologies and the Biological Bottom Line." *Reassembling Motherhood. Procreation and Care in a Globalized World,* edited by Yasmine Ergas et al., Columbia University Press, 2017, pp. 38–54.

Mamo, Laura. *Queering Reproduction: Achieving Pregnancy in the Age of Technoscience.* Duke University Press, 2007.

Nyong'o, Tavia. "Situating Precarity between the Body and the Commons." *Women & Performance: A Journal of Feminist Theory,* vol. 23, no. 2, 2013, pp. 157–61.

Phillips, Anne. "Inequality and Markets: A Response to Jessica Flanigan." *Political Theory,* vol. 41, no. 1, Feb. 2013, pp. 151–55.

———. *Our Bodies. Whose Property?* Princeton University Press, 2013.

Rapp, Rayna. "Reproductive Entanglements: Body, State and Culture in the Dys/Regulation of Child-Bearing." *Social Research,* vol. 78, no. 3, Fall 2011, pp. 693–718.

Robotham, Michael. *The Night Ferry.* Sphere, 2007.

Roy, Modhumita. "Foreign Babies/Indian Make: Outsourcing Reproduction in the Age of Globalization." *Locating Cultural Change: Theory, Method, Process,* edited by Partha Pratim Basu and Ipshita Chanda, SAGE India, 2011, pp. 54–72.

Rudrappa, Sharmila and Caitlin Collins. "Altruistic Agencies and Compassionate Consumers: Moral Framing of Transnational Surrogacy." *Gender and Society,* vol. 29, no. 6, 2015, pp. 937–59.

Spar, Deborah, and Ana M. Harrington. "Building a Better Baby Business." *Minnesota Journal of Science and Technology,* vol. 10, no. 1, 2009, pp. 41–69.

Thompson, Charis. *Making Parents: The Ontological Choreography of Reproductive Technologies.* MIT Press, 2005.

Tomc, Sandra. "Questing Women: The Feminist Mystery after Feminism." *Feminism in Women's Detective Fiction,* edited by Glenwood H. Irons, University of Toronto Press, 1995, pp. 46–63.

CONTRIBUTORS

ZARENA ASLAMI is associate professor in the Department of English at Michigan State University. She is the author of *The Dream Life of Citizens: Late Victorian Novels and the Fantasy of the State* (Fordham University Press, 2012) and is at work on a book project on nineteenth-century British representations of Afghanistan, currently titled *Sovereign Anxieties: Victorian Afghanistan and the Margins of Empire.*

DIANA YORK BLAINE is professor of gender studies and writing and director of undergraduate studies in the Department of Gender and Sexuality at the University of Southern California. She teaches feminist theory, thanatology, rhetoric, and media literacy. Her work focuses on representations of the dead body in American culture, examining the ways in which gendered and raced narratives produce normative subjectivity in the US. She has published, presented, and taught seminars on the ideology of the body in William Faulkner, Thomas Pynchon, the Jon Benet Ramsey murder case, the Dr. Phil show, the Mummies of the World Exhibit, Michael Jackson's memorial service, and yoga in advertising. Her current project seeks to identify and define categories of death narratives in mainstream American culture.

JULIETA CHAPARRO-BUITRAGO is a PhD candidate in the Department of Anthropology at the University of Massachusetts–Amherst. She also holds a graduate certificate in advanced women, gender, and sexuality studies. Her areas of interest are human rights and gender, reproductive justice, decolonial and transnational feminisms, and Latin American studies. Her work looks at the cases of forced sterilization in Peru to analyze how victims (mainly peasant and indigenous women), feminist groups, and the Peruvian state make these cases simultaneously legible and not pursuable within the legal system. Currently, she is developing two journal articles, tentatively titled "Performing Human Rights: Feminist Activism and the Cases of Forced Sterilization in Peru" and "Making Sense of Harm: Women's Narratives and the Limits of Human Rights."

RACHEL FENTON is senior lecturer in law at the University of Exeter, UK. Her research interests include gender and the law, with a specific focus on assisted reproduction and legal regulation, and the prevention of violence against women. She has written extensively on both subjects.

MELISSA HARDESTY is assistant professor in the Department of Social Work at Binghamton University (State University of New York). Her ethnographic research of child welfare workers at a concurrent planning foster care and adoption agency in the Midwestern US focuses both on the nature of the job and on the micropolitics of assessing parents on behalf of the state. Other research interests include feminist and antifeminist selfies and the visual narrative content of prospective adoptive parent profiles. She is also a faculty affiliate in the Binghamton University Sexualities Lab.

REBECCA HOWES-MISCHEL is associate professor of anthropology in the Department of Sociology and Anthropology at James Madison University. She conducted ethnographic research in Oaxaca, Mexico, and in the US between 2005 and 2013 about how public clinics, activist agendas, and policy initiatives shape the material and symbolic care of indigenous women's reproductive bodies and prenatal experiences. Her current research project tracks the emergence of basic science and popular narratives about the gendered and raced body in human microbiome research. Previous research publications have focused on the use of heartbeat diagnostic technologies to make fetal personhood claims and negotiations among activists, health professionals, and policy makers over maternal mortality statistics in Oaxaca, Mexico.

HEATHER MOONEY is a PhD candidate in the Sociology Department at Boston University, focusing on gender, race, and place. Her background is in education and crisis intervention counseling for teenagers. Her work has been published in *Distinktion: A Journal of Social Theory* and *Women's Studies Quarterly.* Currently, she is preparing a comparative study that explores death, race, emotion, and space.

MODHUMITA ROY is associate professor of English at Tufts University. She teaches and writes on global English literatures, environmental justice, and reproductive politics, focusing especially on questions of imperialism, class, and gender. Most recently, she coedited *Sharing the Earth: An International Environmental Justice Reader* (Georgia University Press).

VALERIE STEIN earned her ThD in Hebrew Bible / Old Testament from Harvard University. She is an associate professor of religion and chair of the Department of Philosophy and Religion at the University of Evansville. Her teaching and research explore the intersection of religion and culture in the context of social diversity. She is especially interested in the history of biblical interpretation and the ways in which the biblical text has functioned to marginalize or oppress certain groups. She has presented and published on the Bible's role with respect to issues of gender, Jewish-Christian relations, colonialism, and race.

MARY THOMPSON is associate professor of English and coordinator of the Women's, Gender, and Sexuality Studies Program at James Madison University. After completing her doctoral degree, she worked for several years in abortion providing. Her research examining literary and popular representations of reproductive justice issues has appeared in *GENDERS, Frontiers, Journal of the Motherhood Initiative for Research and Community Involvement,* and several edited volumes.

ROSALYNN A. VEGA is assistant professor of medical anthropology and global health at the University of Texas Rio Grande Valley. Her research explores issues of citizenship and transnationalism, intersectionality and critical race theory, political economy, and knowledge production and circulation. She is the author of *No Alternative: Childbirth, Citizenship, and Indigenous Culture in Mexico* (University of Texas Press, 2018). Her works in progress analyze medical migration across the US-Mexico border, corruption in the Mexican healthcare system, and anthropological instruction within Mexican medical schools.

KAREN WEINGARTEN is associate professor of English at Queens College, City University of New York. Her first book is *Abortion in the American Imagination: Before Life and Choice, 1880–1940* (Rutgers University Press, 2014). She is currently writing a book on the cultural history of pregnancy, disability, and the anxiety of inheritance.

INDEX

good birth and, 98; humanized birth for affluent women, 82, 83, 93, 98; indigeneity and, 93–94; intersectional inequalities in, 93–95; livelihoods for midwives, 89–91; medicalized birth *versus*, 82–83, 89, 96–97, 98; Millennium Development Goals and, 87–88; NGO funding and, 87–88; *nivel cultural* and, 93; referral and reimbursement for, 88; research methods on, 83–84, 83n1, 84n2; target population of, 87, 88; threat of imprisonment, 82, 94

midwifery in Mexico. *See* Mexico, midwifery in

Millennium Development Goals (MDGs), 87–88

Miller, Nancy, 1

Mirren, Helen, 230

Mitchell, David, 158n5

money: commodification anxiety in adoption, 172–88; financial incentives to forgo abortion, 175; moral valence in social relationships, 173–74

Moore, Russell, 43n1, 55–56

moral categories, 14, 16

Morales Canduelas, Magna, 138–39

Morton, Rick, 43n1, 56

Moses, 46–48, 46n4

motherhood: biosocial ideology of, 9; collectivity and, 116; construction and reconstruction of, 8; entanglement of reproduction, motherhood, and state, 3; feminine/mediated, 106–7; gendered identity *versus* action, 115; in *Juno* (2007 film), 128–30; marginalized women *versus* elite, 115–16; materialistic maternity, 132–33; maternity as escape hatch, 108–15; neoliberal, 103–8; opting-out and work, 20, 101–18; pronatalism and, 14, 119, 169, 239; redefinition and understanding of, 3; reentering workforce, 102, 112–14; responsibility for healthcare in Oaxaca, Mexico, 190, 194–96, 199n7; *Revolutionary Mothering* (Gumbs), 115–16; technology of transformation, 116

Mujeres Aliadas, 91

Multi-Ethnic Placement Act of 1994 (MEPA), 175, 182

National Health Service (NHS), United Kingdom, 210–14, 210n2

National Institute for Clinical Excellence (NICE), United Kingdom, 211–14

National Tay–Sachs and Allied Diseases (NTSAD), 165–66

Necochea López, Raul, 149

neoconservatism, 5

neo-eugenics, 12–13, 20, 158. *See also* eugenics

neoliberal feminism, 106

neoliberal motherhood, 103–8

neoliberalism: adoption and, 175–76; austerity programs of, 5–7; choice-marketplace connection in, 15, 20; commoditization in, 5, 7–8; definition and development of, 4, 104–5; dismantling of welfare programs, 6, 104–5, 121, 175–76; disproportionate impact on women, 5–8; economization of life, 103–4; evangelical adoption and, 58–59; governing rationality in, 4; labor practices and, 63–64; Mexican commercial surrogacy and, 63–65; normalization of values, 20; paradoxes in healthcare (Oaxaca, Mexico), 21, 189–205; precarity produced in, 5; reshaping of economies and intimacies, 1, 2–3; Seguro Popular (Mexico) and, 84–86, 91–92; "slow violence" of, 4–8; US, 6; vulnerability under, 21

New International Version Bible, 45, 49n8

New Life Mexico, 62, 69

New Revised Standard Version Bible, 49n8

New Testament, adoption in, 42, 48–49

Nigeria, baby factories/farms in, 17, 233

Night Ferry, The (Robotham), 21, 225–40; alternative family in, 229, 237; baby hunger in, 21, 227, 229, 231–32, 236–38; ethical issues in, 226, 227; "evil trade" in, 236–37; intimate labor in, 226; medical rape in, 235–36; metaphoric confusion between victim and detective in, 229–31; precarity in, 21, 227–28; race and class in, 229

Nixon, Rob, 5

nonpersons, 235

normalization of adoption, 20–21, 183–85, 186

norms, neoliberalism and acceptance of, 151, 192–93

North American Free Trade Agreement (NAFTA), 191, 191n2

Nyong'o, Tavia, 21, 227–28